The Great Grammar Book

Mastering Grammar Usage and the Essentials of Composition

Second Edition

Marsha Sramek

ARCH PRESS

HOUSTON, TEXAS

The Great Grammar Book

Arch Press, http:www.thegreatgrammarbook.com
4 Summit Tower Circle , Asheville, NC 28804
Order @ www.thegreatgrammarbook.com
Second Edition Copyright © 2020 by Marsha Sramek, Arch Press

Library of Congress Control Number: 2009909231

International Standard Book Numbers
978-0-9841157-2-3

Printed in the United States of America

Introduction

You hate the idea of studying grammar, but you realize that others, whether they are teachers or bosses, are judging you whenever they read something you have written. Using clear, step-by-step instructions and exercises, *The Great Grammar Book* is the answer to your grammar anxiety.

This book is fun to read, with fascinating, arcane information that could make you a trivia champion. More important, *The Great Grammar Book* uses and explains only those grammatical terms which are necessary to avoid mistakes or improve writing skills. Whether you are a student or professional, this book will help you write more effectively and clearly.

This book focuses on the most frequent errors in English and how to correct these errors. Unlike other grammar texts, there are enough practice sentences and exercises to overcome long-standing bad grammatical habits.

Get started by taking the diagnostic test to discover your areas of strength and weakness. Soon you'll be able to banish your grammatical errors and write with confidence and style.

Acknowledgments

The book interior layout was done by Deb Tremper of Six Penny Graphics. She is also responsible for the cover art, from a concept by Rich Chiburis.

Thanks to Helen Warning and John Neighbors for proofreading, editing, and being good friends.

Special thanks to my husband, Wayne Sramek, for tireless proofreading and extra special encouragement.

Table of Contents

Chapter Three   Pronouns

Chapter Four   Capital Letters

Chapter Five   **Using Apostrophes Correctly**

Chapter Six   **Complete Sentences**

Chapter Seven   **Punctuation**

Chapter Eight   Commas

Chapter Nine   Irregular Verbs

Chapter Ten **Usage Glossary**

Circle the correct word choice.

1. A necklace made from the claws of a grizzly bear and a Colt .45 six-shooter once owned by "Buffalo Bill" Cody **was/were** sold at an auction in Dallas for more than $40,000 each.

2. A high fat diet, obesity, and lack of exercise **increases/increase** the risk of developing heart disease and Type 2 diabetes, even in young people.

3. **Here's/Here are** news articles about computers being given to a Brazilian jungle tribe.

4. The profit margins at a typical warehouse club **is/are** between 11% and 14%, compared with 25% to 30% at a typical grocery store.

5. A wound infested with maggots **heals/heal** quickly without any threat of infection or gangrene.

6. American consumers have learned that the days of unlimited low cost energy **is/are** over.

7. **There's/There are** 251 school days in China a year, which is 71 more days than in American schools.

8. *Battlefield 3* or *Crysis 2* **has/have** the most realistic game graphics.

9. The pattern of stars that looks like twin boys **is/are** called Gemini, or the Twins.

10. Did you know that **its/it's** the moon that causes the tide to rise and fall?

11. In Texas **its/it's** illegal to shoot a buffalo from the second story of a hotel.

12. For nearly 100 years the Coca Cola Company has been using legal means to protect **its/it's** trademark name.

13. In 1958 a nuclear bomb was lost somewhere along the swampy coast of Georgia and **its/it's** whereabouts remain a mystery to this day.

14. On the island of Santorini, Greece, donkeys are often used in place of taxis for transporting tourists and **their/there** luggage.

15. Teddy Roosevelt, **who's/whose** life was dramatically altered by the tragic deaths of his mother and wife on the same day, went on to become the 26th president of the United States.

16. When **your/you're** in Florida, remember the special law that prohibits unmarried women from parachuting on Sunday.

17. A woman who was looking for shells on a Washington state beach found a prosthetic leg **their/there** instead and was able to return it to the owner after posting a description on Facebook.

18. The U.S. is one of the windiest **country's/countries** on the planet, sometimes called "the Saudi Arabia of wind."

19. In California, Maryland, Pennsylvania, and Wisconsin, it's against the law to hold a "**Ladys/Ladies/Ladies'** Night" because it's deemed gender discrimination.

20. Humpback **whales/whale's/whales'** low frequency calls are the loudest noise made by living creatures.

21. Men process other **men's/mens'** voices with the part of the brain that processes simple sounds such as car engines and machinery, but they process female voices with the part of their brain that processes music.

22. The question on **everyones/everyone's/everyones'** mind was, "How could a jetliner just disappear?"

23. The reporters waited impatiently for the **voter's/voters'** ballots to be counted.

24. Is that convertible **yours/your's**?

25. Maudie and **them/they** discovered a year is actually 365 days, 5 hours, 48 minutes, and 46 seconds.

26. According to psychologists, people make a subconscious judgment about someone that **he or she/they** (has, have) just met within 90 seconds.

27. Provided there is water, an average person could survive one or two months without food, depending on **his or her/their** body fat.

28. Neither Mark nor Christopher liked **his/their** seat assignments.

29. Carrie and **him/he** named their goldfish Jaws.

30. Brittany whispered, "This is strictly between you and **I/me**."

31. I didn't know whether to make the check out to Roger or **he/him**.

32. Researchers have demonstrated that people want more choices and information than **they/you** can actually process.

33. Todd and **he/him** discovered in their research that an average person in the U.S. receives 41 pounds of junk mail a year.

34. By the time a child is six, **he or she/they** can recognize almost 200 company logos.

35. Convincing **us/we** students that we need more testing is a difficult task.

36. Brandon told Annie and **I/me** that his father is serving on board the USS Sterett, a $1.3 billion missile destroyer.

37. Since the Bennets buy gourmet cereals, are always in Starbucks, and constantly wear designer clothes, they spend a lot more money than **we/us**.

38. From the Internet's humble beginnings in the 1980s, usage has **rose/risen** dramatically.

39. The ozone layer is a layer of the upper atmosphere that **lies/lays** about 12-15 miles above the earth's surface.

40. Recent research on vitamin D has **showed/shown** that taking this vitamin can cut cancer rates and reduce the risk of heart attacks.

41. This thermos has **sprang/sprung** a leak.

42. Lucy **come/came** in third in the last race.

In the following "sentences" write 'F' beside each sentence fragment (incomplete sentence), write 'R' beside each run-on sentence, and write 'C' beside each of the sentences that is already correct.

_____43. First we laughed, then we cried.

_____44. Please speak softly.

_____45. As long as you remember how to get there.

_____46. A study at the University of Toronto found that individuals who identified themselves as conservatives were higher in the personality trait of orderliness, while those who self-identified as liberals were higher in empathy.

_____47. If you really want to be a better employee.

_____48. The left side of your brain controls the right side of your body, the right side of your brain controls the left side of your body.

_____49. The first son of a U.S. president to also become a president was John Quincy Adams, whose father was John Adams.

_____50. Hurry!

_____51. Since members of Congress must run for re-election every two years and successful candidates, on average, spend over a million dollars on the campaign.

_____52. Seen Carson lately?

In the following sentences add commas and quotation marks where they are needed.

53. Since the NCAA basketball tournament moved to the 64 game format there has never been a year that all four #1 seeds made it to the Final Four.

54. The world's largest outdoor food festival Taste of Chicago takes place annually in Chicago's downtown Millennium Park.

55. Al McGuire said The only mystery in life is why the kamikaze pilots wore helmets.

56. In 2002 Philadelphia Eagles' star Brian Dawkins became the only player in history to have an interception sack a quarterback recover a fumble and make a touchdown in one game.

57. According to a recent survey many kids in the U.S. are too busy too distracted and too tired to read a book for fun.

58. For days it seemed likely that Hurricane Rita would hit Houston Texas and more than a million people evacuated but the storm veered into Louisiana.

59. Terry Pratchett said The trouble with having an open mind of course is that people will insist on putting things in it.

60. Mr. Barnes said Laptop computers use up to 90% less energy than desktop models.

61. The economic rebound so many experts have predicted including the Federal Reserve chairman is starting to look doubtful.

62. David said Vinny get lost.

63. Although U.S. life expectancy recently rose to more than 78 years the country still lags behind 30 other countries in estimated life span.

64. Before you assume something learn the facts.

65. Claire Danes has a swing in her apartment and she said My parents had a swing a trapeze and a trampoline in their apartment.

66. Rick Shenkman author of _Just How Stupid Are We? Facing the Truth About the American Voter_ states that only 40 percent of voters can name the three branches of American government.

In the following sentences add capital letters and underlining (to indicate italics) where they are needed. (One sentence is already correct.)

67. John Steinbeck's novel the grapes of wrath tells how poor oklahoma farmers traveled to california during the great depression of the 1930s.

68. The restoration is an english historical period during which the monarchy was restored, following a period known as the commonwealth, when england had no king or queen.

69. Weather forecasters are predicting heavy spring rains, which will help fill our reservoirs to meet the heavy demand of summer and fall.

70. Bryan Cranston, portraying President Lyndon Johnson, won the 2014 Tony Award for best actor in the Broadway play All the Way.

71. Hundreds of native american reservations and pueblos are open to the public including taos pueblo in new mexico, pine ridge reservation in south Dakota, and hopi villages in arizona.

72. The six official languages of the united nations are english, french, arabic, chinese, russian, and spanish.

73. Blake said that the band destiny's child was a loser on star search.

74. Angel falls, which plunges 3,212 feet into the churun river in eastern venezuela, has a longer drop than any other waterfall in the world.

75. As a young, struggling dancer in new york city, madonna worked as a counter clerk at dunkin' donuts in times square.

76. Jay gatsby, the main character in f. scott fitzgerald's novel the great gatsby, hopelessly attempts to revive an old romance.

In each of the following sentences, correct the one grammatical mistake by crossing out the error and making the correction above it.

77. I'm not going in that cave because it's to spooky in there.

78. President James Monroe's daughter was the first member of a presidents family to be married in the White House.

79. You never realize how boring you're life is until someone asks you what you do for fun.

80. In Tokyo riding a bicycle for short trips is alot faster than taking a car.

81. Please give me there e-mail address as soon as possible.

82. I should have knew that it was Isaac Newton, the English physicist, who discovered the law of gravity.

83. He ain't afraid of heights.

84. The pioneer settlers were almost froze by the time they made it through the mountains.

85. Britains secret spy agency is recruiting people who speak Mandarin, Arabic, Persian, Dari, and Pashto.

86. We seen that Raju the elephant cried tears of joy after he was rescued from 50 years of being chained and tortured by his owners.

87. The jeans I bought on sale must of been defective because one of the pant legs is shorter than the other.

88. By reading history we come to understand that civil wars have occurred in many countries including England, Spain, and Russia.

89. Scott's mother has spoke to him about moving his head-banging band's rehearsals to someone else's house.

90. Katie said to her mother, "please take me to the carnival, so I can see the man who eats fire."

91. There's three golf balls on the moon.

92. Us two believe that taking notes with the old-fashioned pen and paper method helps us remember more information than taking notes on a laptop.

93. One in every four Americans have appeared on television at least once.

94. Some widely advertised "Speed up your computer" programs work really good, and others don't work at all.

95. Neither of us remember how the argument started.

96. Vikings, the ancestors of todays Norwegians, lived during the Middle Ages.

97. Oh I didn't see you standing there.

98. Since EPA standards for tap water are much stricter than FDA standards for bottled water tap water is usually cleaner than bottled.

99. Binh and Natalie are confident about winning the tennis championship because they have won every previous match against Jillian and she.

100. If a person can't follow simple directions, you're likely to get lost frequently.

Diagnostic Test Answer Key

1. were	27. his or her
2. increase	28. his
3. Here are	29. he
4. are	30. me
5. heals	31. him
6. are	32. they
7. There are	33. he
8. has	34. he or she
9. is	35. us
10. it's	36. me
11. it's	37. we
12. its	38. risen
13. its	39. lies
14. their	40. shown
15. whose	41. sprung
16. you're	42. came
17. there	43. R
18. countries	44. C
19. Ladies'	45. F
20. whales'	46. C
21. men's	47. F
22. everyone's	48. R
23. voters'	49. C
24. yours	50. C
25. they	51. F
26. they	52. F

53. Since the NCAA basketball tournament moved to the 64 game format, there has never been a year that all four #1 seeds made it to the Final Four.

54. The world's largest outdoor food festival, Taste of Chicago, takes place annually in Chicago's downtown Millennium Park.

55. Al McGuire said, "The only mystery in life is why the kamikaze pilots wore helmets."

56. In 2002 Philadelphia Eagles' star Brian Dawkins became the only player in history to have an interception, sack a quarterback, recover a fumble, and make a touchdown in one game.

57. According to a recent survey, many kids in the U.S. are too busy, too distracted, and too tired to read a book for fun.

58. For days it seemed likely that Hurricane Rita would hit Houston, Texas, and more than a million people evacuated, but the storm veered into Louisiana.

59. Terry Pratchett said, "The trouble with having an open mind, of course, is that people will insist on putting things in it."
60. Mr. Barnes said, "Laptop computers use up to 90% less energy than desktop models."
61. The economic rebound so many experts have predicted, including the Federal Reserve chairman, is starting to look doubtful.
62. David said, "Vinny, get lost."
63. Although U.S. life expectancy recently rose to more than 78 years, the country still lags behind 30 other countries in estimated life span.
64. Before you assume something, learn the facts.
65. Claire Danes has a swing in her apartment and she said, "My parents had a swing, a trapeze, and a trampoline in their apartment."
66. Rick Shenkman, author of *Just How Stupid are We? Facing the Truth About the American Voter*, states that only 40 percent of voters can name the three branches of American government.

67. John Steinbeck's novel <u>The Grapes of Wrath</u> tells how poor Oklahoma farmers traveled to California during the Great Depression of the 1930s.
68. The Restoration is an English historical period during which the monarchy was restored, following a period known as the Commonwealth, when England had . . .
69. Correct
70. Bryan Cranston, portraying President Lyndon Johnson, won the 2014 Tony Award for best actor in the Broadway play <u>All the Way</u>.
71. Hundreds of Native American reservations and pueblos are open to the public including Taos Pueblo in New Mexico, Pine Ridge Reservation in South Dakota, and Hopi villages in Arizona.
72. The six official languages of the United Nations are English, French, Arabic, Chinese, Russian, and Spanish.
73. Blake said that the band Destiny's Child was a loser on <u>Star Search</u>.
74. Angel Falls, which plunges 3,212 feet into the Churun River in eastern Venezuela. . .
75. As a young, struggling dancer in New York City, Madonna worked as a counter clerk at Dunkin' Donuts in Times Square.
76. Jay Gatsby, the main character in F. Scott Fitzgerald's novel <u>The Great Gatsby</u>, . . .
77. I'm not going in that cave because it's **too** spooky in there.
78. President James Monroe's daughter was the first member of a president's family . . .
79. You never realize how boring **your** life is until someone asks you what you do for fun.
80. In Tokyo riding a bicycle for short trips is **a lot** faster than taking a car.

81. Please give me **their** e-mail address as soon as possible.
82. I should have **known** that it was Isaac Newton, the English physicist, . . .
83. He **isn't** afraid of heights.
84. The pioneer settlers were almost **frozen** by the time . . .
85. Britain's secret spy agency is recruiting people who speak Mandarin, Arabic, Persian, Dari, and Pashto.
86. We **saw** that Raju the elephant cried tears of joy after he was rescued from 50 years of being chained and tortured by his owners.
87. The jeans I bought on sale **must've (must have)** been defective because one of the pant legs is shorter than the other.
88. By reading history we **came** to understand that civil wars . . .
89. Scott's mother has **spoken** to him about moving his head-banging band's rehearsals to someone else's house.
90. Katie said to her mother, "**P**lease take me to the carnival . . .
91. There **are** three golf balls on the moon.
92. **We** two believe that taking notes with the old-fashioned pen and paper method helps us remember more information than taking notes on a laptop.
93. One in every four Americans **has** appeared on television at least once.
94. Some widely advertised "Speed up your computer" programs work really **well**, and . . .
95. Neither of us remember**s** how the argument started.
96. Vikings, the ancestors of today's Norwegians, lived during the Middle Ages.
97. Oh, I didn't see you standing there.
98. Since EPA standards for tap water are much stricter than FDA standards for bottled water, tap water is usually cleaner than bottled.
99. Binh and Natalie are confident about winning the tennis championship because they have won every previous match against Jillian and **her**.
100. If a person can't follow simple directions, **he** or **she** (or just **he**) **is** likely to get lost frequently.

Subject-Verb Agreement

Parts of Speech

Traditional grammar classifies words based on eight parts of speech: the *verb*, the *noun*, the *pronoun*, the *adjective*, the *adverb*, the *preposition*, the *conjunction*, and the *interjection*.

Each part of speech explains not what the word *is*, but how the word *is used*.

Verbs do one of two things in sentences: they either ***show action*** or ***link*** a subject to the rest of the sentence.

Action verbs most often show physical action such as *talked, freezes, jump, arrives, and threw.* But action verbs can also show mental action. Verbs such as *remember, considered, thinks, realize*, and *learns* are also action verbs.

Examples:
Nearly 10% of Americans ***dress*** their pets in Halloween costumes.
Nearly 90% of Americans ***consider*** pets in Halloween costumes ridiculous.

Linking verbs link the subject to a noun, a pronoun, or an adjective that describes it. The most common linking verbs are the forms of *"be,"* which are *am, is, are, was, were*, and *been.* The verbs *becomes, appears, seem*, and *remain* are some other examples of linking verbs.

Example:
Actor Robert Pattinson ***seems*** a very believable vampire.

Nouns are words used to name persons, animals, places, things, or abstract ideas, including concepts or qualities. Anything you can see, hear, touch, taste, or smell is a noun. A few examples of these nouns include: *poet, concert, surface, tomatoes*, and *smoke.* Conceptual nouns include: *loyalty, popularity, achievement, anger, afterthought, justification*, and *neatness.*

Example:
Teachers expect more attractive ***children*** to perform well, leading to more ***attention***, less ***punishment***, and better ***grades***.

Pronouns replace nouns or other pronouns in order to make sentences less cumbersome and repetitive.

Personal pronouns refer to specific persons or things. These are *I, me, you, he, him, she, her, it, we, us, they,* and *them.*

Possessive pronouns are *my, mine, your, yours, his, her, hers, its, our, ours, their,* and *theirs.*

Reflexive and **intensive** pronouns are *myself, yourself, himself, herself, itself, ourselves, yourselves,* and *themselves.*

Demonstrative pronouns point out a particular person or thing: *this, these, that, and those.*

Interrogative pronouns are used to ask questions: *who, whom, which, what, and whose.*

Relative pronouns are used to introduce subordinate clauses: *who, whom, whose, which,* and *that.*

Indefinite pronouns refer generally, not specifically, to persons, places, or things. A few examples include: *all, any, anybody, both, each, either, everybody, few, many, neither, none, one, several,* and *somebody.*

Examples:
Somebody once said that ***you*** should look at the world the same way an optimist does, because ***he*** or ***she*** always sees the positive possibilities in any situation.

Some psychologists argue that people often fall in love with ***someone who*** is similar to the parent with ***whom*** they have unresolved childhood issues, unaware ***they*** are seeking to resolve ***this*** childhood relationship in adulthood.

Adjectives modify or describe nouns and pronouns, usually by explaining *what kind, which one,* or *how many*: ***insufferable*** snob, ***eclectic*** style, ***Russian*** students, ***federal*** court, ***only*** one, and ***four*** fouls.
Predicate adjectives are separated from the word it modifies by a verb.

Examples:
The protests have become ***violent.***
The gift was ***extraordinary.***

Nouns can be used as adjectives: ***film*** director, ***cattle*** business, and ***stone*** cutter.

Adverbs modify verbs, adjectives, and other adverbs as well as phrases and clauses. Adverbs answer such questions as *how, when, where, how often*, and *how much*. Also, while some adverbs can be identified by their characteristic "ly" suffix, most of them must be identified by how they are used within a sentence.

Examples:
A police bomb squad in India *carefully* dismantled a 1,000-pound bomb that had been dropped during World War II but *never* exploded. (describes *how* and *when*)

To fly *there regularly* would be *too* expensive. (explains *where, how often*, and *how much*)

Prepositions usually indicate locations in space or time. Prepositions are always part of a prepositional phrase and show the relationship between a noun or a pronoun (the object of a preposition) and another word or group of words in a sentence. For a detailed list of prepositions, see page 9.

Examples:
People (*with* blue eyes) see better (*in* the dark.)
It would take (*over* an hour) (*for* a heavy object) to sink 6.7 miles down (*to* the deepest part) (*of* the ocean).

Conjunctions link words, phrases, and clauses to one another. There are three kinds of conjunctions: *coordinating, correlative,* and *subordinating*. **Coordinating conjunctions** are *for, and, nor, but, or, yet,* and *so*. Some people use the acronym *fanboys* as an aid to remember what these conjunctions are.

Example:
Prince Albert and Queen Victoria were born in the same year *and* delivered by the same midwife, *but* they didn't meet until they were teenagers.

Correlative conjunctions occur in pairs: either . . . or,   neither . . . nor,   both . . . and, not only . . . but (also),   whether . . . or.

Examples:
One business manager said, "If I had an employee spending an hour or more a day surfing the net, I'd *either* be increasing this person's workload, *or* reducing his or her hours."

When the United Kingdom went through its mad cow mess, it had to *not only* safely bury the dead animals, *but also* change its butchering methods.

Subordinating conjunctions connect main (independent) clauses with subordinate (dependent) clauses.

Commonly Used as Subordinating Conjunctions

after	before	than	when
although	how	that	where
as	if	though	wherever
as much as	since	unless	while
because	so that	until	

Examples:

Around 800 babies take part in an annual crying contest in Hiroshima, Japan, **where** some believe **that** children's wailing wards off evil spirits.

Because metal was scarce during World War II, the Oscars during that period were made of wood.

Interjections are words that express emotion and have no grammatical relation to other words in the sentence.

Examples:
Oh, Hey, Wow, Ouch, Well. . .

Identifying Verbs in Sentences

Remember, verbs do one of two things in sentences: they either show action or link a subject to the rest of the sentence.

Action Verbs: These verbs most often show physical action such as *runs, laughed, shouted, sang,* and *danced.* But action verbs can also show mental action. Verbs such as *considered, decided, recognizes, understands, believes,* and *hoped* are just as much action verbs as the more obvious physical action verbs.

Examples:
One-third of Russians **believe** that the sun revolves around the earth.
Cleo **understands** the situation.

Linking Verbs: These verbs link the subject to a noun, a pronoun, or an adjective that describes it. The most common linking verbs are the forms of "be," which are *am, is, are, was, were,* and *been.* The verbs *looks, feels, seem, appear, grows, remain, smells, taste,* and *become* are also frequently used as linking verbs.

Examples:
All of the students **appear** worried about the test.
This cashmere sweater **feels** soft.

Helping Verbs: Sometimes a verb needs the help of one or more other verbs to precisely express the meaning intended. These verbs are called helping verbs.
Study this short list:

be, am, is, are, was, were, been	shall, should	can, could
have, has, had	will, would	must
do, does, did	may, might	ought

The complete verb, including helping verbs, might consist of two, three, or four words.

Examples:
Tony *has* not *been working* very long. (The word *not* is not a verb.)
All gondolas in Venice, Italy, *must be painted* black, unless they belong to high government officials.

Recognize that adverbs are not part of the complete verb:

Common Adverbs:

barely	extremely	quickly	not
carefully	frequently	quite	really
definitely	generally	never	terribly
differently	hardly	no	visibly

Exercise One

Underline the complete verb in the following sentences.

Example:
Centipedes *do* not really *have* 100 legs. (*Not* and *really* are adverbs.)

1. Laughter has definitely been shown to relieve stress and to promote a healthy immune system.

2. Bank of America was originally called Bank of Italy.

3. Paper cannot be recycled more than six times.

4. The air pollution in China has caused school closures and traffic problems.

5. A beautician successfully defended herself from a knife-wielding robber by throwing hot wax into his face.

6. Jehovah's Witnesses do not celebrate Easter, Christmas, or birthdays.

7. Two-thirds of the world's population has never seen snow.

8. Nelson Mandela was not removed from the U.S. terror watch list until 2008.

9. The majority of people can still identify 90% of their classmates thirty-five years after leaving school.

10. One of Mr. Roger's sweaters is often displayed at the National Museum of American History, a part of the Smithsonian Institution.

11. Lafitte's Blacksmith Shop Bar in New Orleans is supposedly haunted by the pirate Jean Lafitte.

12. Black cats are usually considered bad luck in the U.S., but not in Japan.

13. Drivers of government vehicles in Cuba are legally required to pick up hitchhikers.

14. Our memories are actually reconstructed and not terribly accurate.

15. Months that begin on a Sunday will always have a Friday the 13th.

Exercise Two

Underline the complete verb in each of the following sentences.

Example: Research *has shown* the negative effects of artificial sweeteners in diet sodas.

1. Daft Punk's "Get Lucky" from the album *Random Access Memories* has become a best seller in more than 30 countries.

2. Matthew Brady, one of America's earliest photographers, is remembered for his famous Civil War photographs.

3. Earth is traveling through space at 660,000 miles an hour.

4. Silly Putty was created accidentally in 1945 by workers at the General Electric Corporation.

5. In spite of everything, our coach appears confident of victory in tonight's game.

6. Red blood cells are created in a person's bone marrow at the rate of 120 million per minute.

7. Jordan Belfort, the real-life "Wolf of Wall Street," served 22 months in a federal prison.

8. Natalie Portman has been published in two scientific journals.

9. Quotation marks should be used to enclose the exact words of a speaker.

10. Legislation was passed during World War I to make it illegal to say "gesundheit."

11. The poem "OCD" by Neil Hilborn, a National Poetry Slam Champion, has had more than 5 million views on YouTube.

12. "Wild Bill" Cody presented the first Wild West Show in North Platte, Nebraska, as part of a Fourth of July celebration in 1883.

13. Men get hiccups more often than women.

14. *Duck Dynasty* receives more mentions on Facebook than any other TV series.

15. The composer Wolfgang Amadeus Mozart was writing music by the age of five.

Identifying Subjects in Sentences

There are several ways to find subjects in sentences. The best method is to find the verb (action) in a sentence and first ask *who?* of the verb. If that doesn't make any sense, then ask *what?* of the verb.

Examples:

A) The Romans constructed military roads, aqueducts, bridges, and marble buildings.

   The verb is **constructed**. **Who** constructed? The **Romans**, which is the subject of the sentence.

B) Does our vacation include seeing Pike's Peak?

   The verb is **does include**. **What** does include? Our **vacation**, which is the subject. **Recognize that *there, here,* and *where* are sentence starters and not subjects of sentences.**

Examples:

A) There are mysterious stone heads on Easter Island which stand 30 to 40 feet high.

   Heads is the subject of the sentence.

B) Here is the answer to the question.

   Answer is the subject of the sentence.

Another way to find the subject of a question sentence is to rewrite the question in the form of a statement.

Examples:

A) Why does China have only one time zone?
   China does have only one time zone.

   The verb is **does have.** **What** does have? **China**, which is the subject.

Identifying Subjects and Verbs in Sentences

Exercise Three

In each sentence, underline the subject once and the verb twice.

Example: Did you know couples argue about money more than anything else?

Turn the sentence around: You did know couples argue about money more than anything else.

You **is the subject and** *did know* **is the verb.**

1. Mosquitoes have teeth.

2. Did you know that a new skyscraper is built in China every five days?

3. Feelings and emotions are stored in the brain, not the heart.

4. Boring, Oregon, has become a "sister community" with Dull, Scotland.

5. Recycling can reduce household garbage and save resources.

6. North Carolina is nicknamed the Tar Heel state.

7. Shakespeare never attended a college or university.

8. There are no rivers in Saudi Arabia.

9. Each human foot has 26 bones, 32 joints, and a network of more than 100 tendons, ligaments, and muscles.

10. The artist's sketch looked exactly like Joey.

11. Here is the sports section.

12. Lightning strikes the Earth 8.6 million times a day or about 100 times a second.

13. Do you have an extra five dollars?

14. An average human loses nearly two hundred head hairs a day.

15. Justin Timberlake is now more successful as an actor than as a singer.

Identifying Prepositional Phrases

Also recognize that the subject of a sentence cannot be in a prepositional phrase.

Examples:

A) During the prison uprising some guards were held hostage.
   During the prison uprising is a prepositional phrase. The subject of the sentence is ***guards***.

B) Of the five longest rivers in the world, the Nile is the longest.
   (***Of the five longest rivers***) (***in the world***) are two prepositional phrases. The subject is ***Nile***.

Remember that prepositional phrases begin with a preposition and end with a noun or pronoun. Review the most commonly used prepositions:

about	by	down	of	throughout
at	before	during	off	to
above	behind	for	on	toward
across	below	from	onto	under
after	beneath	in	out	until
against	beside	inside	outside	up
along	between	into	over	upon
among	beyond	like	since	with
around	concerning	near	through	without
				within

The prepositions that students most often fail to recognize as prepositions are *with, within,* and *without*.

These are also common compound prepositions:

according to	**because of**	**in spite of**
across from	**far from**	**instead of**
along with	**in front of**	**on account of**
aside from	**in place of**	**on top of**

Don't confuse a prepositional phrase with an infinitive, which is *to* plus a verb.
Examples: to get, to plan, to run, to follow, to see, etc.

Exercise Four

Put parentheses around each prepositional phrase in the following sentences. The number in parentheses is the number of prepositional phrases in each sentence.

Example: Each (of the contestants) was asked a different question.

1. All business signs in the province of Quebec, Canada, must be written in French. (3)

2. The first automated teller machine was installed by the Chemical Bank at Rockville Center, Long Island, in January 1969. (3)

3. All pilots on international flights identify themselves in English. (2)

4. Both men and women prefer an attractive face over an attractive body for a long-term mate. (2)

5. During a sunstroke body temperature is abnormally high. (1)

6. Anne Boleyn, the second wife of Henry VIII, was born with six fingers on her right hand. (3)

7. Bill Gates said, "By 2018 an estimated 63 percent of all new jobs will require workers with an education beyond high school." (4)

8. The Pan-American Highway, the longest highway in the world, starts in northwest Alaska and stretches all the way to Chile. (3)

9. In many North African countries, children ride to school on donkeys. (3)

10. *The Great Gatsby* by F. Scott Fitzgerald is considered one of the top 100 American novels of the 20th century. (3)

11. Between 1895 and 1905 the millionaire Andrew Carnegie spent 25 million dollars on fossil collecting trips. (2)

12. Ancient Egyptian women painted black eye makeup around their eyes both for beauty and to reduce the glare of the sun. (3)

13. People born under the sign of the dog in Chinese astrology are considered to be loyal and discreet, although slightly temperamental. (3)

14. Throughout Europe, people eat with the fork in the left hand and the knife in the right. (4)

15. The first live, televised presidential news conference occurred on January 25, 1961, when President John F. Kennedy answered 31 questions in 38 minutes. (2)

Exercise Five

Put parentheses around each prepositional phrase in the following sentences. The number in parentheses is the number of prepositional phrases in each sentence.

1. In Turkey the color of mourning is violet. (2)

2. The Sky Dome's Hard Rock Café in Toronto, Ontario, is the home of the largest electric guitar in North America. (3)

3. One of the best values at a warehouse club is orange juice. (2)

4. According to the Commerce Department, nearly one third of the U.S. economy is affected in one way or another by the weather. (4)

5. In China the death penalty can be given for 68 different crimes including bigamy, Internet hacking, stealing gasoline, and tax evasion. (2)

6. Most varieties of snakes can go a year without eating a single morsel of food. (3)

7. In California it is illegal for anyone to shoot at any kind of game from a moving vehicle unless the target is a whale. (5)

8. The footprints of astronauts who landed on the moon could last 10 million years because the moon has no atmosphere. (2)

9. The band UB 40 got its name from an unemployment form in England. (2)

10. Chop suey was created by a Chinese cook who worked in a California mining camp in the 1800s. (3)

11. Owners of monkeys in Indonesia must have an identity card for the animal, complete with a photo of the monkey. (5)

12. The number of people alive on earth right now is higher than the number of all the people who have died. (3)

13. The roar of a lion can be heard from five miles away. (2)

14. The Gulf Stream could carry a message in a bottle at an average of four miles an hour. (3)

15. Dry breakfast cereal was invented by John Henry Kellogg at the beginning of the 20th century. (3)

Subject-Verb Agreement with Intervening Phrases

Singular subjects must have singular verbs and plural subjects must have plural verbs. It's that simple. Remember that singular verbs often end in *s* and plural verbs do not.

Keep your eye on the subject!

The subject and verb must always agree in number, whether or not phrases come between them. Even expressions such as *along with*, *in addition to*, *as well as*, *together with*, *including*, and *no less than* do not make an otherwise singular subject plural.

Examples: (Intervening phrases are italicized)

1. a) One **is** my brother.
   b) One ***of the boys in the third row of the bleachers* is** my brother.

2. a) Every worker **is** present.
   b) Every worker ***on the assembly line* is** present for the union vote.

3. a) *Christina's World* **was** selected for the Andrew Wyeth exhibition.
   b) *Christina's World*, ***along with several of the Helga paintings***, **was** selected for the Andrew Wyeth exhibition.

To help avoid confusion, put parentheses around any phrases or expressions that come between the subject and the verb, and read the sentence *without* the phrase or expression.

Examples:

Sentence: Each (of the girls) has/have finished her assigned work.

Solution: Each **has** finished her assigned work.

Sentence: One (of the supposed sightings) (of the Abominable Snowman) was/were actually reported by a blind couple.

Solution: One **was** reported by a blind couple.

Sentence: Each (of the parallel sides) (of a trapezoid) is/are called a base.

Solution: Each **is** called a base.

Exercise Six

Enclose in parentheses *all prepositional phrases* and phrases that begin with *along with, together with, in addition to, as well as, including,* and *no less than* in each sentence. Then read the sentence *without the phrases.* Underline the subject once in each sentence and circle the correct verb.

Example:

Sentence: The mysterious Stonehenge in England as well as the Bermuda Triangle almost always **excites/excite** people's curiosity.

Solution: The mysterious Stonehenge (in England) (as well as the Bermuda Triangle) almost always ***excites*** people's curiosity.

1. The tractor-trailer with a full load **was/were** overturned on the freeway.

2. The paintings from Picasso's famous "Blue Period" **is/are** called that because of the mood of the paintings, not because of their color.

3. A large group of people **makes/make** poorer and more emotional decisions than a small group or a single individual.

4. Each of the ten most venomous snake species in the world **lives/live** in Australia.

5. One of the Puritans' two ships **was/were** severely damaged.

6. The computer model for weather forecasts **predicts/predict** a 60 percent chance of rain for both Saturday and Sunday.

7. The movements of the plankton **was/were** studied by a group of scientists.

8. Elizabeth Cady Stanton, one of the most famous feminist leaders of the nineteenth century, **is/are** now almost unknown.

9. Josh Berry, together with his brother Jeff, **was/were** responsible for the research which revealed that women rate a man more attractive if other women are smiling at him.

10. One of my friends **was/were** convinced the e-mail from the Nigerian man was a genuine big money opportunity.

11. Deforestation in Sudan, Zambia, and Tanzania **makes/make** a significant contribution to global greenhouse gasses.

12. The style of Greek and Roman statues **is/are** similar, and for many people they are not easy to tell apart.

13. Sigmund Freud, together with his daughter Mathilde Hollitscher, **is/are** responsible for some of psychiatry's most important writings.

14. Mexican drug lord Joaquin Guzman, along with his beauty queen wife Emma Coronel, **was/were** captured in the Mexican beach resort town of Mazatlán.

15. The earliest surviving examples of Chinese printing **was/were** produced in the second century A.D.

16. A pound of any combination of dimes, quarters, and half dollars **is/are** worth $20.

17. The most common time for romantic breakups **is/are** around three to five months.

18. The woman in 75% of American households **manages/manage** the money and household accounts.

19. A study from researchers at the University of Michigan **reveals/reveal** that the more time people spend browsing their Facebook feed, the worse they feel.

20. Early reports of Einstein's Theory of General Relativity **was/were** covered in the *New York Times* by its golfing correspondent.

Subject-Verb Agreement with Compound Subjects

Study compound subjects carefully.

Two singular subjects joined by *or* or *nor* require a singular verb.
Two or more singular subjects joined by *and* require a plural verb.

Examples:
Paul or Holly *is* usually quick to volunteer.
Paul and Holly *are* usually quick to volunteer.

In a sentence with both a singular and a plural subject joined by *or* or *nor*, make the verb agree with the subject closer to it.

Examples:
Neither the defendants nor the lawyer *is* going to talk to the press.
Neither the defendant nor the lawyers *are* going to talk to the press.

Subject-Verb Agreement with Indefinite Pronouns

The indefinite pronouns *anybody, anyone, each, either, none, neither, somebody, someone, everyone*, and *everybody* are singular and require a singular verb.

Both and *some* are plural and require plural verbs.

Examples:
Either stupidity or stubbornness *is* Joel's most outstanding characteristic.
Both stupidity and stubbornness *are* Joel's most outstanding characteristics.

Exercise Seven

Draw a line through *all prepositional phrases* and phrases that begin with *along with, together with, in addition to, as well as, including,* and *no less than* in each sentence. Then read the sentence *without the phrases.* Underline the subject once in each sentence and circle the correct verb.

1. Neither the players nor the coach **was/were** willing to talk about the unexpected defeat.

2. Either of the digital cameras **is/are** a good choice because they are both highly rated by *Consumer Reports.*

3. Everybody in the bleachers **was/were** wondering what happened.

4. The National Rifle Association and the National Association of Retired Persons **is/are** very influential in Congress.

5. When I worked there, everyone who edited or proofread business communications **was/were** required to suggest at least two changes per page.

6. The exact date and time of the annual stockholders' meeting **has/have** not been decided.

7. Mandarin Chinese followed by Hindustani **is/are** the most widely spoken language in the world.

8. A rain of ashes from the eruption of Mt. Vesuvius on August 24, 79 A.D., **was/were** responsible for the destruction of Pompeii and Herculaneum.

9. Either the professor or her students **deserves/deserve** credit for the theory that people dream about tasks and emotions that they didn't take care of during the day.

10. Neither of the diplomats from Kenya **was/were** present at the ceremony.

11. The traces of copper on a turquoise gemstone **is/are** what produces its distinctive color.

12. One out of every six draftees during World War II **was/were** disqualified due to mental illness.

13. Loneliness and a lack of social connections **has/have** been known to shorten a person's lifespan as much as smoking.

14. Crime, disease, and average walking speed **increase/increases** by 15% as a city doubles in size.

15. A positive attitude and a sense of humor **is/are** important.

16. Neither Marcus nor Noah **earns/earn** enough money to pay for car insurance.

17. During a physicians' strike in Los Angeles, all elective, non-emergency surgery and medical attention **was/were** cancelled.

18. Every student taking freshman English **is/are** required to write a research paper.

19. Management at many retail stores **knows/know** how much time customers are spending at various spots within stores by using customer-tracking technology.

20. Swarms of deadly hornets measuring nearly 2 inches long **has/have** killed more than 40 people and injured an additional 1,600 people in northern China.

Subject-Verb Agreement with Money, Weights, and Time

Use a singular verb with words stating amounts of money, weights, measurements, and periods of time, when you want to express the idea that these items form a single unit.

Example:
Four minutes is usually all it takes to decide whether you like someone or not.

When you want these expressions to mean several separate items, use plural verbs.

Example:
Two weeks *are* required to get the results back.

Subject-Verb Agreement with *Some, Any, All,* and *Most*

The words *some, any, all,* and *most* may be either singular or plural, depending on the noun or pronoun they refer to. If they refer to a singular noun, they are singular, and if they refer to a plural noun, they are plural. Fortunately this is not a real-world problem. Nearly everyone automatically uses correct subject-verb agreement in these cases.

Examples:

All of the ice *is* in the chest.
All of the tickets *are* sold.

Some of the money *has* been lost.
Some of the apartments *have* been rented.

Subject-Verb Agreement with Fractions

Sometimes confusion does arise when written-out fractions are the subjects of sentences. Again, if they refer to a singular noun they are singular, and if they refer to a plural noun they are plural.

Examples:

One quarter of the advertising space *is* sold.
One quarter of all web transactions *are* abandoned at the payment screen.

Subject-Verb Agreement with Titles

Use a singular verb with the title of a poem, book, play, or movie, even though the words in the title may be plural.

Example:
Vampire Diaries *was* first a novel, and later it became a popular TV show on the CW network.

Subject-Verb Agreement in Turned-Around Sentences

In turned-around sentences where the subject comes after the verb, especially when the verb is part of a contraction, be especially careful to make sure the subject and verb agree.

Examples:
There *are* lots of chances to win. (Not: There's lots of chances to win.)
Where *are* your seats? (Not: Where's your seats?)

Chapter Review One

Enclose in parentheses *all prepositional phrases* and phrases that begin with *along with, as well as, together with, in addition to, including,* and *no less than* in each sentence. Then read the sentence *without the phrases.* Underline the subject once and circle the correct verb.

Example:
Sentence: In the jungle, one out of every four lion cubs **starves/starve** to death.
Solution: (In the jungle,) <u>one</u> (out of every four lion cubs) <u>starves</u> to death.

1. Not one of the President's closest advisors **was/were** willing to tell him he was making a mistake.

2. Neither of us **wants/want** to believe that Minneapolis has a law that anyone who double parks a car will be put on a chain gang with only bread and water to eat.

3. The Consumer Price Index, as well as the Gross National Product and the unemployment rate, **indicates/indicate** trends in the economy.

4. **There's/There are** about 1500 volcanoes on land and 10,000 at sea.

5. Her credit card bill stated that forty dollars **was/were** still past due on her account.

6. **Here's/Here are** some menus for you.

7. Either of these streets **is/are** a quicker route than taking Haywood.

8. Orville Wright, along with his brother Wilber, **was/were** responsible for the first powered airplane flight in history on December 17, 1903, at Kitty Hawk, North Carolina.

9. Oxygen, carbon, hydrogen, and nitrogen **makes/make** up 90% of the human body.

10. **There's/There are** some classrooms on the African continent where 20 children share one textbook.

11. The Ad Council, together with America's Second Harvest, **is/are** educating Americans about the 13 million children who sometimes don't get enough to eat.

12. **Where's/Where are** your passport and credit cards?

13. Water, electricity, and gas **has/have** been free to the residents of Turkmenistan since 1991.

14. One of President Calvin Coolidge's favorite practical jokes **was/were** to press all the call buttons on his desk and then hide behind his door.

15. Each of these commas **needs/need** to be removed.

Chapter Review Two

Enclose in parentheses *all prepositional phrases* and phrases that begin with *along with, together with, in addition to, as well as, including,* and *no less than* in each sentence. Then read the sentence *without the phrases.* Underline the subject once and circle the correct verb.

Example:
Sentence: Each of the passengers **was/were** required to participate in the evacuation drill.
Solution: <u>Each</u> (of the passengers) <u>**was**</u> required to participate in the evacuation drill.

1. Flavored milk, including chocolate milk, **has/have** more calories than soft drinks.

2. One of the most persistent beliefs from the ancient Romans onward **is/are** that the number 13 is unlucky and perhaps dangerous.

3. Overweight children with high cholesterol or high blood pressure **is/are** much more likely than children with normal readings to have heart disease or strokes by their 30's or 40's.

4. According to historians, one third of the cowboys in the early American West **was/were** African-American.

5. In Finland long periods of silence in a business meeting **is/are** common.

6. Former National Security Agency contractor Edward Snowden says neither Russia nor China **has/have** had access to the sensitive documents he took from the spy agency.

7. Certain parts of the very expensive Japanese puffer fish **contains/contain** a powerful nerve poison that can kill people who accidentally eat it.

8. Though Christina Aguilera is of Ecuadorian descent and recorded an album in Spanish, she **doesn't/don't** speak the language.

9. Each of the soldiers in Genghis Khan's army **was/were** made into an executioner after every battle.

10. One of the girls on the top row of the bleachers **was/were** using binoculars to see her boyfriend on the football field more clearly.

11. The most common name for the fear of open spaces **is/are** agoraphobia.

12. Each of these coats of arms **has/have** a unique combination of colors and symbols.

13. The most frequent complaint of working people **is/are** noisy co-workers.

14. Neither of the dragons in this story **seems/seem** really scary.

15. Either the subway system of Tokyo or Moscow **carries/carry** the greatest number of passengers per year.

Chapter Review Three

Draw a line through *all prepositional phrases* and phrases that begin with *along with, together with, in addition to, as well as, including,* and *no less than* in each sentence. Then read the sentence *without the phrases.* Underline the subject once and circle the correct verb.

1. The fingerprints of a koala bear **is/are** similar in pattern, size, and shape to the fingerprints of a human.

2. The report about conditions in China's factories **was/were** controversial.

3. The most important job of English teachers **is/are** to insist students learn how to function in the real world.

4. One of the most unusual customs in Greece **is/are** that children toss their baby teeth onto the roof of their home to bring good luck and a healthy replacement tooth.

5. In one of the stalls at the Farmers' Market, one of the vendors **was/were** selling puppies along with the usual fruits and vegetables.

6. In the Caribbean one out of every ten boats **is/are** supposedly operated by pirates.

7. Every one of your subject-verb errors **is/are** easy to correct.

8. Either Megan or Rachel **is/are** going to drive us there.

9. One of three men in Britain of Bangladeshi origin **work/works** as a waiter.

10. Research on monkeys, dogs, and humans **has/have** proved that if one yawns, so do those around them.

11. Neither of the conspiracy theories about the death of Princess Diana **seems/seem** likely to me.

12. Miss Tennessee, along with her chaperone, **is/are** traveling to Atlantic City for the Miss America contest.

13. The nutritional value of squash and pumpkin seeds **improves/improve** as they age.

14. A working person today faced with the difficult housing market as well as the lack of pension plans, **needs/need** to exercise good financial judgment.

15. **There's/There are** experts who believe that although a person's mood levels and well-being are partially determined by factors like genetics and upbringing, roughly 40 percent of happiness is under a person's own control.

Chapter Review Four

Draw a line through *all prepositional phrases*. Then read the sentence *without the phrases*, underlining the subject once and circling the correct verb.

Example:

Sentence: The range and number of instruments in a modern orchestra **varies/vary** widely.

Solution: The <u>range and number</u> (of instruments) (in a modern orchestra) **vary** widely.

1. Only one of the Seven Wonders of the Ancient World still **survives/survive**.

2. Some houses in the countryside of Nepal **is/are** made of cow dung, mud, sand, and clay.

3. The quality of our relationships **is/are** determined by the depth and honesty of our conversations within them.

4. Each of the coin tosses **has/have** landed on tails.

5. Research shows that brains of healthy but physically inactive people who exercise 45 to 60 minutes three times a week **increases/increase** in size.

6. **Here's/Here are** one of the best definitions of semi-annual: twice a year, every six months.

7. One in every four Americans **has/have** appeared on television at least once.

8. In the picture, the size of his hands **looks/look** enormous.

9. According to United Nations' officials, the spread of deadly superbugs that evade the most powerful antibiotics **is/are** no longer just a prediction.

10. The demand for oil and natural gas **is/are** constantly increasing.

11. From Rio de Janeiro, Brazil, to London, England, each of the best attended rock concerts **has/have** taken place outside the United States.

12. Neither of these paths **lead/leads** directly to the beach.

13. The flight attendant, along with the passengers, **was/were** calm during the emergency evacuation.

14. The number of nuclear warheads held by various countries **is/are** estimated to be 27,600.

15. Each of the Seven Wonders of the Modern World **was/were** built during the 20th century.

Chapter Review Five

Correct each of the following sentences. One sentence is already correct.

Sentence: Truckloads of merchandise arrives at the outlet center each week.
Solution: Truckloads (of merchandise) **arrive** at the outlet center each week.

1. Either of the high definition television sets is a good choice because they both have excellent customer satisfaction records.

2. One of these hot dogs are all that I can eat.

3. There's more rain forests in Brazil than in any other country.

4. Neither Jenny nor Marcus were impressed by the fact that most doctors consider ice cream, artificially colored foods, and cold cuts extremely unhealthy.

5. At one time in 1964, every one of the top five singles on the Billboard chart were by the Beatles.

6. Each of the correct answers are worth five points.

7. Here's the results of the study which shows that homicide rates rise during a full moon and fall as the moon wanes.

8. One of the earliest streetcars in San Francisco were made to resemble a horse, so that actual horses wouldn't be afraid of it.

9. Each of us were surprised to learn that Americans owe $1 trillion in student loan debt, even more than they owe in credit card debt.

10. A friendly smile and a firm handshake was working well for Eric.

11. About 13,000 years ago, an entire "zoo" of animals, including wooly mammoths and giant sloths, were suddenly rendered extinct, probably by an asteroid.

12. Corporations that display corporate social responsibility is particularly appealing to younger employees.

13. Every one of the items in a dollar store sell for one dollar or less.

14. The carpenter, along with his assistant, expect to be working here all week.

15.   A good attitude in an interview and an excellent resumé is needed to get the job you want.

Final Chapter Review

Correct each of the following sentences. One sentence is already correct.

1. Someone, either a utility worker or a local resident, have turned in an alarm about the natural gas leak.

2. The roach races at the annual "Bug Fest" at the Academy of Natural Sciences in Philadelphia is worth seeing.

3. Neither of the theories about cosmic rays make sense to me.

4. Abigail, along with her sister, is taking a pledge to stick to a vegetarian diet for 30 days.

5. The head of the department and one of her employees has come up with some new ideas for the company.

6. One out of four second opinions by doctors fail to confirm the first doctor's opinion.

7. The one million inhabitants of the Chinese city of Zhuji makes 8 billion pairs of socks a year—35% of the total worldwide sock production.

8. Where are my stack of books?

9. Every one of the Russians interviewed believe "it is a great misfortune that the Soviet Union no longer exists."

10. Matt's brother or sister attend every game.

11. Either fog or ice or snow make driving dangerous.

12. A mass of lava and ashes were responsible for burying Pompeii in A.D. 79.

13. Despite economic uncertainty, political unrest, and natural disasters, there's lots of reasons to believe that in today's world the good outweighs the bad.

14. Either an epidemic, a lack of water, or fear of enemies were what caused some ancient cities to disappear.

15. The simplest of all the possible writing systems use pictures or pictograms.

Common Errors
(Errors that drive educated people crazy)

Their, There, They're

Their **is possessive. It states a relationship.**

Examples:

It was ***their*** idea.

Their allergies are making them miserable.

There **is either a sentence starter or a place.**

Examples:

There was no access road to the lighthouse.

An alligator is over **there** on the bank of the lake.

They're **is a contraction of** *they are.*

Examples:

They're thinking about visiting the Grand Canyon.

They're both going to get Lasik surgery.

Its, It's

Its **is possessive.**

Examples:

A frightened bear cub got ***its*** head stuck in an oversized cookie jar and had to be tranquilized so that firefighters could gingerly cut the jar off the bear's head.

Its chemicals get broken down by heat.

It's **is a contraction of it is.**

Examples:

It's physically impossible for a pig to look up at the sky.

It's true that the planet Venus was named after the Roman goddess of love.

Your, You're

Your **is possessive.**

Examples:

Your credit card payment is overdue.

Your phone number is hard for me to remember.

You're **is a contraction of** ***you are.***

Examples:

When you wish upon a star, ***you're*** a few million light years late, because that star is dead.

You're foolish to pay such a high interest rate when you could apply for a lower one.

Whose, Who's

Whose **is possessive**

Examples:

Whose side are you on?

A researcher discovered that people ***whose*** brains were exposed to cell phone radiation not only slept less, but also didn't reach a state of deep sleep.

Who's **is a contraction of** *who is.*

Examples:

Who's going to pay for the gas to get there?

Who's aware that Tokyo has the world's largest bowling alley?

Exercise One

Circle the correct word choice.

1. Car buyers now have **there/their** choice of gas, diesel, or hybrid engines.

2. Jennifer Aniston, **who's/whose** real name is Jennifer Anastassakis, established a successful movie career after starring on *Friends.*

3. **There/Their** is strong evidence that people who have dark colored cats are more likely to develop allergies than people who have light colored cats.

4. **Who's/Whose** going with me to Starbucks?

5. **Your/You're** belief that a poinsettia plant could kill a pet is untrue, but fresh lilies could be lethal.

6. Jerome, **who's/whose** mother is French, can speak English and French fluently.

7. This gum has lost **its/it's** flavor.

8. Robert Frost wrote in a poem, "**Who's/Whose** woods these are I think I know."

9. Samantha said, "As an outsider, what's **your/you're** opinion of the human race?"

10. The war in which more Americans lost **their/there** lives than any other was the Civil War, which is estimated to have cost 920,000 lives.

11. The ad asked, "Do glasses or contacts rule **your/you're** life?"

12. **Its/It's** a simple system to upload your photo images.

13. The bank has increased **its/it's** lending to minority businesses.

14. **Who's/Whose** aware that keeping a romantic relationship secret intensifies feelings for one another?

15. Sixty percent of all U.S. professional athletes have filed for bankruptcy five years after retiring, regardless of how much money they made in **there/their** careers.

Exercise Two

Study the definitions for *their, there, they're, its, it's, your,* and *you're* and write 2 sentences for each, and write 3 sentences each for *who's* and *whose*. (Total: 20 sentences.)

Exercise Three

Circle the correct word choice.

1. Both meditation and aerobic exercise can sharpen **your/you're** memory.

2. Border collies are prized by dog owners for **their/there/they're** intelligence.

3. **Its/It's** possible to prevent an infection by putting a dab of honey on a cut before applying a bandage.

4. Most people text faster when **their/there/they're** texting someone they like.

5. The National Guard spent $26.5 million to sponsor NASCAR racing to bolster its marketing and recruitment but failed to sign a single new soldier to **its/it's** ranks.

6. British politician John Montagu, **who's/whose** official title was the Earl of Sandwich, is credited with naming the sandwich.

7. The company's sales of **its/it's** Nintendo games have remained remarkably steady.

8. If everyone in the world washed **their/there/they're** hands properly, a million lives a year could be saved.

9. Aztec emperor Montezuma had a nephew, Cuitlahac, **who's/whose** name meant "plenty of excitement."

10. **There/Their/They're** are various explanations for how Stonehenge, a huge ring of stones set in place 4,000 years ago in southern England, came to be.

11. The company said **their/there/they're** not dumping chemicals in the river.

12. **Who's/Whose** going to introduce the speaker?

13. The rarest of all tigers is the South China tiger, and **its/it's** population is down to only 23-30 in the wild.

14. If **your/you're** listening to the news while you try to answer e-mail, you may not be doing either very well.

15. **Its/It's** true that video games can actually be good for your brain because they can improve your ability to focus.

Good/Well

Good **is always an adjective used to modify a noun.**

Examples:

Seeing a *good* book made into a movie is often a disappointment.

I think I made a *good* impression on the interviewer.

Well **is usually an adverb.**

Example:

The lawyers argued their case *well*.

Occasionally *well* is used as an adjective to refer to health.

Example:

I am feeling *well*. (It's also correct to say, "I am feeling good.")

To/Too

To **is generally used to express direction, aim, or purpose.**

Examples:

Bees are attracted *to* dark colors.

Researchers have noted that mothers sometimes give more attention *to* their most attractive children.

Too **means also, in addition, more, extremely, or very.**

Examples:

When Julius Caesar was captured by pirates, he insisted they raise his ransom because he felt it was *too* low.

I think so *too*.

Exercise Four

Circle the correct word choice.

1. It was Philip Stanhope, a British statesman and man of letters who first said, "Whatever is worth doing at all is worth doing **good/well."**

2. Economists stated that it's **to/too** late for China to stop its inflation in the near future because of its recent monetary policy and fiscal stimulus.

3. A workaholic may not feel **good/well** about leisure.

4. George Clooney sometimes sleeps in the walk-in closet of his LA mansion because, he says, "The bedrooms are **to/too** light."

5. According to Christopher Marley three ingredients for a **good/well** life are learning, earning, and yearning.

6. I'll do it, even though I don't want **to/too**.

7. Mark Zuckerberg, the founder of Facebook, chose the color blue for the Facebook website because he is colorblind, and blue is one of the few colors he can see **good/well**.

8. In an attempt to make Americans feel **good/well** about their country in the depths of the Depression, President Franklin D. Roosevelt said, "The only thing we have to fear is fear itself."

9. Shakira was banned from her school choir because her music teacher didn't think she could sing **good/well**.

10. After being very sick with pleurisy, my aunt is now **good/well**.

11. The ice skater executed her difficult spin very **good/well**.

12. Morocco was the first country **to/too** officially recognize the United States in 1789.

13. Michael plays computer games really **good/well**, but he's not good at making friends.

14. During World War II, U.S. Army soldiers used lace curtains to camouflage their helmets as they marched through the snow in Luxembourg, and it worked really **good/well**.

15. Ryan kept telling Amir he was driving **to/too** fast.

Exercise Five

Study the definitions of *good* and *well* and write 5 sentences for each.

Should of, would of, could of, must of, might of, may of, etc.

Don't misuse:

should of for *should've*
would of for *would've*
could of for *could've*
must of for *must've*
might of for *might've*

Remember:
Should've is a contraction of **should have.**
Would've is a contraction of **would have.**
Could've is a contraction of **could have.**
Must've is a contraction of **must have.**
Might've is a contraction of **might have.**
May've is a contraction of **may have.**

Alot, Alright

'Alot' and 'alright' are words that don't exist in standard English. **A lot** should always be written as two words, and this usage is informal and shouldn't be used in formal English.

Alright should always be written as **all right.**

Incorrect: Laurie has alot of friends.
Correct: Laurie has **a lot** of friends.
Better: Laurie has **many** friends.

Incorrect: If it's alright with you, I'd like to borrow your notes.
Correct: If it's **all right** with you, I'd like to borrow your notes.

Them, Those, These

Don't use 'them' as an adjective. Use **these** or **those.**

Incorrect: Please bring me one of them muffins.
Correct: Please bring me one of **those** muffins.

Exercise Six

Correct the errors in each of the following sentences.

1. That word is alright, but if you had used a thesaurus, you could have found a better one. *[all right]*

2. The Industrial Revolution, which for the first time mass-produced goods by machine, brought about alot of changes in the way people lived.

3. Alot of times I've noticed that it is hardest of all to forgive the people we love the most. *[a lot]*

4. I would of never guessed it, but recent research has shown that men and women gossip equally. *[have]*

5. It takes them plastic containers fifty thousand years to start decomposing.

6. Karen should of known that Nelson Mandela was South Africa's first black prime minister. *[those]*

7. Alot of people think that Key West, Florida, is the southernmost piece of land in the U.S., but South Cape on the island of Hawaii is actually farther south. *[a lot]*

8. I didn't know alot of prospectors had a hard time supporting themselves in the 1850s during the California Gold Rush. *[a lot]*

9. I think I could of guessed that there are 10,000 times more photographs on Facebook than in the U.S. Library of Congress. *[have]*

10. It's amazing that Egyptians slept on them stone pillows. *[those] [have]*

11. In Washington state it's illegal to walk around in public if your suffering from the common cold.

12. Its surprising that over half of all single people in America have not had a date in over two years.

13. Each of them snow crystals is unique. *[those]*

14. I must of forgotten that each state has two senators, but the number of representatives depends on the population of the state. *[have]*

15. Gorillas often show they are nervous by beating there chests. *[their]*

Improve Your Spelling

Become familiar with the major spelling rules.

> **Use *i* before *e* except after c, when the sound is long *e*.**
>
> **Examples:**
> believe, niece, relieve

> **Use *e* before *i* *after c,* *or* when the sound is not long *e*.**
>
> **Examples:**
> neighbor, weigh, receipt

> **When adding the suffix –ly or –ness, do not change the spelling of the original word.**
>
> **Example:**
> usual + ly = usually

> **Generally drop the final silent *e* before a suffix beginning with a vowel:**
>
> **Examples:**
> arrive + -al = arrival
> dine + -ing = dining

> **Change the final *y* to *i* before a suffix unless the suffix begins with *i*.**
>
> **Examples:**
> happy = happiness
> funny=funnier

Chapter Review One

Correct each of the following sentences.

1. Laura would of been here earlier if the gas gauge on her car had been working.

2. Hallie visited their and especially enjoyed seeing Graceland, the home of Elvis Presley.

3. Fish oil capsules, noted for there role in protecting heart health, can also improve a person's mood.

4. I need one of them paper clips.

5. The Mongol emperor Genghis Khan, who's original name was Temuji, started out as a goat herder.

6. It's alright to eat armadillos because Native Americans once hunted them for food.

7. Hooch, a young hound mix, swallowed a mixture of nails, screws, and staples from a building project, but he is doing good after surgery.

8. Its true that President Jimmy Carter once sent a jacket to the dry cleaners with the nuclear detonation codes still in the pocket.

9. Researchers in Scotland found that when women left voicemail messages for men they found attractive, there voices shot up in pitch.

10. Marco Polo, the author of *Travels of Marco Polo*, gave 14th century Europeans there first accurate information about China and Asia.

11. In Venezuela if you are invited to someone's home for a meal, it's recommended that you arrive 10-15 minutes later than the requested time because if you arrive on time you are viewed as being to eager.

12. We should of read the directions before we started.

13. Them performers at the Hampton Jazz Festival are some of the best in the country.

14. Whose aware that New Zealand was the first country to grant women the right to vote?

15. Bicyclist Mack Temple of Pendleton, Oregon, discovered he was riding to close to a hawk's nest when a male hawk dive-bombed his helmet so hard it felt "like getting hit with a baseball bat."

Chapter Review Two

Correct each of the following sentences.

1. Its good that midsized cars produced today generate only about 5% of the pollution generated by cars of fifty years ago.

2. You should of known that at the time of his death in 1980, John Lennon was one of the most famous men in the world.

3. At repairpal.com your able to find out what typical car repairs should cost, based on car make, model year, and ZIP code.

4. There discovery was that men in love are more willing to take unnecessary risks to impress a romantic partner.

5. During the discussion there were alot of comments about the fact that more than half of the world's population is under 25 and bilingual.

6. Whose going to believe that before beginning his movie career Keanu Reeves managed a pasta shop in Toronto, Canada?

7. Listening to music works good in reducing chronic pain, and it can also help lessen depression.

8. Students at West Linn High School in Santa Barbara, California, hired a mariachi band to follow there principal around the school for an hour.

9. We saw them totem poles in Seattle.

10. In 1908 the Grand Canyon changed it's status from game preserve to national monument, and in 1919 it became a national park.

11. The London Underground has made more money from it's famous map than it ever has from running trains.

12. The driver was alright after the accident, but the car was badly damaged.

13. Warren can't see good without his glasses.

14. He should of known that polar bears can run 25 miles an hour.

15. Buffalo were brought to Italy in the 7th century, and cheese made from there milk began appearing around the 1300s.

Chapter Review Three

Correct each of the following sentences.

1. Some people believe that their [*there*] was a city and island of Atlantis, perhaps in the Mediterranean Sea, that was destroyed by an earthquake and flooding 12,000 years ago.

2. A chimpanzee showed it's [*its*] killer instinct as it hunted smaller monkeys.

3. Allison shouted, "Your [*You're*] it!"

4. I should of [*should've*] known that men have a much easier time burning fat than women.

5. In the contiguous United States (excluding Alaska and Hawaii) their [*there*] are 1,654 landfill sites.

6. Most observers believe Russia is striving to modernize it's [*its*] military.

7. It's alright if you don't believe me, but a man who was lost in the woods chopped down some power lines so that workers would have to come and rescue him.

8. Learn how to protect you're [*your*] home computer from viruses.

9. Jacob did really good in memorizing the Gettysburg Address.

10. I could of [*couldn't've*] never guessed that the people of India speak nearly a thousand different languages.

11. We're studying a whose who [*who's who*] of warriors: Amazons, Vandals, Vikings, Conquistadors, and Cossacks.

12. Hotel guests complained that there [*they're*] were to [*too*] few elevators for the number of rooms in the hotel.

13. According to New York law, couples cannot [*can't*] dissolve a marriage on grounds of irreconcilable differences, unless there [*they're*] both in agreement about it.

14. The article explains how to eat good for less money.

15. I would of [*would've*] never guessed that 50 milligrams of nicotine would kill an adult within minutes.

Final Chapter Review

Correct each of the following sentences. One sentence is already correct.

1. When a massive star burns out, it collapses on itself, and the resulting densely compacted mass is known as a black hole, because no light can escape its intense gravitational field.

2. The President, who's veto was overridden by both the House and the Senate, said he was disappointed.

3. There are alot of forests cut down every year to obtain lumber or to clear land for farming.

4. Them bright red shoes from *The Wizard of Oz* are famous.

5. Your correct that even Interstate numbers run east-west, while odd Interstate numbers run north-south.

6. You should of seen the look on the chimp's face when she recognized herself in the mirror.

7. The Swiss Guard, who's function is to guard and protect the Pope in Vatican City, was formed in the 15th century.

8. Military dogs are heroes to, since they have saved the lives of thousands of American soldiers.

9. Its illegal for boys in ninth grade to grow a mustache in Binghamton, New York.

10. They're are more than four dozen reigning monarchs in the world today.

11. Alexandre Gustave Eiffel, who's most famous creation was the Eiffel Tower, also designed the inner structure of the Statue of Liberty.

12. Your absolutely right that ostriches can be trained to herd sheep.

13. Its true that North Dakota is the only U.S. state which has never had an earthquake.

14. It's alright if you daydream, since most people daydream about 30% of the time.

15. One of them oil spills killed sea turtles, birds, and fish.

As a final tip, make a list of words that you know you frequently misspell and try to discover why you have trouble with these words. Then practice one word each day to master the correct spelling. Study the following list to see which words might be giving you trouble.

absence	cemetery	existence	license	prejudice
accessible	changeable	extremely	maintenance	restaurant
accommodate	column	February	mischievous	reminisce
acknowledge	commitment	forty	necessary	rhythm
acquaintance	committee	gauge	noticeable	ridiculous
acquire	conscience	ghost	occasion	sergeant
amateur	decision	grammar	occurred	similar
appearance	definitely	humorous	pamphlet	suspicious
arithmetic	develop	hypocrite	parallel	technical
athlete	disastrous	incidentally	particularly	unanimous
athletics	discipline	independence	permissible	undoubtedly
attendance	embarrass	initiate	prairie	vacuum
bureau	entirely	irrelevant	playwright	vengeance
calendar	especially	irresistible	preferred	villain

Pronouns

Pronoun Agreement with Antecedents

Pronouns must agree with their antecedents. (Antecedent means what came before.)

Example:
A reporter saw the **accident** and filed a report about **it**. (The *accident* is the antecedent of *it*.)

A Pronoun Must Agree in Number with its Antecedent.

Singular antecedents must have singular pronouns and plural antecedents must have plural pronouns.

Examples:
A) Beth or Sarah will perform **her** (not their) comedy routine.

B) Frederic Chopin and Franz Liszt had a powerful influence on **their** (not his) generation of composers.

C) In Thailand a person can be fined the equivalent of $600 if **he** or **she** (not they) throws away used gum on the sidewalk.

D) To get a green card, a legal immigrant must prove there are no qualified American citizens suitable for the job that has been offered to **him or her** (not them).

In formal English use singular pronouns to refer to *somebody, everybody, anybody, someone, anyone, everyone, each, either, neither,* **and** *any,* **when used with a singular noun.**

Examples:
A) Body language experts say a person will subconsciously point *his* or *her* (not their) feet toward whomever or whatever is most interesting.

B) Everyone can improve *his* or *her* (not their) driving etiquette.

C) Everybody must bring **his** or **her** (not their) picture I.D. to the airport.

D) A person with low self-esteem is more likely to criticize and put down others in order to make *himself* or *herself* (not themselves) feel better.

E) Neither of the streets has had **its** (not their) potholes filled.

Exercise One

Circle the correct answer in each sentence.

1. One of the scientists demonstrated **her/their** theory that four seconds of awkward silence in a conversation creates a feeling of rejection in a human brain.

2. The average person will spend two weeks during **his or her/their** lifetime waiting for a traffic light to change.

3. According to Match.com 48% of women and 38% of men say they research someone online before they go out with **him or her/them**.

4. During the first summer, each tree should be watered regularly to prevent **it/them** from dying during a long, hot summer.

5. An inventor cannot create new ideas unless **he or she/they** can "think outside the box."

6. An ancient Greek would throw a coin into **his or her/their** well for good luck.

7. To create an instant link with a date, say **his or her/their** name at least twice in a conversation to show attentiveness and connectedness.

8. One of the research scientists stated **his/their** belief that America is now falling behind other technologically advanced countries in bio-medical research.

9. Neither of the girls ate **her/their** popcorn.

10. The Red Cross provides swimming classes and everyone is encouraged to enroll in **it/them**.

11. All parents suppose that **his or her/their** child has wonderful manners.

12. No one at Exxon would permit **himself or herself/themselves** to be quoted by the reporter.

13. The average person will go out on at least 100 dates before **he or she/they** finally (marry, marries).

14. When a person is happy with **his or her/their** accomplishments, there's no need to feel jealous of someone else's success.

15. In Kentucky it is illegal for people to carry an ice cream cone in **his or her/their** pockets.

Exercise Two

Circle the correct answer in each sentence.

1. Every elected representative at the debate defended **his or her/their** voting record.

2. An average smoker fails three or four times before **he or she/they** can successfully stop smoking.

3. To get the job you want, always ask yourself, "What can I give to the employer that would add to **his or her/their** success?"

4. Carmakers are testing devices in **its/their** cars to prevent drunk drivers from operating the vehicles.

5. If a student is serious about a classical music career, **he or she/they** should consider attending the Curtis Institute in Philadelphia.

6. Nearly everyone tends to be more truthful in face-to-face conversations than if **he or she/they** phone(s) or text(s).

7. If an accountant has a busy tax preparation business, **he or she/they** can expect to work many hours of overtime during tax season.

8. In order to see a diamond more clearly, ask a jeweler for **his or her/their** loop to examine the stone under a magnifying glass.

9. Currently the United Nations is troubled by previous financial scandals and tensions among **its/their** 192 member nations.

10. Every day a giant Sequoia tree consumes enormous quantities of water through **its/their** roots.

11. One of the actors on *General Hospital* had a short in **his/their** microphone during the broadcast.

12. It's a waste of energy when people spend all of **his or her/their** free time blogging.

13. In Canada it is illegal for people to remove **his or her/their** bandages in public.

14. For anyone curious about measuring **his or her/their** carbon footprint, check out carbonfootprint.com.

15. According to education experts, using a time-out room in school is effective if it provides space for a child to calm down and reflect on **his or her/their** behavior.

Exercise Three

Correct the pronouns in the following sentences.

1. The insurance company claimed their adjusters were the best trained and fairest in the business.

2. *The Game of Thrones* season one episodes are among its most watched shows.

3. Neither the governor nor the state senator would explain their previous comments about immigration.

4. According to most financial advisors, if a person wins a lottery, they should take the lump sum and invest it.

5. The difference between a vegan and a vegetarian is that a vegan not only eliminates all animal products from their diet, but also dairy products as well.

6. If a driver won't obey traffic rules and speed limits, they will collect a lot of traffic tickets.

7. When a child uses a swimming pool, they must be accompanied by an adult.

8. The car company had to explain their executive compensation plan to members of Congress.

9. Each species of animal has their own personality, with preferences, behaviors, and quirks that persist throughout life.

10. The World Health Organization recommended that every passenger on long air flights exercise their legs to reduce the risk of dangerous blood clots.

Writing tip:
If you are uncomfortable with the "Everyone must pay his or her deposit in the next thirty days" usage, change the antecedent to a plural so that you can use a plural pronoun.

Example:
All travelers must pay their deposits in the next thirty days.

Pronouns Must Also Agree with Their Antecedents in Person.

First person pronouns are *I, my, me, we, our,* and *us.*

Second person pronouns are *you* and *your.*

Third person pronouns are *he, him, she, her, it, they, their,* and *them.*

All nouns (such as *Jenny, the boys,* and *people)* are in the **third person.**

Examples:
Whenever a *person* gets really angry, *he or she* (not you) should count to ten.

If a *person* accidentally swallows poison, *he or she* (not you) should call the poison control.

Exercise Four

Circle the correct pronoun.

1. If a customer experiences rude service in a store, **he or she/you** should notify the store manager.

2. Does anyone want to add **his or her/your** name to the petition that proposes term limits for elected officials?

3. For someone who wants to quit smoking, **he or she/you** should try chewing gum.

4. If a person doesn't know how to properly install a computer, **he or she/you** could call the Geek Squad or Staples' Easy Tech.

5. Amish carpentry is known worldwide for **its/their** fine craftsmanship.

6. A person with a creative mind tends to have a harder time falling asleep at night, and **he or she/they** prefer(s) to stay up late.

7. A "friend" in the Facebook sense represents someone who says things we want to hear, for as long as we wish to hear from **him or her/them**.

8. Unless someone has experience selling on Ebay, **he or she/you** should do some research on how to do it successfully.

9. Applicants are urged to limit **their/your** resumes to just one page.

10. Each of the famous NASCAR drivers thrilled **his/their** fans by posing for pictures and answering questions.

Exercise Five

Circle the correct pronoun choice.

1. When a driver has a fender bender, **he or she/you** should move the car to the shoulder and wait until police arrive.

2. Anyone who visits Luxembourg, Switzerland, or France, should give up **his or her/their** habit of chewing gum in public because this behavior is considered vulgar and highly unattractive.

3. Each country should require **its/their** diplomats to obey New York's parking and traffic laws.

4. If someone wants to make a good impression on a job interview, **he or she/you** should dress conservatively.

5. Neither Tracy nor Lauren liked **her/their** tacos.

6. A person's eye pupils expand up to 45% when **he or she/you** look(s) at a loved one.

7. Every step a person takes places 1.5 times **his or her/their** body weight on each foot.

8. National Public Radio has included Bob Dylan and Tom Waits in **its/their** list of the ten greatest living songwriters.

9. If an American is traveling to a foreign country, **he or she/you** should apply for a passport.

10. When someone doesn't recharge **his or her/your** cell phone, it's likely to go dead at the worst possible moment.

11. Every lobbyist in Washington D.C. uses **his or her/their** huge expense account for wining and dining members of Congress.

12. Anyone who reads *The Poisonwood Bible* by Barbara Kingsolver will increase **his or her/their** understanding of missionary life in Africa.

13. Everyone arrested twice for shoplifting will receive a jail term for **his or her/their** crime.

14. Each of the radio stations lost **its/their** power during the storm.

15. In Russia a person usually gives an odd number of flowers to **his or her/their** friends because an even numbered amount of flowers is considered proper only for funerals.

Exercise Six

Correct the pronouns in the following sentences. One sentence is already correct.

1. An Internet buyer needs to be especially careful when they purchase any type of medicine online because many pills are dangerous, counterfeit products.

2. If a student can't figure out which pronoun to use, you won't do well in college.

3. The clothing manufacturer projects a life expectancy of 50 washings for their products.

4. The placebo effect is demonstrated when a person takes an aspirin and their headache improves in seconds, which can't be the drug, because it takes at least 15 minutes to kick in.

5. A car buyer should consider your driving habits before deciding what car to buy.

6. A law in Virginia allows a driver to keep their road kill as long as the incident is reported within 24 hours.

7. If someone wants to improve your balance, take a yoga class.

8. Any consumer who is concerned about the greenhouse effect should modify their lifestyle to better protect the environment.

9. According to the United Nations' Convention on the Rights of the Child, every child has the right to live with their parents unless it is against the child's best interest.

10. Harvard University studies show that when domestic differences arise, it's usually the spouse who does most of the talking who gets their way.

11. Neither Amanda nor Elizabeth could explain their habit of putting ketchup on mashed potatoes.

12. To avoid the possibility of the potentially fatal Reyes Syndrome, parents should avoid giving aspirin to your sick children.

13. According to the Sixth Amendment, people have the right to a speedy trial, to legal counsel, and to confront his or her accusers.

14. When an astronaut returns from space, his or her body must readjust to the earth's gravity.

15. Every visitor to Asia needs to adjust their handshake to last much longer than in the U.S., to as long as ten to fifteen seconds.

Pronoun Agreement in Case

Pronouns Have Two Cases: Nominative and Objective.

1. Use the nominative case of a pronoun (*I, he, she, who, we, and they*) when it is used as the subject of a verb.

   Examples: Keith and *he* (not him) were standing in line about an hour.
   We (not us) cat owners aren't surprised by anything our pets do.

2. Use the nominative case after the verb *to be*.

   Example: This is *she* (not her). (When someone asks for you on the phone.)

   Note: Although it is technically correct to write:
   "It could have been they who were the donors," it sounds bizarre.
   To avoid stilted language, rewrite the sentence: "They could have been the donors."

Use the objective case of a pronoun (*me, him, her, whom, us, and them*) when it is used as the object of a verb or the object of a preposition.

Examples: Mr. Price told Mandy and *me* (not I) that a rat can tread water for three days.
Vote for Luke and *him* (not he).

Errors are more likely to occur when pronouns are used in pairs or used with a noun than when they are used alone. Therefore, **test each pronoun choice separately.**

Example: He/Him and I/me watched Thomas do card tricks.
Read: *He/Him* watched Thomas do card tricks.
Read: *I/Me* watched Thomas do card tricks.
The answers, *He and I,* are then obvious.

Example: I asked Tina and she/her for better directions or a map to the skate park.
Read: I asked *she/her* for better directions or a map to the skate park.
The answer *her* is then obvious.

Example: We/Us two are on top of the situation.
Read: *We/Us* are on top of the situation
The answer *We* is then obvious.

Always remember that "between you and *me*" is the correct pronoun choice.

Exercise Seven

Circle the correct pronoun choice.

1. **We/Us** performers appreciated the generous applause.

2. By the time the movie was over, Cody and **I/me** had learned that only two people signed the Declaration of Independence on July 4: most signed on August 2.

3. A police report shows Paul made the 911 call that led to the arrest of **him/he** and his wife on disorderly conduct charges.

4. Adrian told Alex and **they/them** about celebrating Bastille Day when he was in Paris last July.

5. Jared explained to Matt and **I/me** that statistically tornadoes are most likely to occur between 3 p.m. and 9 p.m., but they can happen all hours of the day.

6. **We/Us** two discovered that the McIlhenny Company is the only licensed producer of Tabasco sauce.

7. **He/Him** and **I/me** agree that the eldest children in families tend to develop higher IQ's than their siblings.

8. If you have any trouble locating our house, ask Cassidy or **us/we**.

9. For their roles in *Winter's Bone,* Jennifer Lawrence and **she/her** learned how to skin squirrels.

10. The kitchen smells bad because **her/she** and Jasmine burned popcorn in the microwave.

11. Ask Aunt Alana or **she/her** about our ancestors who settled in Kentucky in the early 1800s.

12. Molly and **we/us** listened to the street musicians in front of Faneuil Hall Market when we visited Boston.

13. **We/Us** four discussed our professor's comment that creative people have short attention spans, are easily distracted, and tend to talk to themselves more often.

14. Kyle and **I/me** took pictures of the sky divers as they formed a circle.

15. Cade and **we/us** saw wreaths and plaques made of human hair.

Exercise Eight

Circle the correct pronoun choice.

1. Mr. Kerns told Abby and **I/me** that men are six times more likely to be struck by lightning than women.

2. Ava and **I/me** did research on the Iolani Palace in Honolulu.

3. When you answer the telephone and someone who doesn't recognize your voice asks to speak to you, the correct response is, "This is **him/he** or **her/she**."

4. Just between you and **I/me,** William always tries to buy Park Place when he's playing Monopoly.

5. It was news to Olivia and **I/me** that smelling green apples can help us lose weight.

6. Mrs. Burton told Edward and **us/we** that one gallon of used motor oil can ruin approximately one million gallons of fresh water.

7. We told Aaron and **they/them** that studies show that before a man even speaks a word, his posture counts for over 80% of a woman's first impression.

8. Taylor told Hannah and **us/we** that bulls are colorblind and will charge at any colored cape a matador waves at it.

9. Isabella and **she/her** discovered that robots in Japan pay union dues.

10. Janie told Joshua and **us/we** to study words that have the letter "q" to become better Scrabble players.

11. Sammy and **they/them** weren't too impressed to hear that unhappy people watch more TV.

12. It's up to Gavin and **they/them** to work on their resumés and cover letters.

13. Scott insisted to Mattie and **us/we** that dueling in Paraguay is legal as long as both parties are registered blood donors.

14. **He/Him** and Suzanne said that recycling one glass jar saves enough energy to power a TV for three hours.

15. Madison and **I/me** couldn't believe that nose prints are actually used to identify dogs.

Exercise Nine

Correct the following sentences. One sentence is already correct.

1. Me and Amy stayed in the back of the ship because the stern is more stable than the bow in rough weather.

2. The dramatic flamenco dancers provided an unusual evening's entertainment for Frida and I.

3. When there was such a rare opportunity to learn from experts, us two had no choice but to take advantage of it.

4. Me and Zach are joining forty million other Americans who use online dating services.

5. The e-mail from my brother and he said they'd be staying on another two days.

6. Just between you and I, when Jonathan was in Egypt, he accidentally insulted his host family by sprinkling salt on his food.

7. Us four were surprised to learn that the opposite sides of a dice cube always add up to seven.

8. Trisha and me shuffle the cards carefully when we play with them.

9. Samuel and him charmed their way into an area with a breathtaking view of the launch pad.

10. This is something you and me should consider carefully.

11. I'll bet you and he didn't know the average person blinks more than 10 million times a year.

12. I was standing in line after actor Jack Black and he.

13. I wondered when Dylan and him would explain their research that most women take longer to make a decision than men do, but once they make a decision, they are more likely to stick to it.

14. Us economics students discovered that kids in North America spend close to half a billion dollars a year on chewing gum.

15. Her and me remembered that in the U.S. military and in most European countries, official time is based on a 24-hour clock, making 6 p.m. 1800 hours.

Using *Who, Whom, That,* and *Which*

Use the Pronouns *Who* and *Whoever* as the Subjects of a Question or Clause.

Examples:

Who left?
Whoever did this should be held responsible for the damages.

Use the Pronouns *Whom* and *Whomever* as Direct Objects or Objects of Prepositions.

To *whom* should I address this letter?

You can bring *whomever* you want to the party.

1. Be sure to use *who* and *whom* only to refer to people.

2. Use *which* to refer to animals or things.

3. Use *that* to refer to animals, things or people.

Examples:

I will always remember the U.S. women soccer players *who* celebrated so exuberantly.

The bald eagle, *which* is the official national bird of the United States, is found only in North America.

The ferry *that* sank in the English Channel had just passed its safety inspection.

Chapter Review One

Circle the correct pronoun choice.

1. Most people **who/which** get sick after traveling by air do so not because of what they breathe but because of what they touch, such as the tray table and the button to push back the seat.

2. Do you know with **who/whom** they're staying?

3. **Whoever/Whomever** discovered that left-handed men who graduate from college make 26% more than their right-handed counterparts?

4. Wolves **who/that** roamed the prairies terrified early American settlers.

5. Crispis Attucks is often considered the first person **who/whom** was killed in the Revolutionary War.

6. **Who/Whom** was the person who discovered that a can of Diet Coke will float in water while a can of regular Coke sinks?

7. **Whoever/Whomever** said, "Well, if I called the wrong number, why did you answer the phone?"

8. To **who/whom** did you speak about competing on *Wheel of Fortune*?

9. **Whoever/Whomever** signs up for a marathon must be willing to put in long hours of training.

10. A restaurant in L.A. gives 5% off to patrons **that/which** give up their phones before being seated.

Intensive and Reflexive Pronouns

The intensive and reflexive pronouns *myself, himself, herself, ourselves,* and *themselves* have only very limited and specific uses.

Do not use these pronouns in place of regular objective pronouns.

Examples:

Give the credit to Casey and *me* (not myself).

It's up to Justine and *me* (not myself) whether we want to go or not.

Use these pronouns in rare instances to indicate that the subject performs and receives action or for special emphasis.

Examples:

They did it themselves.

She pictures herself becoming a great ballerina someday.

He himself couldn't believe the news.

Chapter Review Two

Circle the correct word choice.

1. I can't wait to watch Andy and **he/him/himself** play charades.

2. **She/Her** and **I/me** had to stay at the office to answer the phone and take messages.

3. **Whoever/Whomever** spent time discovering that, on average, there are eight peas in a pod should find a more productive research project.

4. Every stock market investor expected **his or her/their** investment to increase.

5. People **who/whom** live in glass houses shouldn't throw stones.

6. Don't blame Jason and **I/me/myself** because we didn't lose the tickets.

7. Remembering the difference between Fahrenheit and Celsius temperature scales is difficult for Rica and **I/me/myself**.

8. From **who/whom** did you learn that women have a stronger sense of smell than men and are attracted to musk and black licorice smells?

9. **She/Her** and Janie couldn't decide whether to take a karate or a kung fu class.

10. Neither Craig nor Jesse reviewed **his/their** history notes before the exam.

11. Customers **which/who** are not wearing shirts and shoes are not allowed in the store.

12. Scarlett and **I/me** know that crows recognize human faces and hold grudges against ones they don't like.

13. Spencer and **I/me/myself** learned that in most parts of Asia, it is taboo to touch people's heads, especially those of children.

14. When a person looks at a new love, **his or her/their** brain suppresses the instinct to make critical judgments.

15. Divide the money between Hector and **he/him/himself**.

16. Kip and **I/me** learned that in a recent Boise, Idaho, mayoral election, there were four write-in votes for Mr. Potato Head.

17. If a child has no interest in reading, **his or her/their** parents are generally to blame.

18. It's up to James and **he/him/himself** to get used to eating army food.

19. Find the camera and take a picture of Christy and **he/him**.

20. **Whoever/Whomever** called didn't leave a message on my voicemail.

Personal Pronouns after *Than* or *As*

Sentences that end with phrases like ***than him*** and ***as he*** often contain incomplete comparisons. In other words, these sentences are elliptical, meaning that unnecessary words of the comparison have been omitted.

There are two patterns to recognize:

A) Katie likes Michael more than I.
Katie likes Michael more than I (like him).

B) Katie likes Michael more than me.
Katie likes Michael more than (she likes) me.

Study the following patterns to discover which words you need to add in your own mind to choose the correct pronoun in an elliptical sentence:

1. Ronny is much more likely to get a headache from flying than **I/me** am.

2. Picasso is considered a more influential painter than **he/him** is.

3. Shannon is the oldest child in our family, so my parents give her more attention than they do **I/me**.

4. Swimming is easier for Sean than it is for **he/him**.

5. Reese Witherspoon is a better actress than **she/her** is.

6. Jane Austen flatters readers into believing they're as intelligent as **she/her** is.

7. They weren't as successful getting petitions signed as **we/us** were.

8. Brazilians drive more fuel efficient cars than **we/us** do.

9. They are more likely to become clients of the 4M Multimillionaire Matchmaking Club than **we/us** are.

10. Driving in heavy traffic is easier for Yvonne than it is for **I/me**.

Exercise Ten

Mentally supply the omitted phrase in each sentence in order to select the correct pronoun.

Examples:

Silas Marner worked more hours a day than **he/him**.
The thought behind the sentence is: Silas Marner worked more hours a day than *he* did.

Lifting weights is easier for Warren than **I/me**.
The thought behind the sentence is: Lifting weights is easier for Warren than for *me.*

1. Correctly reading subtle facial and verbal expressions is easier for Sofia than **I/me**.

2. She seems more knowledgeable about the origin of the woven rugs than **they/them**.

3. They were more surprised than **we/us** to discover that on game day Cowboy Stadium uses more electricity than in all of Liberia on the same day.

4. Captain Bligh was more inflexible than **he/him/himself**.

5. The passport application process is easier for you than **he/him**.

6. The loan committee was more prudent than **they/them**.

7. According to *New Scientist,* someone like Addison, who is meticulous and organized, is less likely to get Alzheimer's than someone messy like **I/me**.

8. Leonardo Di Caprio has gotten more Oscar nominations than **he/him**.

9. Norah likes Alice Walker's books better than **she/her**.

10. Mr. Williams was more conscientious in paying his employees than **they/them/themselves**.

11. Expressing gratitude in words and actions is easier for Maggie than **she/her/herself**.

12. We enjoyed the stories in the science fiction anthology more than **they/them/themselves**.

13. Talking to the wedding planner is more fun for Christine than **he/him**.

14. My friend Fergie subscribes to almost as many magazines as **I/me/myself**.

15. In Chicago Jane Addams was more famous than **she/her/herself**.

Exercise Eleven

Mentally supply the omitted phrase in each sentence in order to select the correct pronoun.

Examples:

Finny was a better athlete than **he/him**.
The thought behind the sentence is: Finny was a better athlete than *he* was.

Accepting the truth was harder for Finny than **he/him**.
The thought is: Accepting the truth was harder for Finny than it was for *him*.

1. Getting out of his cell phone contract was less difficult for Aaron than **he/him**.

2. Monica is not nearly as involved in social networking as **she/her/herself**.

3. Dr. Sanchez has a busier medical practice than **he/him/himself**.

4. Kim is more knowledgeable about life on the American frontier than **I/me**.

5. The female astronaut Sally Ride got more questions from reporters than **they/them/themselves**.

6. After his pet alligator started snapping and making loud noises, Jeremy was just as eager to turn it into animal control officers as **I/me**.

7. President Barack Obama has more Facebook fans than **he/him**.

8. Yolanda is much more successful at winning fantasy football than **she/her**.

9. The lawyers for the prosecution don't have as many years' experience as **they/them**.

10. The vice president spoke longer than **he/him**.

11. The possibility of a hurricane worried them more than **we/us/ourselves**.

12. Remembering joke punch lines is harder for me than **she/her**.

13. Public speaking is more intimidating for me than **she/her**.

14. Believing that Greyson could catch a 15 pound lobster by himself was harder for us than **they/them**.

15. We were as confused by our professor's assignment as **they/them**.

Chapter Review Three

Choose the correct pronoun in each sentence.

1. Everyone who fails to vote loses **his or her/their** right to complain about how badly the country is run.

2. When Scott and **he/him** were in Thailand, they learned the hard way that it was considered rude to sit in a way that showed the soles of their shoes.

3. Although he didn't notice us, Jayson sat near Adam and **I/me**.

4. Shawn is more susceptible to ragweed pollen than **she/her/herself**.

5. We thought Evelyn and **he/him** would be interested to learn that people who have recently fallen in love are less able to focus and perform tasks that require attention.

6. The guide told Jennifer and **I/me** that Gary Cooper, Clark Gable, and Jean Harlow had been a few of the famous guests at Hearst Castle.

7. After a person gets bitten by a snake, **you/he or she** should wrap the area in a loose dressing, keep the area above the heart, if possible, and head to a hospital.

8. People generally believe that others are more easily influenced than **they/them**.

9. Bob and **she/her** were hired to work on the Senator's re-election campaign.

10. To **who/whom** did the police give the speeding ticket?

11. Studying for the economics test was harder for Jeremy than **he/him**.

12. Everybody here thinks **he or she/they** (is, are) a better songwriter than John Lennon.

13. Bobbie doesn't know any more about Dutch history than **I/me/myself**.

14. By the 1760s American colonists **who/which** were far removed from England, tended to forget their need for the British government.

15. Everyone bought Girl Scout cookies except Reggie and **he/him**.

16. Making good decisions about a person's physical health helps **him or her/them** emotionally as well.

17. Mrs. King told Valerie and **I/me** that several men not only robbed a neighborhood gas station, but they also tied up the attendant and stayed around to pump gas for customers to collect additional money.

18. Maria pays less for her automobile insurance premiums than **he/him**.

19. The Liz Claiborne clothing firm became known for **its/their** quality materials, comfortable fit, and good construction.

20. Wallis had a harder time passing the state-licensing exam than **I/me/myself**.

21. The king **which/who** was most responsible for the Magna Carta was King John.

22. On World Youth Day 2013 **she/her** and Tim joined millions of young religious pilgrims in Rome to flash dance to the song "Francis" in honor of Pope Francis.

23. According to scientists, a sheep can distinguish facial differences of **its/their** fellow sheep.

24. Magazine editors **which/who** select feature articles must have special training.

25. Chinese dairy companies involved in the tainted milk scandal have apologized for the harm **its/their** products caused to the affected children and society.

Final Chapter Review

Circle the correct word choice.

1. Larissa and **she/her** volunteered to work on a Habitat for Humanity project.

2. Because of her attention deficit disorder, getting to class on time is harder for Talia than **I/me/myself**.

3. A spokesman for the Lehman Brothers Corporation said **its/their** executive bonuses were completely justified.

4. The elephant Mila spent most of her life in solitude performing in a circus, but she was moved to the San Diego Zoo where zookeepers say Mila was surprised to see another elephant as big as **her/she**.

5. **He/Him** and **I/me** don't understand Payton's fascination with President McKinley's parrot.

6. Avery told Cody and **I/me** that when a man spots a woman he finds attractive, he stares at her for an average of 8.2 seconds.

7. Kirstie lost more weight than **she/her/herself**.

8. The campaign committee asked Warren Buffett and **them/they** for sizable donations.

9. Hunter told Noah and **I/me** that some countries have actually banned plastic bags.

10. According to Eileen and **she/her**, gray is the most fashionable wall color of all.

11. A U.S. family **which/that** tried to spend a year without Chinese goods found it so nearly impossible that they wrote a book about it.

12. Kaitlyn and **he/him** are arguing for stricter immigration laws.

13. We were all surprised when Nathaniel won the chess championship, but no one was more surprised than **I/me/myself**.

14. Dr. Fields said, "Nobody wants to have a patient die from a medication **he or she/they** wrote a prescription for."

15. French teenagers are expected to learn more languages than **we/us**.

16. After a person is overcharged in a restaurant, **he or she/you** should point out the mistake to the server.

17. According to a Princeton study, making more money makes a person happier up to $75,000 a year, but after that, higher pay does not increase **his or her/their** happiness.

18. The monkeys **who/that** were in the experiment were given low fat diets.

19. A representative from the moving company said **its/their** estimates are usually accurate.

20. If a person really wants to be more environmentally friendly, **he or she/you** should cut down on driving.

21. In Indonesia a person points with **his or her/their** thumb, since it's considered rude to point with a forefinger.

22. Verne Troyer, the actor who plays Mini-Me in the Austin Powers franchise, has to do his own stunts because it's impossible to find a stunt double the same size as **he/him**.

23. Some students in China tie their hair to the ceiling to prevent **them/themselves** from falling asleep while studying.

24. Until its 2013 surge in popularity, the single largest consumer of kale in the U.S. was Pizza Hut, **who/which** used the leafy vegetable not for food, but to decorate its salad bar.

25. Statisticians have discovered that when people spend more than 45 minutes commuting to work **they/you** are 40% more likely to get divorced.

Capital Letters

Capitalize the First Word of Every Sentence, Including the First Word of Every Complete Sentence Inside a Quotation.

Examples:

A) Please sign here.

B) President Theodore Roosevelt said, "Speak softly, but carry a big stick."

Capitalize Place Names

Capitalize all proper place names including the names of countries, states, cities, streets, oceans, lakes, rivers, parks, highways, etc.

Examples:

Myrtle Beach, South Carolina	the Indian Ocean
Ward Parkway	Acadia National Park
the Mississippi River	Fort Hood
Pike County	Washington Reagan National Airport
State Street	Ninety-sixth Street
Lake Ontario	Silver Dollar City
Guam Island	the Pacific Trust Territories
the Orient	the Roman Empire

Do not capitalize words like street, river, lake, etc. unless they are part of a proper name.
Do not capitalize the second part of a hyphenated word.

Examples:

Their house is actually on the lake, across the street from our house.
Visiting Forty-second Street in New York City is an adventure.

Capitalize North, East, South, and West and combinations of these words when they name geographical sections of the country. Use lower case letters when they indicate directions on the compass.

Examples:

North (region)	east (compass direction)	Far West (region)
South (region)	west (compass direction)	Pacific Coast (region)

Further example:

We drove west for 16 hours until we got to the West Coast.

58

Capitalize Proper Nouns and Proper Adjectives

Capitalize proper nouns and proper adjectives that apply to people, nationalities, languages, races, religions, and religious terms. Also capitalize all words that relate to God.

Examples:

John Webster	Grandfather Jones	African-American	Buddhist
the Almighty	Indian	Protestant	Jehovah's Witnesses
God	Eskimo	Roman Catholic	German
the Holy Ghost	Caucasian	Hindu	Muslim
the Koran	Native American	Aztec	Christian Scientist

Nouns:	Asia	Jew	Italy	Christ	Tao	France	Rome
Adjectives:	Asian	Jewish	Italian	Christian	Taoist	French	Roman

However, do not capitalize the *devil, heretic, atheist, agnostic, divinity,* or the word *god* when it refers to the gods of ancient mythology. The names of specific gods within mythology, however, are capitalized as all proper nouns are. Do not capitalize common nouns following proper adjectives.

Examples:

A) In Roman mythology Jupiter was the god who ruled over all other gods and people.

B) I ordered a slice of Boston cream pie.

Capitalize Historical Events and Eras

Capitalize the days of the week, months, eras, holidays, special events, and historical events, but not seasons.

Examples:

Saturday	Memorial Day	spring
August	Kentucky Derby	autumn
Christmas	Stone Age	the Louisiana Purchase
Yom Kippur	the Renaissance	World War II
the Twenties	Lent	Panama Canal Treaty
B.C.	Battle of Gettysburg	the Holocaust

Further example:

Julius Caesar was assassinated in 44 B.C., not A.D. 44. (B.C. always follows the year, while A.D. precedes it.)

Exercise One

Add capital letters where they are needed.

1. The castle where count dracula was born is still standing in the town of sighisoara in the transylvania region of romania.

2. In a.d. 432 ireland was converted to christianity by a romanized briton named patrick.

3. In norway people hide their brooms on christmas eve to prevent witches from taking them for a spin.

4. Carl sandburg, american poet and journalist, was born in galesburg, illinois, on january 6, 1878.

5. Drive three blocks south to forty-first street.

6. Near our hotel in athens was a huge temple dedicated to the greek god zeus.

7. A San Diego fourth of july fireworks display malfunctioned and the show, which was expected to last 18 minutes, went up in smoke within 15 seconds.

8. We're spending a week in the south for spring vacation.

9. In medieval times knights wore heavy, uncomfortable armor into battle.

10. During the war of 1812, the white house was burned by the british.

11. Anthony lives on forty-eighth street, half a block north of wilson avenue.

12. Ralph Waldo Emerson wrote, "the first wealth is health."

13. I'm looking forward to march 21, the first day of spring.

14. It was alexander pope who wrote, "a little learning is a dangerous thing."

15. Oklahoma state goal kicker Ben Grogen scored a field goal during a 4.5 magnitude earthquake at boone pickens stadium.

16. In the netherlands students are expected to be fluent in other languages besides dutch.

17. The ghost town bodie, california, is a former gold mining town in the sierra nevada mountains which boasted nearly 10,000 residents in the late 1870s.

18. The golden gate bridge was shrouded in fog.

19. Montezuma II, the last aztec ruler of mexico, was overthrown by cortez.

20. Montauk point lies on the eastern tip of long island.

Capitalize Businesses and Organizations

Capitalize the names of businesses, buildings, organizations, and institutions such as schools, hospitals, and places of worship.

Examples:

Congress	Duke University
Loews Theatres	Beth Israel Synagogue
Petrones Towers	Home Depot Corporation
the Mayo Clinic	the MGM Grand Hotel
Dallas Cowboys	Barbara Bush Elementary School
Laura's Draperies	Metropolitan Museum of Art

Do not capitalize words like hotel, corporation, school, or theater, unless they are part of a proper name.

Example:
Charles did not start college immediately after high school, but he graduated from Drake University before he was 25.

Capitalize Titles of Books, Movies, Poems, etc.

Capitalize the first word and all other words except articles within the title (a, an, the) short prepositions, and conjunctions in the titles of books, stories, articles, movies, poems, works of art, musical compositions, and the names of ships, trains, and planes.

Do not capitalize the article *the* in the title of newspapers.

Examples:
the Mississippi Queen (boat)
Scientific American (magazine)
"The Jilting of Granny Weatherall" (short story)
Air Force One (plane)
The Hunger Games (movie)
The Thinker (statue)
An Inquiry into the Nature and Causes of Wealth of Nations (book)
The Merry Widow (opera)
the Baltimore Sun (newspaper)

Further examples:
In 1497 Leonardo di Vinci completed *The Last Supper* on the wall of a convent in Milan, Italy.

We attended the New York Philharmonic's opening night performance of Handel's *Messiah*.

Exercise Two

Add capital letters where they are needed.

1. The golden globe awards each january are sponsored by the hollywood foreign press association.

2. The first city in which girl scout cookies were sold was philadelphia, pennsylvania.

3. Maya angelou first read her poem "on the pulse of morning" at president clinton's inauguration in 1993.

4. Although most people consider ladybugs cute, each year residents in the south are not amused when they face swarms of these insects trying to enter their homes to ride out the winter.

5. William h. prescott stated in his book *the history of the conquest of mexico* that the aztec calendar was eleven days more accurate than that of the conquering spaniards.

6. The saxons complained that after william the conqueror defeated them, they were forced to live in poor huts, while the normans lived in castles.

7. No visit to washington, d.c. is complete without a trip to mount vernon, the home of our nation's first president, george washington.

8. Because of our interest in native american handicrafts, alex, meg, and I visited the heard museum in phoenix, arizona.

9. The pacific ocean is not only the world's largest ocean but it's also the deepest, with an average depth of 14,000 feet.

10. Six states are considered new england states: maine, new hampshire, vermont, massachusetts, rhode island, and connecticut.

11. President john f. kennedy told a group of nobel prize winners dining at the white house, "the white house hasn't seen such a collection of talent since thomas jefferson dined here alone."

12. The united states entered world war II after the japanese attacked pearl harbor on december 7, 1941.

13. A recent issue of n*ewsweek* included an article about the multinational giant, sony corporation.

14. The huntington library has a copy of geoffrey chaucer's *canterbury tales*, which was printed in the 14th century.

15. On labor day we visited the san diego zoo in balboa park.

16. The navaho indians are known for their handwoven blankets, usually in geometrical designs.

17. Since Mithras was supposedly a God of great courage, he became a popular God for Roman Soldiers to Worship.

18. Eagle high school football stadium near dallas, texas, which made headlines for its $60 million price tag, was officially closed for the 2014 season after engineers found major structural problems.

19. Danny lives on forty-eighth street in buffalo, new york.

20. Lewis and clark attempted to find a waterway between the atlantic ocean and the pacific ocean.

Capitalize Brand Names

Capitalize the brand names of products but *not* the products themselves.

Examples:

Starbucks coffee	Ben and Jerry's ice cream	Burger King hamburgers
Zest soap	Seiko watches	Mitsubishi sedan
Old Navy jeans	Morton salt	Papa John's pizza
Visa credit card	Ford truck	Dell computers

Capitalize Titles with Names, Certain Family Relationships

Capitalize titles showing a person's profession, rank, office, or family relationship such as the President, the Secretary of State, the Governor, captain, doctor, police chief, and senator when they are used with personal names.

When these titles are used alone, they are not capitalized, except titles of high ranking officials, which may be capitalized even when used alone. When words like mother, father, aunt, and grandfather are used with possessive nouns or pronouns, use only small letters. Words like mother, father, and grandfather used in place of names may be either upper or lower case.

Examples:

the President	the Secretary of State	the Governor
Aunt Alice	my father	Grandmother Phillips
Dr. Robert Henderson	Major Randall Reed	the police chief
Captain James	the captain	Chief Jones
Mother	Grandfather	Ambassador Carey

Capitalize Specific School Subjects and Languages

Do not capitalize the names of school subjects except 1) when followed by numbers that make them specific or 2) when they name languages or are derived from a proper name. Also do not capitalize class years.

Examples:

Biology II	physical education	choral music
History I	European history	economics
art	French	physics
freshman	senior	American literature

Capitalize certain well-known abbreviations.

Examples:

D.C. (District of Columbia)	TV (television)
IRS (Internal Revenue Service)	I.O.U. (I owe you)
CNN (Cable News Network)	I.D. (Identification)

Do Not Over-Capitalize

Do not capitalize the common names of trees, flowers, birds, fish, occupations, diseases, foods, or games.

Examples:

minister	apples	cardinal	tennis
interior designer	pizza	purple martin	measles
oak	geranium	bass	cancer

Some once-proper adjectives are now no longer capitalized.

Examples:

oxford cloth	india ink	gothic	french fries
china plates	puritanical	madras cloth	plaster of paris

When you are in doubt, always consult a dictionary.

Exercise Three

Add capital letters where they are needed and remove capitals where they are not needed.

1. The petrified forest is a section of the Painted desert in Eastern Arizona known for its Fossilized Trees dating from the Triassic period more than 200 million years ago.

2. That activity center is at the intersection of Decker avenue and Seventy-Ninth street.

3. Pocahontas, a plowshare princess, befriended English Colonists at Jamestown and is said to have saved captain John Smith from Execution.

4. In the south black-eyed peas are eaten on New Year's day for good luck.

5. During world war II, before telephones were used, carrier Pigeons took messages between ships at sea.

6. The takabisha roller coaster at the fuji-highland amusement park in japan has the steepest roller-coaster drop in the world, a 141-foot single vertical fall.

7. Pointillism, a type of 19th Century Painting, was characterized by applying small dots of paint on Canvas instead of using brush strokes.

8. I like burger king hamburgers better than wendy's hamburgers.

9. Members of a mosque in paris helped jews escape nazis by giving them muslim id's during world war II.

10. Brad got a vaccination against german Measles.

11. Eight very expensive corvettes fell into a 40-foot-wide, 30-foot-deep sinkhole under the national corvette museum in bowling green, kentucky.

12. In ancient rome as well as modern european and American Folklore, a hooting Owl warns of an impending death.

13. In the Fall Thomas will be a Senior at Arizona state university.

14. Yolanda needs to see a Doctor to get some medicine for her Allergy problems.

15. Mr. Westcoff said, "the crusades lasted nearly two hundred years, from 1095 until 1290."

Exercise Four

Add capital letters where they are needed and remove capitals where they are not needed. One sentence is already correct.

1. According to legend, when Shakespeare was eleven he watched the pageantry associated with Queen elizabeth I's visit to kenilworth castle near his home in stratford, and later he re-created the scene in several Plays.

2. Lisa Kudrow has a degree in Biology from vassar College.

3. Duran duran band member simon le bon can trace his family tree to a french family that emigrated to england after the family was chased out of france by catholics for its protestant Beliefs.

4. We bought Starkist Tuna, mrs. baird's bread, and breyer's ice cream at krogers.

5. Benjamin Franklin wasn't trusted to write the declaration of independence because some of his colleagues feared he would put a joke in it.

6. Beyonce knowles' hit single "crazy in love" was the best-selling cell phone ring tone in england in 2003.

7. Sammie is a very smart border collie who can herd sheep expertly.

8. Mila Kunis was born in ukraine and spoke no english until she was seven.

9. Stephen Hopkins said when he signed the declaration of Independence, "my hand trembles, but my Heart does not."

10. Our next door neighbors bought a black Ford Pickup Truck.

11. The actor billy bob thornton at one time worked for eighteen months in a los Angeles Pizza Parlor.

12. Mr. Morrison is the vice president of the room store corporation.

13. The national history museum in london, england, held a "darwin day" on february 12, 2009, to celebrate the 200th anniversary of charles darwin's birth.

14. During his first semester at college, tyler failed freshman English, but he got an A in Physics.

15. My Aunt and Uncle visited the automotive hall of fame in dearborn, michigan.

Chapter Review One

Add capital letters where they are needed and remove capitals where they are not needed.

1. To enter mexico we crossed a Bridge over the Rio Grande river.

2. James Garfield, 20th president of the u.s., could write greek with one hand and latin with the other.

3. Next semester I'm certainly taking european history, calculus 201, environmental sciences, and english.

4. The Trojan marching band performed at half time at the Rose bowl.

5. Every year on March 17 the irish celebrate Saint Patrick's day in honor of the Patron Saint of Ireland.

6. The old man whispered, "this is the work of the Devil."

7. The wind changed from the West to the South.

8. The Architecture of the American southwest is influenced by its Spanish History.

9. During world war II, the very first bomb dropped by the allies on berlin killed the only elephant in the berlin zoo.

10. Navajo, the native american language, was used successfully in world war II as a U.S. military Code.

11. Gavin told us his uncle ryan often volunteers for the red cross.

12. In the bible, Bathsheba married king david, after he sent her first husband, Uriah, to death in battle.

13. For her birthday on Thursday, we're going to surprise mother with a sony tv.

14. Morris works for the department of defense in Washington, d.c.

15. In 1947 Norwegian Explorer thor Heyerdahl and a small crew successfully sailed 4,300 miles from Callao, peru, to the Tuamotu islands of Polynesia in 101 days on a raft named kon-tiki.

Chapter Review Two

Add capital letters where they are needed and remove capitals where they are not needed.

1. The city of buffalo, new york, gets lots of snow because of its location near lake erie.

2. Dr. Meyers suspects Gabriella has german measles.

3. An alarmed passenger alerted security officers at chicago's o'hare airport that an alligator was slithering through the terminal.

4. My father said, "Ireland is called the emerald isle because of its green countryside, not because of its Gemstones."

5. In an attempt to rid guam of an infestation of brown snakes that kill exotic birds and ravage local crops, two thousand poisoned, dead mice were dropped in tiny cardboard parachutes over anderson air force base for the snakes to eat.

6. Nick Cannon might be a multi-millionaire record producer and rapper, but he began his career doing stand-up comedy on the baptist TV channel run by his dad.

7. In roman mythology juno was the goddess of marriage and queen of the gods.

8. We bought a used maytag washer and dryer for the apartment.

9. It took 150 years, but the *patriot-news* of harrisburg, pennsylvania, recently retracted a negative editorial that had described abraham lincoln's 1863 gettysburg address as "silly remarks" that deserved a "veil of oblivion."

10. Uncle Phil and Aunt Rhoda both work at white star cleaners, which is on the south side of spruce street.

11. The boston tea party of 1773 was actually boston citizens, disguised as native Americans, dumping tea off british merchant ships to protest british taxes on tea.

12. The governor insists he will not engage in mudslinging in this Campaign.

13. The great wall of china is so big and long that it can be seen from the moon.

14. The Springfield City Council supports the Mayor's Proposal.

15. Alisha said, "we're going to McDonald's for some Hamburgers, Cokes, and French Fries."

Final Chapter Review

Add capital letters where they are needed and remove capitals where they are not needed. One sentence is already correct.

1. The first continental congress met in 1774 to express colonists' anger against the british Colonial policy.

2. The plane took off 40 minutes late from O'Hare airport, but landed on time at new york's Kennedy.

3. Carlsbad caverns national park, located in the foothills of the Guadalupe mountains in Southeast New Mexico, is one of the largest Subterranean Caverns in the World.

4. Lindsey doesn't want to drive her parents' Volvo station wagon.

5. I ordered my Salad with Caesar Dressing, not Blue cheese.

6. Two math majors at reed college in portland, oregon, lost control of a massive snowball that rolled into a dorm, knocking out part of a bedroom wall, but fortunately not injuring anyone.

7. We took an elevator to the top of the empire state building and got a great view of manhattan.

8. My Aunt and Uncle took me to dinner at olive garden restaurant for my Birthday.

9. Researchers at beth israel medical center in new york reported that people who play video games for three plus hours a week make better surgeons.

10. The dome in monticello, Thomas Jefferson's home, concealed a billiards' room because in Jefferson's day, billiards were illegal in Virginia.

11. The overweight mayor of the italian town of varallo has put the whole community on a group diet and will pay men $68 dollars if they lose eight pounds and pay women $68 if they lose six pounds.

12. Columbia university is the second largest landowner in new york city, after the catholic church.

13. During the war of 1812, many african-american soldiers fought in the battle of lake erie.

14. A poll by the national sleep foundation revealed that 69% of children have sleep problems.

15. The coachella valley music and arts festival in indio, california, attracts nearly 700,000 indie/rock music fans each year.

 # Using Apostrophes Correctly

Use an Apostrophe To Show Possession

1. Add an apostrophe and an *s* to a singular noun to make it possessive.

Examples:

The boy's dog	a policeman's badge	Poe's poems
David's cousin	tomorrow's class	the suspect's location
Our car's gas mileage	the speaker's remarks	anyone's guess

2. Add only an apostrophe to a plural noun to make it possessive

Examples:

Olsens' house	customers' complaints
teachers' meeting	candidates' speeches
the girls' team	mayors' convention

3. Add an apostrophe and an *s* to the few plural nouns that do not end in s. The most common nouns are *men, women, children*, and *people*.

Examples:

The men's organization	the children's toys
The people's choice	the women's shoe department

Use an Apostrophe For Contractions

Use apostrophes to indicate where letters have been omitted in contractions. Be sure to put the apostrophe exactly where the letters have been omitted.

Examples:

I'd	(I had)	hasn't	(has not)	I'll	(I will)
we're	(we are)	you're	(you are)	mustn't	(must not)
could've	(could have)	isn't	(is not)	let's	(let us)
won't	(will not)	we'll	(we will)	don't	(do not)

Exercise One

Circle the correct choice.

1. The **miner's/miners'** wildcat strike wasn't authorized by their union.

2. The **Presidents'/President's** State of the Union address was heard by millions of listeners around the world.

3. The **Fitzhenry's/Fitzhenrys'** house is one of the oldest in the city.

4. The **journalists'/journalist's** notes and her newspaper article were subpoenaed by the district court judge.

5. An estimated 7,000 Americans die each year as a result of **doctor's/doctors'** bad handwriting.

6. Although Rip Van Winkle thought he'd had just one **night's/nights'** sleep, it actually lasted 20 years.

7. For centuries, **children's/childrens'** clothes were simply miniature versions of adult clothing styles.

8. The **lawyer's/lawyers'** conference, which lasted four days, took place in Honolulu, Hawaii.

9. Last **night's/nights'** paper included the information that all of the money Honey Boo Boo earns is going into a college fund.

10. The IRS **employee's/employees'** tax manual has instructions for collecting taxes after a nuclear war.

11. Cats have evolved enough to recognize their **owner's/owners'** voices, but they haven't evolved enough to care.

12. Ancient Chinese artists would never paint pictures of **women's/womens'** feet.

13. Michael **cant/can't** understand that a change in the average global temperature by even a degree or two can lead to serious consequences around the globe, including lower crop yields and an increased risk of storms and flooding.

14. Derek said the **bands'/band's** sound system cost well over $100,000.

15. The new **girls'/girl's** name is Whitney, and she's from Miami Beach.

Use an Apostrophe for Omissions.

Use an apostrophe to show where a number or numbers have been left out.

Examples:

Spirit of '76 (1776)   Class of '16 (2016)   Gold Rush of '49 (1849)

Use an Apostrophe for Plurals of Letters and Numbers.

Use an apostrophe to show the plurals of alphabetical letters and the plurals of numbers.

Examples:
Cross your t's and dot your i's.
They didn't have any more size 9's.

Use an Apostrophe for Certain Expressions.

A few expressions require an apostrophe, even though actual possession may be unclear. Again, for singular nouns add an apostrophe and an *s*, and for plural nouns simply add an apostrophe.

Examples:
at wit's end   writer's block
a stone's throw   a year's subscription
fifty cents' worth   two weeks' work

When Not to Use an Apostrophe

1. Never add an apostrophe to *his, hers, its, ours, yours,* or *theirs.* These are personal pronouns that already show possession.

   Remember that *it's* means *it is.* (*It's* a lot of fun.)

   Its is the possessive of *it.* (*Its* lid was chipped.)

2. Never add an apostrophe to a simple plural noun.

   Example: For more than three weeks I have been waiting for a reply to my letter.

3. Do not use apostrophes for the plurals of years.

   Example: The late 1960s was a time of social unrest in many countries.

Exercise Two

Correct the following sentences by adding apostrophes where they are needed. Three sentences are already correct.

> Please note: The greatest number of apostrophe errors occur when writers attempt to form the possessive of *men, women, children, people, everyone,* and *everybody.*
>
> The correct possessive forms are always *men's, women's, children's, people's, everyone's,* and *everybody's.* The apostrophe always comes **before** the s.

1. The jury delivered its verdict to a packed courtroom of eager reporters and spectators.

2. The officers club offers a beautiful formal dining room featuring steaks, seafood, and pastas.

3. The upside down ketchup bottle earned its inventor 13 million dollars.

4. Since everyones time is valuable, I'll get straight to the point.

5. According to experts, it's impossible to predict weather more than three weeks ahead of time with any degree of certainty.

6. Sam said he had writers block and couldn't finish his theme.

7. Womens hearts beat faster than mens hearts.

8. To no ones surprise, car accidents are the leading cause of accidental deaths in the U.S.

9. We had two weeks worth of laundry to do when we got back.

10. You're ugly and your mother dresses you funny.

11. Mr. Rogers said, "Discovering the truth about ourselves is a lifetimes work, but it's worth the effort."

12. A county sheriff said he replaced the jail inmates orange jumpsuits with black-and-white stripes because the former were viewed as fashionable because of TV shows such as *Orange is the New Black.*

13. Thousands of years ago cats were worshipped as gods, and they have never forgotten.

14. Ohio State offers a course called "Sports for the Spectator," where students learn how to be "an informed and appreciative sports spectator."

15. Jayden graduated in the class of 13.

Use Apostrophes for Compound Possessives

In compound possessives, only the final name takes the possessive form.

Example:
Ben and Jerry's butter pecan ice cream is my favorite.

However, this applies only when the possession is truly collective.

Example:
My parents' and grandparents' houses both need to be painted.

Exercise Three

Correct the following sentences by adding apostrophes where they are needed and removing apostrophes where they are not needed. No sentence will have more than one error. Three sentences are already correct.

1. At this years New York Auto Show the big news was greater horsepower.

2. This sweatshirt must be your's.

3. Goldilocks certainly made herself at home at the three bears house.

4. The childrens petting zoo was the most popular attraction.

5. I don't think tomorrow's cafeteria selections will be any better than the ones we had today.

6. Economists predict a severe shortage of workers such as welders and machinists who are needed to build petrochemical plants across the country.

7. This is worth several minute's of your time.

8. A credit union is a non-profit organization owned by it's members that passes along earnings to members in the form of lower fees and higher customer service.

9. Angie and Bens story about the ghost aroused everyone's curiosity.

10. Vikings, who were the ancestors of todays Norwegians, lived during the Middle Ages from A.D. 720 to A.D. 1200.

11. If you find a lost drivers license, you can drop it in any mailbox and the Postal Service will deliver it to its owner.

12. U.S. women's history has been full of pioneers who have worked hard to make gains in the fields of science, politics, sports, literature, and art.

13. The U.S. has 30 percent of the world's 50 million motor vehicles.

14. I would like two dollars' worth of dimes, please.

15. Miss Piggy's dieting advice is that you should never eat more than you can lift.

16. The show's top dog was a grey standard poodle named Bravo.

17. The pilots' union called for a strike in an effort to gain greater job security and an annual 2.5 percent pay raise.

18. St. Jude Children's Research Hospital is internationally recognized for its pioneering work in finding cures and saving children with life-threatening diseases.

19. The entrance to the men's locker room is the second door on the left.

20. A small amount of stress helps people remember things better, but a large amount hinders people's memories

21. Happy, shouting children crowded into the children's playground.

22. England's prime minister is a strong supporter of U.S. foreign policy.

23. Since we had to work, we couldn't watch the People's Choice Awards show.

24. The tree kangaroo has returned to the habitat of its ancestors, the tree.

25. Adam and Melinda's house is for sale.

Chapter Review One

Correct the following sentences. Add apostrophes where they are needed and remove apostrophes where they are not needed. Sentences may have more than one error. One sentence is already correct.

1. The consumer's frequent complaints about the safety of this particular product have led to it's being removed from store shelves.

2. Sherrys rude behavior seemed to be testing everyones' patience.

3. The military dictatorships' oppression of Haitians led to the United State's military action in 1994.

4. By 2014 bluegrass music festivals were being held in 45 states and in more than a dozen countries'.

5. Supposedly, if a groundhog sees it's shadow on February 2, Ground Hog Day, there will be six week's more winter.

6. The prisoner's cells' were even smaller than I expected.

7. We are facing a drought because this years' total rainfall is far less than last years'.

8. We are celebrating Jack and Dianes wedding anniversary next week.

9. Loraine Hansberry's play *A Raisin in the Sun*, tells the story of Lena Younger, who received $10,000 from her recently deceased husbands' life insurance.

10. There were more than half a million U.S. troops in Vietnam in the late 1960s.

11. Varanasi, India, one of the worlds' oldest cities, is deeply associated with the sacred River Ganges.

12. What's your fathers' first name?

13. Amelia Earharts' disappearance on June 1, 1937, during her attempt to complete a round the world flight, has aroused peoples' curiosity ever since it happened.

14. In forty minutes time, all the tickets for the concert were sold.

15. Parents worries about their children being injured in car accidents are well-founded, but worries about children being abducted by strangers are not nearly as realistic.

Chapter Review Two

Correct the following sentences. Add apostrophes where they are needed and remove apostrophes where they are not needed. Sentences may have more than one error. One sentence is already correct.

1. The city councils decision was widely criticized for it's haste and failure to let neighborhood residents speak.

2. The car dealers showroom was filled with people.

3. Samsons face turned bright red with embarrassment.

4. Its really nobodys' business.

5. Produce at a farmers market is sometimes cheaper than at a grocery store.

6. The painters' drop cloth had about 20 different paint colors on it.

7. Lawrence insists this isn't another of his publicity stunts.

8. The Vietnamese boat peoples' determination enabled many to flee from Vietnam to other countries.

9. A high school in Michigan has illogically ruled that student backpacks must remain in students lockers at all times.

10. We told Katie to put on her p.j.s.

11. Thomas Hardy's novels, frequently set in Englands' remote countryside, often deal with the part fate plays in peoples' lives.

12. The Senates' version of the energy bill calls for automakers to increase fuel economy in all their cars to 35 miles per gallon.

13. Is it possible that Amber actually passed her drivers test?

14. After exercising several months, Armandos weight loss became obvious to everyone.

15. Keishas' research paper about the UFO Museum in Goreme, Turkey, aroused everyones curiosity.

Chapter Review Three

Add apostrophes where they are needed and remove apostrophes where they are not needed. Sentences may have more than one error. One sentence is already correct.

1. The fans excitement increased as they sensed an upset victory.

2. Louis Pasteurs achievements included developing a vaccine against rabies and discovering that heating milk to high temperatures destroys bacteria.

3. The mens karate class meets twice a week.

4. In 2014 Scottish voters rejected a referendum that would have declared Scotlands independence from England by a margin of 55% to 45%.

5. A Chicago personal lawyer is offering students' a $1,000 scholarship to pursue an education in any field but law, because of the economic reality that there are many more lawyers than there are jobs.

6. An elephant broke out of it's stall, causing panic and drawing crowds of curious residents as it wandered through the streets before being cornered by police.

7. Experts have warned that getting sufficient sleep is critical to childrens' health.

8. Charlie Sheens advice to Lindsay Lohan was, "Work on your impulse control."

9. Most evenings Arthurs family sits down together for dinner and discusses the days happenings.

10. The astronauts bizarre behavior was recorded on video surveillance tape.

11. In the United States today, just 6.5% of our nations' electricity is generated at hydroelectric plants.

12. I found someones keys on the counter.

13. Generally, good liars are good at detecting other peoples lies.

14. The sign said, "Restrooms are for customer's use only."

15. The building's windows are triple glazed which allows sunlight to enter, but not heat.

Final Chapter Review

Add apostrophes where they are needed and remove apostrophes where they are not needed. Sentences may have more than one error. One sentence is already correct.

1. General Motors reported an operating loss of $35 billion in its 2009 first quarter statement, but the company earned $4.7 billion in 2010.

2. Gabby didn't follow her parents advice about which colleges she should apply to.

3. Maria Shriver offers five tips for letting go of other peoples' expectations about what you should do with your life.

4. Madison is majoring in womens' studies.

5. Claire said, "I'd appreciate everyones' ideas on whether the Kindle is really worth the price."

6. *Esquire* is one of the oldest mens' magazines in America.

7. The President answered the reporters questions at the news conference.

8. Two years work went into the project.

9. George Washington created the Purple Heart in 1782, making it the nations oldest military decoration.

10. Pediatricians, responding to parents concerns about the safety of vaccines, have insisted that childhood vaccinations are safe.

11. Jackson asked, "Can it be possible that everybodys' relatives are as crazy as mine?"

12. The term "childrens literature" generally refers to literature suitable for readers and listeners up to the age of twelve, and books are often illustrated.

13. Are these notebooks her's?

14. No high jumper in the history of mens' track and field has ever been able to stay off the ground for more than one second.

15. Advertising is designed to attract attention, so that the product stays in customers minds.

Complete Sentences

Some Sentence Fragments Lack a Subject

A complete sentence must express a complete thought and have at least one subject and one complete verb.

Some sentence fragments lack a subject.

Examples:
Fragment: Think that employees who find meaning in their work are more likely to work hard and stay loyal to their companies.
Complete: *They* (*We* or *I*) think that employees who find meaning in their work are more likely to work hard and stay loyal to their companies.

Fragment: Blew his whistle after he saw the foul.
Complete: *The referee* blew his whistle after he saw the foul.

As you may know, in request or command sentences, the subject is usually not stated. This is an *understood subject* and the subject is the *unwritten you*. A sentence with an understood subject is still a *complete sentence*.

Examples:
Complete: Put the dirty dishes in the sink = (You) put the dirty dishes in the sink.
Complete: Ask her to go with us. = (You) ask her to go with us.

Don't confuse a sentence with an understood subject with an incomplete sentence.

Exercise One

Read each of the following "sentences" and decide which are complete sentences and which are fragments. Write 'C' beside each complete sentence. Write 'F' beside each fragment.

1. Discovered there is a scale for measuring the spiciness of food called the Scoville Heat Index.   F

2. Listened to a science lecture where I learned that the risk of a person being struck by a falling meteorite is one occurrence every 9,300 years.   F

3. Please stay calm.   C

4. In Dyersburg, Tennessee, is against the law for a girl to telephone a boy to ask for a date.   F

5. Watch your step here because the sidewalk is uneven.   C

6. Discovered that Calvin Klein's *Obsession for Men* is used by researchers to attract animals to cameras   F
   in the wilderness.

7. Think your problem through before you decide what to do.   C

8. Had a strange discovery that Hallmark sells a line of "encouragement" cards that can be sent to   F
   people who lose their jobs.

9. Remember that couples usually wait six to eight dates before they are willing to enter into an   C
   exclusive relationship.

10. Enthusiasm dropped after the first test.   C

11. Hurry up.   C

12. Really enjoyed reading about Thomas Jefferson's children.

13. Just lost his head about it, I guess.

14. Consider the fact that music lessons have been shown to boost brain organization in
    children and adults.

15. Blew his trumpet as loud as he could.

Some Sentence Fragments Lack All or Part of a Verb

Some sentence fragments either have no verb at all, or a part of the verb is missing.

Examples:

Fragment: Seashell fossils found high in the Himalayan Mountains, suggesting the land was
       once underwater.

Complete: Seashell fossils ***have been*** found high in the Himalayan Mountains, suggesting the
       land was once underwater.

Fragment: The filmmaker James Cameron, who directed *Avatar*, *Titanic*, and *Aliens*, also a deep
       sea explorer.

Complete: The filmmaker James Cameron, who directed *Avatar*, *Titanic*, and *Aliens*, ***is*** also a
       deep sea explorer.

Exercise Two

**Write 'F' before each sentence fragment and rewrite it so that it becomes a complete sentence.
Write 'C' before the two sentences that are already correct.**

1. A survey of over 1,000 Americans finds that almost everyone annoyed by some lapse of phone
   etiquette either at work or in public places.

2. Rihanna's hit "The Only Girl in the World" the 2011 Grammy Award winner for Best Dance Record.

3. Beautiful women less likely to get asked out because men tend to be intimidated by them.

4. Hasn't been any anthrax in this county for years.

5. Betsy Ross the only real person to have been the head on a Pez dispenser.

6. Tell me about your blog.

7. Benjamin and Sydney naming their son Mohammed.

8. Canada a Native American word meaning "Big Village."

9. Lend me a dollar.

10. The Japan Railway and other connecting subway and train systems well-known for their incredibly punctual schedules.

11. The average L.A. commuter in traffic 136 hours a year.

12. Michael Jackson's 1988 autobiography *Moonwalk* edited by Jacqueline Kennedy Onassis.

13. The Robertsons using solar energy to heat their house.

14. In the Philippines a strong handshake considered extremely aggressive behavior.

15. Honolulu the only place in the United States that has a royal palace.

Some Sentence Fragments Lack Both a Subject and a Verb

Some sentence fragments lack both a subject and at least part of a verb.

Examples:

Fragment: A country with many interesting things to see and do.
Complete: *Portugal is* a country with many interesting things to see and do.

Fragment: A long walk from here, about two and a half miles.
Complete: *It's* a long walk from here, about two and a half miles.

Exercise Three

Write 'F' before each sentence fragment and rewrite it so that it becomes a complete sentence. Write 'C' before the three sentences that are already correct.

Examples:

Fragment: Water the earth's most valuable resource.
Sentence: Water *is* the earth's most valuable resource.

Fragment; Looking for a new digital camera?
Sentence: *Are you* looking for a new digital camera?

1. Have any suggestions?

2. Persistence counts.

3. Hoping to find out today whether I got the job or not.

4. The swastika, which has been around for over 3,000 years, used by cultures all over the world to symbolize goodness and luck, up until its use by the Nazis in Germany.

5. Your body creating and killing 20 million red blood cells per second.

6. Ask her if she knows how to get there.

7. Vatican City the only place in the world where cash machines offer instructions in Latin.

8. I understand.

9. Baseball the first sport to be pictured on the cover of *Sports Illustrated* magazine.

10. Looking for a new romance?

11. Really need to get your answer about this very soon.

12. In Saudi Arabia women forbidden by law to drive cars, and girls are only rarely allowed to ride bicycles.

13. No pearls of value ever found in North American oysters.

14. In the 16th century Paris home to more than a thousand tennis courts, both indoor and outdoor.

15. Having a hard time believing that men are more attracted to women whose bone structure is similar to their mother's.

Some Sentence Fragments Lack a Complete Thought

Examples:

Fragment: As long as you understand my problem.
Complete: *It's all right*, as long as you understand my problem.

Fragment: When she told me, "You're my best friend."
Complete: *I believed her* when she told me, "You're my best friend."

Exercise Four

Write 'F' before each sentence fragment and rewrite it so that it becomes a complete sentence. Write 'C' before each of the four correct sentences.

1. If the phone rings.

2. Whenever I want some fresh gossip.

3. If you get offered the part of Tinkerbell.

4. Have a taco.

5. Until the governor campaigning for reelection sent out a fundraising flyer that misspelled the state's name as "Neveda" instead of "Nevada."

6. After all the times I've warned you not to tease the dog.

7. Because Air Force One can only be called that when the President of the United States is on board.

8. As soon as you left, she called.

9. When I need help, I'll ask for it.

10. Since hip-hop emerged from the South Bronx in the 1970s and has become an international multi-billion dollar phenomenon.

11. Though she didn't appear to notice me.

12. Since camels have three eyelids to protect themselves from blowing sand.

13. As if we weren't already tired of reading all their Facebook postings.

14. Before class we played chess.

15. As if we hadn't already made big enough fools of ourselves.

As you may have already realized, a *complete sentence* can be transformed into a *sentence fragment* simply by adding a subordinating conjunction at the beginning of the sentence.

Sentence: Mr. Jenkins arrives here at 7:30.

Fragments: After Mr. Jenkins arrives here at 7:30.
Although Mr. Jenkins arrives here at 7:30.
As long as Mr. Jenkins arrives here at 7:30.
Because Mr. Jenkins arrives here at 7:30.
Before Mr. Jenkins arrives here at 7:30.
If Mr. Jenkins arrives here at 7:30.
Since Mr. Jenkins arrives here at 7:30.
Unless Mr. Jenkins arrives here at 7:30.
Until Mr. Jenkins arrives here at 7:30.

Chapter Review One

Write 'F' before each sentence fragment and rewrite it so that it is a complete sentence. Write 'C' beside each of the three correct sentences.

Example:
Fragment: Since most of the first human settlements began near rivers, lakes, and springs.
Sentence: Most of the first human settlements began near rivers, lakes, and springs.

1. Give me a bite of your Snickers.

2. Herbert Hoover President of the United States from 1929 to 1933 when Franklin Roosevelt replaced him.

3. If Americans spend more money per year on beauty enhancements than they do on education.

4. Can't wait to get my new iPhone.

5. People 14% more likely to die on their birthday than any other day.

6. Duke Ellington, who brought jazz into concert halls for the first time, one of the most respected figures in the history of jazz.

7. Budget your time wisely.

8. Since a family was forced to relocate to a hotel so their house could be fumigated to kill dangerous spiders that got into the house on the bananas they bought at a neighborhood grocery store.

9. Robinson Crusoe shipwrecked for 28 years.

10. Although there are 35,112 golf courses in the world, and half of them are in the U.S.

11. Just under the water, the submarine waiting to attack the battleship.

12. The population of Ireland still 2 million less than it was before the potato famine 160 years ago.

13. Get well soon.

14. Didn't sack the quarterback the whole game.

15. If you say so.

16. Approximately 1300 new blended families created every day in the United States.

17. Fascinated learning that nearly 90% of 18-29 year- olds are active on social media.

18. Displayed on the wall a complicated-looking weather map.

19. Until we knew for sure Marty was moving to Australia to work on a sheep ranch.

20. Because I didn't read the paper, watch TV, or get online last night.

Chapter Review Two

Write 'F' before each sentence fragment and rewrite it so that it is a complete sentence. Write 'C' beside each of the four correct sentences.

1. Wonder if Riley knows that General Motors' most recalled car is the Chevrolet Malibu.

2. Heart disease the leading cause of death in the United States.

3. Westminster Abbey, noted for its beautiful stained glass windows.

4. After the earthquake struck and we discovered everyone was safe.

5. Remember that there is a garbage swirl in the ocean twice the size of Texas.

6. Lucky no one was on the bridge when it collapsed.

7. Kevin hoping Dr. Thurston will remove his cast so he can play in the golf tournament.

8. Before you enter class, turn off your cell phone.

9. When George Washington delivered the nation's first State of the Union Address in 1790.

10. Forget it!

11. In Africa more people killed by crocodiles than lions.

12. Carthage an ancient Roman city on the northern coast of Africa, near modern Tunis.

13. Have any money?

14. Learned that the world's population spends about 500,000 hours a day typing Internet security codes.

15. After I found the registration card I needed to apply for my insurance.

16. After Helen Keller lost her sight and hearing as a young child.

17. Unless you have a better idea.

18. The most common time for a bank robbery on a Friday, between 9 and 11 a.m.

19. If I see you, I'll wave.

20. Amelia Earhart the first woman to fly across the Atlantic in 1931.

Run-on Sentences

Run-on sentences occur when two complete sentences are incorrectly written as one sentence. In one type of run-on sentence, a *fused* sentence, there is no punctuation at all between two independent clauses.

Examples:
Fused: Firstborn children are given more responsibility at home they can be quick to take charge.
Correct: Firstborn children are given more responsibility at home. They can be quick to take charge.

Another kind of run-on sentence is the comma splice, which incorrectly links two sentences with only a comma between them.

Examples:
Comma splice: Quotation marks have been in existence only about 300 years, they're the youngest punctuation marks.

Correct: Quotation marks have been in existence only about 300 years. They're the youngest punctuation marks.

You can correct both types of run-on sentences three different ways.

1. **You can separate the two sentences with a *period*.**

2. **You can separate the two sentences with a *semicolon*.**

3. **You can separate the two sentences with a *comma and a coordinating conjunction* (such as *and, or, but,* or *for*.)**

Examples:

Run-on: We saw the play, then we got something to eat.

Correct: A) We saw the play; then we got something to eat.
            B) We saw the play. Then we got something to eat.
            C) We saw the play, and then we got something to eat.

Don't confuse long sentences with run-on sentences.
Parade Magazine wrote in 2008, "Saratoga National Historical Park in New York hosts a statue of the boot of Benedict Arnold, who led a charge in one of American history's most important victories and was wounded in the leg not long before he became America's most notorious traitor." This is **not** a run-on sentence.

Exercise Five

Correct each of the following run-on sentences, using all of the alternate types of corrections in the course of the exercise. Three sentences are already correct.

1. Wars often kill more civilians than soldiers, in a war the safest place to be is usually in the army.

2. Hamlet does not trust Rosencranz and Guildenstern he thinks they are spying on him.

3. Don't use credit cards, they charge too much interest.

4. A U.S. ton is 2000 pounds, a British ton is 2400.

5. When Rachelle saw flames shooting out of her neighbor's window, she first tried a fire extinguisher, but when that failed, she used her snow blower to pour snow on the flames and successfully put out the fire.

6. Both John Adams, our second president, and Thomas Jefferson, our third president, died July 4, 1826, the 50th anniversary of the signing of the Declaration of Independence.

7. Central Africa is one of the world's poorest regions, AIDS is epidemic there.

8. You can use pine cones to predict the weather, if the scales are closed, rain is on the way.

9. Buckle up it's the law.

10. She didn't like the photograph, she blinked.

11. Our eyes never grow our nose and ears never stop growing.

12. A cat has four rows of whiskers, it uses them to determine if a space is large enough to crawl through.

13. Winona Ryder's real name is Winona Horowitz, Tom Cruise's real name is Thomas Mapother IV.

14. Florence Nightingale was an English nurse who reorganized a Crimean War hospital by instituting strict discipline and improved sanitation, reducing the death rate from 42% to 2%.

15. A peanut is not a nut or a pea it's a legume.

Many students incorrectly assume a conjunctive adverb such as *then, therefore, instead, meanwhile, still, also, nevertheless, for example,* or *however* can connect two independent clauses. They can't, unless you use a semicolon after the first clause.

Examples:
Run-on sentence: Very few of the ancestral Pueblo villages that were built in the American Southwest in the sixth century still exist, however, an example of this architecture can be seen in Mesa Verde National Park.

Corrected: Very few of the ancestral Pueblo villages that were built in the American Southwest in the sixth century still exist; however, an example of this architecture can be seen in Mesa Verde National Park.

Exercise Six

Correct each of the following run-on sentences, using all of the alternate types of corrections in the course of the exercise. Three sentences are already correct.

1. Get the keys friends don't let friends drive drunk.

2. During Puritan times people only took baths a few times a year, they thought it was unhealthy.

3. Delaware is one of the smallest states however, Rhode Island is even smaller.

4. Denver, Colorado, is a mile above sea level, therefore it is known as "the mile high city."

5. Foreign correspondents are well traveled they fly from one continent to another.

6. Since natural gas has no odor, the smell is added later so that leaks can be detected.

7. You can always be right or you can stay married take your pick.

8. Lake Ontario is the smallest of the Great Lakes Lake Michigan is the largest.

9. The Eiffel Tower was built for the 1889 Paris Exposition at the time many people considered it ugly.

10. After an 89-year-old woman used her cane to dent the car of the two people who stole her friend's purse authorities were able to track down the getaway car, based in part on the cane's imprint.

11. A fresh egg will sink in water a stale egg will float.

12. Mike was sure the Lakers would win instead, they lost in overtime.

13. When Taliban commander Mohammed Ashap saw his face on a wanted poster, he grabbed one of the fliers and went to a police checkpoint in the Sar Hawza district of Afghanistan where he demanded the $100 reward, but Afghan officials arrested him instead.

14. You should hang that picture a little lower it's too high the way it is.

15. Police found the bomb it wasn't connected properly so it wouldn't have gone off anyway.

Exercise Seven

Correct each of the following run-on sentences. Each sentence needs just one correction. However, be sure to use each of the three possible corrections at least once in the course of the exercise. Five sentences are already correct.

1. The first cell phones cost $3,000 each, they had a battery life of about 20 minutes.

2. Gabriel said, "Good-bye friends, I'll miss you."

3. The hurricane left most of the residents without electricity for several days, nevertheless, most people overcame the adversity and were able to joke about it.

4. Spaghetti and Venetian blinds both originated in China, isn't that surprising?

5. The Korean War began on June 25, 1950, on that day North Korean troops invaded South Korea.

6. An eagle snatched a video camera that had been set up by wildlife rangers to record crocodiles in northwest Australia, and the camera captured fascinating footage of the eagle's 70 mile journey across the country's remote landscape.

7. I got tired of waiting for the bus, I walked home.

8. *The Color Purple* was first a book, later it became a movie.

9. Since Abby's parents are deaf, she knows sign language.

10. Although the Native American princess Pocahontas was a friend to the colonists of Jamestown in Virginia at a time when they were finding life difficult, she was held captive for a time to exchange for English prisoners, and during this time, she met and married John Rolfe.

11. Debit cards can be used as either a debit card or a credit card, credit cards can only be used as a credit card.

12. The Liberty Bell was cracked as it was being tolled for the death of Supreme Court Chief Justice John Marshall, therefore, it was never rung again.

13. After generations of careful breeding, dairy cows around the world produce more milk than ever, but these cows are less fertile than those of previous generations.

14. The senator gave a talk at the luncheon, more men than women asked questions.

15. The grizzly bear is the official state animal of California, but no grizzlies have been seen there since 1922.

Chapter Review Three

Write 'F' beside each sentence fragment and then correct it. Write 'R' beside each run-on sentence and then correct it. Write 'C' beside the seven correct sentences.

1. Although we didn't expect him to come back with a tattoo.

2. Actually more plastic flamingos in the United States than real ones.

3. Twenty-three American astronauts have gone into outer space, twenty-one were firstborn children and the other two were only children.

4. The stomach-flipping butterflies people feel when they see someone they love the body's physical stress response, caused by the release of adrenalin.

5. Try the pecan pie.

6. In 1990 Ellis Island rebuilt as a museum and officially opened to the public.

7. The wingspan of a Boeing 747 longer than the Wright brothers' first flight.

8. What's the matter with you, do you have spring fever?

9. The defense attorney tried to plea bargain the case, the prosecuting attorney refused.

10. George Elliot the pen name of British writer Mary Ann Evans.

11. When the first movie theater opened in Hong Kong, people had to be paid to go in because most Chinese believed "moving spirits" on the screen had evil powers.

12. Although we tried hard not to laugh at Justine's attempts to speak Spanish.

13. Dublin is the capital of Ireland, Belfast is the capital of Northern Ireland.

14. Singer-songwriter Josh Groban has sold 25 million albums world-wide, but he's also appeared on the TV shows *Glee* and *Saturday Night Live*, and he was in the movie *Stupid Love*.

15. Can you believe a cubic mile of fog is made up of less than a gallon of water?

16. The mineral deposits growing upward in caves are called stalagmites, the ones growing downward are stalactites.

17. Consider my suggestion.

18. After Swiss engineer George de Maestral noticed cockleburs in his dog's hair and studied them, he went on to invent Velcro.

19. Trying to find the receipt so I can take back my sweater and exchange it for something else.

20. The road is full of potholes, the rains are ruining the streets.

21. One of the secrets of getting good grades in college is don't miss class and take careful written notes of everything the professor says, especially anything the professor writes on the board or includes in a Power Point presentation because, in many cases, the major part of the midterm and final comes from the professor's lectures.

22. Luke insists he can make it to the finals of *American Idol*, nevertheless, I think it would take a miracle.

23. I can't hear you we have a bad connection.

24. The plane was scheduled to depart at 7:30 in the morning, however, a storm delayed the departure until almost 10 o'clock.

25. In Carpenter's Hall in Philadelphia, the first Continental Congress met in 1774, also, in Independence Hall in Philadelphia the Declaration of Independence and the Constitution were adopted.

Final Chapter Review

Write 'F' beside each sentence fragment and then correct it. Write 'R' beside each run-on sentence and then correct it. Write 'C' beside the seven correct sentences.

1. Poverty Point, Louisiana, which is an archaeological site dating back to 2200 B.C., contains a geometric earthwork complex, consisting of more than eleven miles of raised terraces.

2. Seen Todd lately?

3. Jody plays tennis twice a week, she runs two or three miles on other days.

4. When Oklahoma was a center of the early cattle industry.

5. The current 50 star flag was designed by then 17-year-old Robert Heft, as part of a school project, for which he received a grade of B-, but when his design was chosen and adopted by presidential proclamation, his teacher changed his grade to an A.

6. Although President George Washington oversaw the construction of the White House, he never lived in it.

7. In class we are studying world capitals, therefore I now know Belfast is the capital of Northern Ireland and Wellington is the capital of New Zealand.

8. Al Capone was a famous gangster in Chicago in the 1920s and 1930s and he often said, "Public service is my motto."

9. A crocodile bit off Captain Hook's hand, that's why he has a hook instead of a hand.

10. Make yourself at home.

11. After the peso was devalued and the prices rose.

12. Most Americans in Northern states call the armed conflict between the North and the South the Civil War, however, many Southerners call it the War Between the States.

13. The Spanish omelette was invented in Spain, there it's eaten as lunch or dinner and is often served cold.

14. If the pizza is moldy, you should throw it away.

15. In Hawaii "Aloha" means hello, it also means goodbye.

16. As long as you know what you're doing.

17. Pilots advise that if you dislike turbulence when you fly, book a morning flight, because the heating of the ground causes bumpier air, and it's more likely to storm in the afternoon.

18. Margaret Thatcher the first woman prime minister of Great Britain.

19. Read in a magazine article that studies show that physically attractive people tend to have better paying jobs in higher–level positions than do their less attractive counterparts, and this preference is collectively referred to as "beauty bias."

20. A person who is myopic can see clearly only at short distances, a person who is hyperopic can see clearly only at long distances.

21. Mickey Mouse is over 50 years old, so is Cinderella.

22. Cinco de Mayo marks an unlikely1862 victorious battle by Mexican troops over larger French forces, however, the holiday is more popular in the U.S. as simply a celebration of the Mexican way of life.

23. Really weird that the 67-year-old president of Uganda said he might release a rap album after a rap he performed in 2011 became a smash hit on the country's radio stations and in night clubs.

24. The basement stairs are creaky, please walk down them carefully.

25. Queen Juliana of the Netherlands abdicated her throne in 1980, then her daughter Beatrix became queen.

There are four types of complete sentences.

A simple sentence consists of a single independent clause without any dependent clauses.

Example:
Lions rub heads to maintain their friendships.

A sentence is classified as simple even when it has a compound subject or predicate or both.
Examples:

Lions and tigers rub heads to maintain their friendships.
Lions and tigers rub heads and cuddle to maintain their friendships.

A compound sentence consists of two or more independent clauses with no subordinate clauses. The independent clauses are usually joined with a comma and a coordinating conjunction (*and, but, or, nor, for, so, yet*) or with a semicolon.

Examples:
In ancient Rome only the most important people wore purple clothes, and purple dye came from a particular shellfish that was very expensive.
Each day about 20 banks are robbed; the average take is $2500.

A complex sentence consists of a single independent clause with one or more dependent clauses.

When you want to indicate that one idea is less important than another, you subordinate the secondary idea to the primary one. Often the main idea is in an independent clause and the less important idea is in a dependent clause. Remember that dependent clauses, introduced by subordinating conjunctions or relative pronouns cannot stand alone.

Examples:
Incorrect: A middle child who marries another middle child desires peace at any price. Which can actually lead to avoidance.
Correct: A middle child who marries another middle child desires peace at any price, which can actually lead to avoidance.

A compound-complex sentence consists of two or more independent clauses and at least one dependent clause.

Example:
Since only children spend so much time alone, they tend to be self-entertainers, and they are often the most creative of all birth orders.

7 Punctuation

Quotation Marks

Use quotation marks to enclose a speaker's exact words, but do not use quotation marks around an indirect quotation.

Examples:

Jada said, "The first box of Crayola crayons was produced with just eight colors: red, blue, yellow, green, violet, orange, black, and brown."

Jada said *that* the first box of Crayola crayons was produced with just eight colors: red, blue, yellow, green, violet, orange, black, and brown.

Use a comma to introduce the quotation. Also capitalize the first word of a complete sentence inside a quotation, and always place a comma or period inside the closing quotation marks.

Example:

Eleanor Roosevelt said, "Nobody can make you feel inferior without your permission."

In question sentences or in sentences that contain an exclamation, put the question mark and exclamation point inside the quotation marks.

Examples:

Mike asked, "What are you doing here?"
Josie screamed, "Fire!"

Exercise One

Add commas, quotation marks, and capital letters where they are needed. *Consider every statement a direct quotation, unless there is clear evidence that it is not.* Four sentences are correct.

Examples:

Incorrect: Cameron asked when did Emma Watson graduate from Brown University?
Correct: Cameron asked, "When did Emma Watson graduate from Brown University?"

Incorrect: Run exclaimed Brad.
Correct: "Run!" exclaimed Brad.

1. The marine biologist said global warming can damage or destroy delicate coral reefs.

2. Samuel said that he didn't know that hypertension had the potential to cause a stroke or heart attack.

3. Mom said turn down the TV.

4. Our history teacher said *Uncle Tom's Cabin* by Harriet Beecher Stowe was the first American novel to sell one million copies.

5. Steven said tigers have striped skin, not just striped fur.

6. Mrs. Coffman said did you know that on average most people fall asleep in seven minutes?

7. Mason said several studies have shown that college students tend to rate their teachers' performance more on the basis of physical attractiveness than on the content of their lectures or ability to communicate.

8. The researcher said that firstborn and last-born children visit therapists and counselors more often than middle children.

9. Am I the only one who has boring dreams asked Sydney.

10. The World Health Organization's report stated about 1 billion people lack access to clean drinking water.

11. Lily said things are going to get a whole lot worse before they get better.

12. Sherlock Holmes never said elementary, my dear Watson.

13. The magazine article stated that more American workers call in sick on Friday than any other day.

14. No eye gouging was the only rule during wrestling matches in ancient Rome.

15. The World Bank reported that Cairo, Egypt, with a population of 11 million people, has the worst air pollution in the world.

Exercise Two

Add commas, quotation marks, and capital letters where they are needed. *Consider every statement a direct quotation, unless there is clear evidence that it is not.* **Four sentences are already correct.**

1. Marley said we saw skeletons of prehistoric animals at the Ashfall State Historical Park in Nebraska.

2. Kyle shouted bring the fire extinguisher!

3. Mr. Chandler said that when the first settlers arrived in America millions of buffalo roamed the plains.

4. Do you understand why I'm reminding you about this asked Mr. Statler.

5. You're out yelled the umpire.

6. Lenny asked do you know how to recognize counterfeit money?

7. Adam said is this the best you can do?

8. Danielle said that Jorge Ramos, the star newscaster of the Hispanic television network Univision, is one of the most famous faces on television.

9. Hunter said sleeping on the job is acceptable in Japan because it's viewed as exhaustion from working hard, so some people fake it to look committed to their job.

10. Foster Meharny Russell said every story has three sides to it—yours, mine, and the facts.

11. Mr. Findley said that on-the-job accidents tend to peak during the greatest incidence of sunspot activity.

12. Chrissy yelled change the channel!

13. Calvin said that ninety-seven percent of the world's water is in the ocean.

14. Let's give it a try said Monty.

15. Kate Winslet said I do think it's important for young women to know that magazine covers are retouched, and people don't really look like that.

Exercise Three

Study the previous examples and write 5 sentences with a speaker's exact words, using correct capitalization, comma usage, and quotation marks. Then write 5 sentences with indirect quotations, also using correct capitalization, comma usage, and no quotation marks.

Split Quotations

In a single quoted sentence that is interrupted by *he said* or *she said*, <u>do not</u> capitalize the first word in the second part of the sentence.

Example: "If you take the expressway," Casey said, "we'll get there faster."

If there are two quoted sentences interrupted by *he said* or *she said*, <u>do</u> capitalize the first word of the second sentence. Also notice that the period comes after the *he said* or *she said*.

Example: "Take the expressway," Casey said. "We'll get there faster."

Exercise Four

Add commas, periods, quotation marks, and capital letters where they are needed. Consider each statement a direct quotation unless there is clear evidence that it is not.

1. I'm so sorry said Jenny but I really do have to leave.

2. If you procrastinate until the last minute said Taylor there's no way you'll do as good a job as if you'd started earlier when you had more time.

3. Drinking black tea said Lisa has the ability to soothe and calm by lowering the stress hormone cortisol.

4. I agree said Brandon let's get started right away.

5. When you see her said Jamie tell her how happy I am for her.

6. I never thought I'd pay eight bucks to see Al Gore give a slide presentation said Lee Iacocca but I did.

Chapter Seven

7. Let's talk somewhere else said Makayla it's bedlam in here.

8. Our mechanic said if you keep the correct air pressure in your tires, you'll save 10 percent on your gasoline bills.

9. All hands on deck said the captain I have an important announcement.

10. Oh, I see said Sally that's fantastic.

11. Dan said some astronomers believe in the existence of living things on other planets.

12. Cate said that most of her baby pictures were recovered after the flood.

13. Britney Spears said I'm rich, freakin' rich.

14. Mountain goats are not goats, but small antelopes said Ben.

15. Mr. Madison said the earth is turning to desert at a rate of 40 square miles per day.

Use Quotation Marks for Single Words and Titles

Quotation marks are also used to enclose single words as well as titles of articles, poems, stories, songs, and speeches. Do *not* use a comma before the quotation marks in these instances.
Examples:

Our professor said that Kinsey's work had been "influential."

Francis Scott Key was a young lawyer when he wrote the poem "The Star Spangled Banner" after watching Americans fight off the British attack of Baltimore during the War of 1812.

One of the main characters in Flannery O'Connor's "The Life You Save May Be Your Own" is a severely retarded young woman.

Robert Frost used the New England countryside as the setting for many of his poems such as "Mending Wall" and "Home Burial."

Use Single Quotation Marks to Enclose a Quotation Within a Quotation.

Examples:

Our teacher said, "President Truman was a plain-spoken man who kept a sign on his presidential desk that said, 'The buck stops here.'"

Our financial advisor said, "There's no difference in the terms 'mean' and 'average.'"

100

Chapter Review One

Add commas, periods, quotation marks, and capital letters where they are needed. Consider every statement a direct quotation.

1. Bring your umbrella, said Jared it's still raining.

2. Mrs. Riley said in Medieval times many people had to contend with rats in their houses eating their food.

3. I love the story of Paul Revere said President Warren Harding whether he rode or not.

4. Take all the selfies you want Maya said but don't post all of them on Facebook.

5. Doing what's right isn't the problem said President Lyndon Johnson it's knowing what's right.

6. Mark Twain said the difference between the right word and the wrong word is the difference between the lightening bug and lightening.

7. Everybody talks about the weather said Charles Dudley Warner but nobody does anything about it.

8. Show me a good and gracious loser said Knute Rockne and I'll show you a failure.

9. England and America said George Bernard Shaw are two countries separated by the same language.

10. I have a doctor's appointment said Sam so I'll be a little late for rehearsal.

11. One of my favorite songs by the Beatles is Eleanor Rigby.

12. Never tell people how to do things said General George S. Patton tell them what to do and they will surprise you with their ingenuity.

13. Matt asked was Jules Verne the first author to specialize in science-fiction books?

14. History said Henry Ford is more or less bunk.

15. Economist John Kenneth Galbraith said more die in the United States of too much food than of too little.

Chapter Review Two

Add commas, periods, quotation marks, and capital letters where they are needed. Consider every statement a direct quotation, unless there is clear evidence that it is not. Two sentences are correct.

1. Travis said I still have a cold but I don't think I'm contagious anymore.

2. Hey said Paige you're walking so fast I can't keep up with you.

3. By channeling my inner heiress, I created a new opportunity for young heiresses said Paris Hilton.

4. Mrs. Freeman said what we call soccer in the U.S. is called football in most of the rest of the world.

5. Kyle said that caged birds are often seen on sale in the cities of Vietnam for followers of Buddhism to buy and release, thus earning them extra merit in life.

6. Make yourself useful said dad wash the dishes.

7. The police officer said the car was going too fast to be able to make the curve.

8. Gus said Thomas made a lot of money repairing air conditioners over the summer.

9. The weather forecaster said these rains we've been having will end soon.

10. Rita Dove said if only sun-drenched celebrities are being worshiped, then our children are going to have a tough time seeing the value in shadows where the thinkers, probers, and scientists are keeping society together.

11. I forgot to use Roman numerals in my outline said Rebecca.

12. Attractive politicians said Ms. Warning typically receive more news coverage than less attractive politicians.

13. The banner read everything on sale!

14. Joanna said that the state sport of Maryland is jousting.

15. My brother said to me don't bring back my car with an empty gas tank.

Italics/Underlining

In handwritten essays use underlining. In print, always use italics.

1. **Use italics or underlining for the titles of books, magazines, newspapers, movies, plays, television shows, and websites.**

   Examples:
   Benjamin Franklin stated in *Poor Richard's Almanac*, "Three may keep a secret if two of them are dead."
   Dustin Hoffman starred as Willy Loman in *Death of a Salesman* on Broadway.

2. **Use italics or underlining for the names of works of art and the names of ships, trains, and planes.**

   Examples:
   The *Queen Elizabeth* is one of the world's largest and most luxurious passenger ships.
   The President of the United States flies around the globe on *Air Force One*.

The Question Mark

1. **Use a question mark after a direct question.**

   Examples:
   Why doesn't Canada have mail delivery on Saturday?
   How fast do shooting stars travel?

2. **Do not use a question mark after an indirect question.**

   Examples:
   Lamar wants to know what time you're going to pick him up.
   I wonder what a woolly mammoth actually looked like.

Parentheses

Use parentheses to enclose nonessential explanations or additions in a sentence. Place a period, question mark, or an exclamation point outside the parentheses if it is part of the sentence.

Examples:
The sky deck view is amazing and worth the money ($7.50 for adults and $5.00 for kids).
In 1898 (fourteen years before the *Titanic* tragedy) Morgan Robertson wrote the novel *Futility*, about the largest ship ever built hitting an iceberg in the Atlantic on a cold April night.

The Colon

The colon is a rather formal punctuation mark that is always used after an independent clause (complete thought).

1. Use a colon to introduce a list.

Example:
The kiwi, the national bird of New Zealand, has a number of unusual characteristics: it can't fly, it lives in a hole in the ground, it is almost blind, and it lays only one egg each year.

2. Use a colon to introduce an appositive.

Example:
My goal is simple: find a job.

3. Use a colon to introduce a formal quotation.

Example:
This is how President George W. Bush began his address to the nation on the evening of 9/11/2001: "Good evening. Today our fellow citizens, our way of life, our very freedom came under attack in a series of deliberate and deadly terrorist acts. The victims were in airplanes or their offices: secretaries, businessmen and women, military and federal workers, moms and dads, friends and neighbors."

The Dash

The dash is a dramatic punctuation mark, so use it sparingly.

1. Use a dash to set off an abrupt interruption in thought.

Example:
When I was still living with my parents--but I told you about that already.

2. Use a dash to emphasize an appositive or parenthetical expression.

Example:
The wedding--planned for months--has been called off.

3. Use a dash to set off an introductory or concluding series.

Example:
Poverty, chastity, and obedience--these are the vows of both priests and nuns.

The Hyphen

Authorities sometimes do not agree on hyphen use. The simplest method to use when deciding when or how to hyphenate, is to check a recent dictionary. If you can't find the hyphenated or compound word in the dictionary, write the words separately. Fortunately, there are some agreed-upon rules, such as the following:

1. **Use a hyphen to join two or more words serving as a single adjective before a noun.**

   Examples:
   This is a quick-acting formula.
   I love chocolate-covered cherries.

   However, do not use a hyphen when the compound modifiers come after a noun.

   Example:
   The cherries were chocolate covered.

2. **Use a hyphen with the prefixes *all, ex, self;* between a prefix and a capitalized word; and with numbers or letters.**

   Examples:
   She drives an all-terrain vehicle.
   They are ex-committee members.
   Please enclose a self-addressed envelope.
   He examined the figure to determine if it was actually pre-Columbian art.
   Televisions have been popular since the mid-1950s.

3. **Use a hyphen with compound numbers.**

   Examples:
   Mia celebrated her twenty-sixth birthday.
   We expect at least fifty-five members.

4. **Use a hyphen to avoid confusion or an awkward combination of letters.**

   Examples:
   Please re-sign your letter of intent to join the firm.
   His teacher concluded that Jake was semi-illiterate.

5. **Use a hyphen to divide words at the end of a line, and make the break only between syllables. Also, for line breaks, divide already hyphenated words only at the hyphen.**

6. **Using a hyphen in written out fractions is optional.**

The Ellipsis

1. **Use the ellipsis mark to indicate omissions within quotations.**

   Example:
   After the fall of France in 1940, Prime Minister Winston Churchill said in part: "we shall defend our island, whatever the cost may be, we shall fight on the beaches, we shall fight on the landing grounds, we shall fight in the fields and in the streets, we shall fight in the hills, we shall never surrender . . . ."

2. **When the ellipsis comes at the end of a sentence, write the period and then add the ellipsis (three dots) as well.**

Exercise Five

Add question marks, hyphens, dashes, colons, parentheses, and underline to indicate italics where they are needed.

1. Katy Perry's album Teenage Dream became the first album recorded by a female artist to produce five number one hits.

2. The most dangerous jobs in the United States are the following sanitation workers, fire fighters, police officers, and leather tanners.

3. Grant Woods' painting American Gothic portrays a primly dressed, stern looking Midwestern farm couple in front of a church.

4. Othello by William Shakespeare is a tragedy partly based on a story in a collection of tales by the Italian author Cinthio.

5. Write "Dear Mayor White" for the salutation of your business letter.

6. We are not anti intellectual.

7. Corn-rowing styling hair in thin braids originated in Africa.

8. Cybersickness cases of headaches, vomiting, and dizziness are now on the rise among people who play 3-D video games.

9. The Queen Mary, a former luxurious British passenger ship, is now a popular tourist attraction docked in Long Beach, California.

10. Near the end of World War II, President Truman addressed the nation with the following statement "The Allied armies, through sacrifice and devotion and with God's help, have wrung from Germany an unconditional surrender."

Exercise Six

Add commas, italics, question marks, hyphens, dashes, colons, and parentheses where they are needed. One sentence is correct.

1. The Mona Lisa by Leonardo di Vinci is probably the most famous portrait ever painted.

2. Her grandmother has maintained a semi independent lifestyle.

3. Mark Wilkinson of Birmingham England had to be rescued from his sinking 16-foot cabin cruiser the Titanic II the first time he took it out on a fishing trip.

4. Researchers at the University of Arkansas-Little Rock said that inmates released from prison lack financial literacy from how to balance a checkbook to the importance of a good credit report to such a degree that it raises the risk for them returning to jail.

5. Pursuing happiness leads not only to happiness itself, but also to success according to Shawn Achor author of The Happiness Advantage.

6. We discovered the lamp was valuable after watching Antiques Road Show.

7. When Kristen Bartkow of Manitoba, Canada, sent her kids off to school with a home cooked meal for lunch, she was astonished to be fined $10 because the meal she packed failed to contain any grain.

8. His desk was cluttered with all kinds of books and papers two dictionaries, three telephone books, note pads, job applications, and a stack of unopened letters.

9. What Tony needed most he never got love.

10. Sending a man to the Moon and finding Osama Bin Laden cost the U.S. government about the same amount of time and money ten years and $100 billion.

11. Did you know that the origin of the military salute goes back to the days when armored knights raised their visors to identify themselves as they rode past their king?

12. The long lost document was discovered inside the bank vault.

13. Maintaining good credit is important for it allows you to qualify for new credit accounts like car loans credit cards and mortgages at the lowest possible interest rates.

14. Lindsay thinks Harry Potter and the Order of the Phoenix is the best book of the series.

15. Every job applicant should be prepared for two questions in a job interview "Tell me about yourself," and "What are your strengths and weaknesses?"

Final Chapter Review

Add commas, quotation marks, and underlining (to show italics) where they are needed. Consider every statement a direct quotation unless there is clear evidence that it is not. One sentence is already correct.

1. Get up said mother you'll be late for work.

2. Get up said mother or you'll be late for work.

3. In 2014 Monet's Water Lilies painting sold for $27 million.

4. Robert Frost said poetry should be common in experience but uncommon in books.

5. We all have flaws, and mine is being wicked said James Thurber.

6. Paul said Beethoven was totally deaf when he composed his Ninth Symphony.

7. Will said that David Beckman got $150 million over a five year period to play for the Los Angeles Galaxy soccer team.

8. Will said David Beckman got $150 million over a five year period to play for the Los Angeles Galaxy soccer team.

9. The opera Aida has often been performed on a grand scale with a huge cast including elephants and other animals.

10. Do you know how fast you were driving asked the policeman.

11. You were speeding said the policeman and I have to give you a ticket.

12. You were speeding said the policeman I have to give you a ticket.

13. Gabriella said, the time spent deleting spam e-mails costs U.S. businesses about $10 billion annually.

14. Man is a complex being said Gil Stern he makes deserts bloom and lakes die.

15. Kevin Bacon said there are two kinds of actors: those who say they want to be famous and those who are liars.

Commas

Commas to Prevent Confusion

There is one general rule to obey: always use a comma when it will prevent confusion.

Examples:
In this department sale goods are marked with red tags. (Possibly confusing on the first reading.)

In this department, sale goods are marked with red tags. (Clearer)

For the photography project I picked Jesse and Chad picked Heather. (Rather confusing)

For the photography project I picked Jesse, and Chad picked Heather. (Clearer)

Exercise One

Read aloud each of the following sentences and decide where commas are needed to make the meaning clearer.

1. I just talked to Alisha and Jody got angry.

2. The day after I leave on vacation to the Bahamas.

3. If Jaclyn had known everything would have been different.

4. Dolly Parton said, "The funny thing is that the poorer people are the more generous they seem to be."

5. By the time we found out about it it was too late.

6. The week before she lost her keys.

7. Trent and I finally got a response from Rodney and Meredith hasn't e-mailed us yet.

8. We're planning a party for Friday and Saturday we're going to a hockey game.

9. I yelled for my cat and my dog came running.

10. In this company rules are very strictly enforced.

Commas in a Series

Use commas to separate words, phrases, and short clauses in a series. According to the Modern Language Association (MLA), use a comma before the *and* in a series.

Examples:

A) It takes the earth exactly 365 days, 5 hours, 48 minutes, and 47.8 seconds to go around the sun.

B) We looked for the costumes under the bed, in the attic, and in the garage.

C) She studied, she memorized, and she worried.

Some words are usually thought of as pairs, like ham and eggs, bread and butter, and yin and yang. When such a pair occurs with other items in a series, set it off with commas as a single item.

Example:
The elegant brunch included Belgian waffles, ham and eggs, smoked salmon, and fresh berries.

If you want to create your own pairs, set them off with commas as well.

Example:
Before we move we'll have to separate and examine, select and discard, and weigh and pack our belongings.

Use no commas when all items in a series are connected by *and* or *or*.

Example:
Josh seems as carefree and jaunty and happy-go-lucky as ever.

Exercise Two

Add commas where they are needed. Two sentences are correct.

1. Research studies show that schools colleges coffee shops and malls are excellent places to flirt because people are more open to meeting people in these places.

2. Ron cleared his throat tried to speak and started laughing.

3. In Hawaii there's not much difference in temperature between spring summer fall and winter.

4. The entire month before the candidates campaigned throughout the state.

5. Most people get rich by inheriting it successfully investing in real estate owning a profitable business or saving a huge amount of money over a long period of time.

6. Colin is timid and shy and very easily embarrassed.

7. Soon after Paige apologized.

8. Four common date blunders include showing up late talking about yourself too much revealing too much about an ex and obvious over-eagerness.

9. At the conference Ms. Bundy appeared poised and regal intelligent and intimidating and steely and arrogant.

10. We cleaned the basement vacuumed the rug and swept off the front steps in our attempt to make a good impression.

11. Efficient people write down their goals prioritize them and spend part of each day working toward reaching them.

12. I called Matt a foolish thing to do.

13. People who worry least are more willing to take chances have a sense of perspective and have confidence they can handle whatever comes at them.

14. The week before Frida lost her glasses.

15. If we had known the rehearsal could have been rescheduled for another time.

16. Some of the better-paying jobs that don't require a college degree are web-developer medical secretary insurance agent and electrician.

17. As you depart the baggage area is on your right.

18. It rained all day Saturday and all day Sunday and all day Monday.

19. Pink said, "I work hard I have talent I'm funny and I'm a good person."

20. We loaded the boat hoisted the sails and set off on our Caribbean adventure.

Commas to Separate Adjectives, Dates, and Addresses

Use commas to separate two or more coordinate adjectives that modify the same noun.

Examples:

Ben is a cheerful, likable person.

In the Netherlands giving sharp, pointy objects like knives or scissors as gifts is considered unlucky.

In both of these examples, **and** can be substituted for the comma. However, if you cannot substitute **and** without changing the meaning, the adjectives are not coordinate, and no comma is needed.

Example:
Lauren knitted a dark brown sweater for her sister.
It makes no sense to say, "Lauren knitted a dark and brown sweater."

When a date or address consists of two or more parts, use a comma after each item, except between the state and the ZIP code.

Examples:

Address the letter to Rita Watson, 520 West Legion, Apartment 8G, Evansville, Wisconsin 53536.

The will was read on Thursday, April 20, 2009.

Exception: When you write just the month and year, do not use a comma.

Example:

The will was read in April 2014.

Do not use commas to set off items separated by prepositions.

Example:

The committee will meet **in** the assembly room **on** Wednesday **at** 9 a.m.

Exercise Three

Add commas where they are needed. Five sentences are already correct.

1. Terry Morgan moved to 110 Peacock Dr. Seattle Washington on December 30 2008.

2. To an ancient mariner the seven seas were the North and South Atlantic the North and South Pacific the Indian the Arctic and the Antarctic Oceans.

3. The meeting is scheduled for 2 p.m. Thursday May 18th.

4. Will Rogers said, "All you need to grow healthy vigorous grass is a crack in your sidewalk."

5. Holding hands with someone can alleviate physical pain and stress and fear.

6. The beautiful simple furniture made by the Shakers in New England is admired around the world.

7. In order to be elected President a candidate must be at least 35 years old a natural-born citizen of the United States and a resident of the U.S. for at least 14 years.

8. College students listed gender studies and religious studies and philosophy as the most useless college majors.

9. The adoring supporters of Mexican President Santa Anna had a funeral for his amputated leg on September 26 1842 in Mexico City.

10. Charlotte starts her new job on June 10th in Kansas City, Missouri.

11. Steady dependable Paul Revere was an important organizer in the American Revolution.

12. At Sequoyah Hills Park in Knoxville Tennessee visitors can jog walk bike or paddle.

13. The company is moving its headquarters to 815 Broad Street San Francisco California 90477.

14. He felt awkward and ill at ease tongue-tied and bumbling and foolish and clumsy meeting his girlfriend's sophisticated wealthy parents.

15. Minnie Munro became the world's oldest bride when she married Dudley Reid at the age of 102 on May 31 1991.

16. All of the hotels and motels and inns are completely booked for the event.

17. We'll see you on Monday at 10 a.m. in the cafeteria.

18. Cheryl's address is 2005 Winona Street Pasadena California 91103.

19. The big smelly ogre made all of the fairy tale creatures leave his swamp.

20. Superman is described as "faster than a speeding bullet more powerful than a locomotive and able to leap tall buildings in a single bound."

Commas for Interrupters

Use commas to set off non-essential phrases and clauses.
Don't confuse "non-essential" with unimportant.

The difference between a non-essential and an essential clause is: **When the clause is removed, does the meaning of the sentence change?**

Examples:

Non-essential: Teenagers, who can't drive properly, should be kept off the highways.
(This means that *all* teenagers can't drive properly and should be kept off the highways.)

Essential: Teenagers who can't drive properly should be kept off the highways.

This means that *only* those teenagers who can't drive properly should be kept off the highways.

Look at other examples:

Essential: Any car that fails the emissions test won't pass the safety inspection.

(Not every car will fail to pass the safety inspection, just the ones that fail the emissions test. It tells *which one*. Therefore, **do not** use a comma.)

Non-essential: Carbon monoxide, *which is an odorless, colorless poison*, can be deadly.

(Although the description is an important element in the sentence, it's not *grammatically* essential because the meaning of the sentence doesn't change without it: *Carbon monoxide can be deadly*. Therefore, a **comma is necessary.**)

Think of it this way: if a clause contains grammatically essential information, *it's too important to be set off with commas.*

Exercise Four

Decide whether the italicized clauses in the following sentences are essential or non-essential. Add commas to the sentences with non-essential clauses.

1. Jumper cables *which are put on backward* can create many serious problems for the car.

2. Plumbers *who are unlicensed* may still be able to do a good job.

3. A new tomato variety, *which contains a powerful antioxidant,* is jet black on the outside and juicy purple-red on the inside.

4. Penelope Cruz, *who as a teenager wanted to become a ballet dancer,* attended ballet classes in Madrid, Spain.

5. The store reimburses parking fees *for anyone who makes a store purchase.*

6. People *who donate a kidney to someone else* can live normal, healthy lives.

7. Bobbing for apples at Halloween originated with the Druids, *who thought fishing apples out of a tub of water, without using any hands guaranteed a prosperous year.*

8. Any letters *that you mail at the post office before 4 p.m.* will be postmarked today.

9. Decades ago, early voting was available only to voters *who stated a reason for not being able to vote on election day.*

10. The Carolina northern flying squirrel, *which is found mainly in western North Carolina,* has been on the endangered species list since 1985.

11. When Harvard College was founded in 1636, it was surrounded by a tall stockade, *which was built to keep out prowling wolves, and hostile Indians.*

12. William Henry Harrison, *who was president of the United States for only 31 days,* caught cold the day of his inauguration and died of pneumonia on April 4, 1841.

13. Every customer *who makes a $50 purchase* will receive a $10 gift certificate.

14. The lunch meat, *which was past its expiration date,* tasted okay to me.

15. Clara Barton, *who was a reformer and nurse of the 19th century,* founded the American Red Cross in the 1880s.

Commas for Appositive Phrases

Use commas to set off appositive phrases, if it's not essential to the meaning of the sentence.

An appositive phrase explains or identifies what comes before it.

Examples of appositives:

In Brazil New Year's Day is celebrated with a bowl of lentil soup, *the symbol of wealth*.

The first test tube baby, *Elizabeth Jordan Car*, was born on December 28, 1981.

Exercise Five

Add or delete commas where necessary in the following sentences. Three sentences are already correct.

1. Attila the Hun who died on the night of his marriage is thought to have been poisoned.

2. Harriet Tubman an escaped former slave was one of the most famous "conductors" on the Underground Railroad.

3. The University of Dublin opened by Queen Elizabeth I in 1592 is the oldest university in Ireland.

4. People who have poor vision need corrective lenses to work, drive, and participate in leisure activities.

5. Food which is too spicy makes me very sick.

6. The Pony Express which lasted only 18 months began in April, 1860, and ended in October, 1861.

7. In Wisconsin a leading milk producer it's illegal to serve butter substitutes in state prisons.

8. The part of the fireplace behind the screen, is called the firebox.

9. Any person working two jobs deserves a night out with friends occasionally.

10. Children who are exposed to even low levels of lead particles released into the air from factories or incinerators suffer losses in learning ability, I.Q., and memory.

11. Savir Mirchandani a 14-year-old student from Pittsburgh Pennsylvania figured out that the U.S. government could save $400 million a year by switching fonts in official documents from Times New Roman to Garamond which would use 25% less ink.

12. William who's embarrassed because he's so skinny just sent off for some body-building equipment.

13. The Taj Mahal which was commissioned in 1630 was built by Shah Jehan to honor his wife who died in childbirth.

14. Izaak Walton said that fishing provides the most calm quiet innocent recreation in the world.

15. All of my classmates who graduated with me in June are now in college.

16. Krystal Smith a 24-year-old Vermont grocery bagger won the $10,000 top prize at the 2011 U.S. Best Bagger National Championship in Las Vegas by filling three grocery bags in 38 seconds.

17. Vanessa who is from Martinique speaks both French and English.

18. Soap which is now universally accepted as a cleanser was originally used only for medical reasons.

19. Manuel who was tired from working all day decided not to go with us.

20. The hand fan the world's most basic air conditioner has been found in Egyptian tombs that date back thousands of years.

Chapter Review One

Add or delete commas where necessary in the following sentences. Five sentences are already correct.

1. The twins were born on July 29 1995 in Sarasota Florida.

2. The world's oldest musical instruments laboriously carved from bone and ivory at least 35,000 years ago were discovered in southwestern Germany in 2009.

3. In Florida a special law prohibits unmarried women from parachuting on Sunday or they risk arrest a fine or a stay in jail.

4. Why is it that people who forget to turn off their car's headlights, always remember to lock their doors?

5. The seven dwarfs are Bashful Doc Dopey Grumpy Happy Sleepy and Sneezy.

6. My best friend Martin Andrew De Salvo was the first to wish me good luck.

7. The heroes of American legends are generally tall big-muscled men with fierce undaunted courage.

8. I have had enough that's all.

9. Pamela Anderson is Canada's Centennial Baby the first baby born on the 100th anniversary of Canada's independence.

10. I start my new job on June 10th at 9 a.m.

11. We need a person who is bilingual for the sales job.

12. Please mail the receipt to Janice Malley 20801 Lansing Lane Littleton Colorado 80124.

13. From the 1500s to the 1700s doctors prescribed tobacco to treat a variety of ailments including headaches, toothaches, arthritis, and bad breath.

14. Steve Jobs the founder of Apple Corporation came to regret the decision he made years earlier to reject potentially life-saving surgery in favor of alternative treatments like acupuncture dietary supplements and juices.

15. Adrian insists he doesn't believe in UFOs aliens or ghosts.

16. Our club met for the first time at 7 p.m. on January 21 2009 in downtown Phoenix Arizona.

17. Before Brad Pitt became an actor he supported himself as a chauffeur a furniture mover and a costumed mascot for the restaurant El Pollo Loco.

18. The gift wrapped in silver paper is for you.

19. Women who report a fair division of housework were happier in their marriages than women who thought their husbands didn't do their fair share.

20. The Declaration of Independence was signed on July 4 1776 in Philadelphia Pennsylvania.

Chapter Review Two

Add or delete commas where necessary in the following sentences. Three sentences are already correct.

1. Mr. Andrews who teaches digital photography is a professional photographer.

2. Check the box on the left side, of the sheet, if you're willing to volunteer.

3. Jesse James Billy the Kid and Butch Cassidy are famous American outlaws.

4. A tramway, which goes straight up a mountain, is called an aerial tramway.

5. The coroner who performed the autopsy said that it was definitely a case of foul play.

6. Colin Marley who is working this month as a fortune teller always has unusual jobs.

7. All of the students who participated in the food drive will receive recognition for their community service.

8. Camel's milk a popular drink in Arab countries has ten times more iron than cow's milk.

9. Buddy the first seeing-eye dog in America was brought to the U.S. from Switzerland in 1928.

10. Shangri-La the first name of the Presidential retreat in Maryland was renamed Camp David for President Eisenhower's grandson David.

11. The singer, who sang at the wedding, won a talent competition last week.

12. The novel a book recommended by Oprah Winfrey is tense exciting and difficult to put down.

13. The Henry Ford Museum located in Dearborn Michigan is well worth seeing.

14. Since the 1940s the American Ad Council a non-profit corporation has been instrumental in raising awareness about important social issues.

15. Yu Youzhen a Chinese millionaire works as a street sweeper for the sanitation department to set an example for her children.

16. Asia the largest of the earth's continents accounts for three fifths of the world's population.

17. The girl, standing at the back of the stage, is my sister.

18. Ulysses Grant, a Civil War hero, of the Northern Army, became the 18th president, of the United States in 1869.

19. The cheetah found in southern Asia and southern Africa can run 45-70 miles an hour for short distances.

20. The color red looks good on you.

Chapter Review Three

Add or delete commas where necessary in the following sentences.

1. A daily dose of aspirin taken by many people to prevent heart attacks may also reduce the risk of colon cancer.

2. The Calvin Klein model was a slim dark dashing figure.

3. Children, who have frequent tonsillitis, may be good candidates for a tonsillectomy.

4. *Notes From a Small Island* written by American author, Bill Bryson was recently chosen by English readers as the best book about England.

5. Craigslist which started in San Francisco in 1995 has become the world's largest classified ad service.

6. Victoria Woodhall an American political reformer ran for president in 1872.

7. The only two Southern state capitals, not occupied by Northern troops during the Civil War, were Austin Texas, and Tallahassee Florida.

8. The restaurant is located at 185 East Bay Street Charleston South Carolina 29401.

9. *Grey's Anatomy* star Patrick Dempsey began his career as a juggling unicycle-riding clown.

10. Children, who are handicapped or who have special needs, pose particular challenges for photographers trying to get expressive and natural portraits.

11. Halley's Comet named for astronomer Edmund Halley appears approximately every 76 years.

12. The term cop comes from constable on patrol a term used in England.

13. Sheila ordered a dainty breakfast, of scrambled eggs bacon wheat toast hash browns orange juice and coffee.

14. We ate the whole bucket of extra crispy, fried chicken.

15. The Pentagon in Arlington, Virginia has five sides and five stories and five acres of land.

16. Kristen carefully washed her shiny new, red, convertible.

17. Maps blueprints and photographs were on the table.

18. Two log cabins were built inside the Twitter headquarters in San Francisco so that employees would have an opportunity to eat and relax in an intimate rustic space.

19. The letter was addressed to Mr. Jack Watson 111 Water Tower Place, Apt 806 Chicago Illinois 60605.

20. The boy wearing the blue raincoat, and red cap, is my brother.

Commas for Parenthetical Expressions and Interjections

1. Use commas to set off parenthetical expressions which interrupt the main thought of the sentence.

Examples:
I will understand, of course, if you are unable to attend.

The children, I suppose, are getting really excited about the holidays.

Common parenthetical expressions are:

to tell the truth	for example	you know	however
on the other hand	nevertheless	it seems	perhaps
as a matter of fact	by the way	therefore	I think

2. Use commas to set off words like *yes, no, well, oh,* and *why* when used at the beginning of a sentence.

Examples:
Well, elephants are the only animals that can't jump.

Oh, I didn't see you standing there.

Commas for Direct Address

Use commas to set off a person's name or other words that stand for a person when they are used in direct address.

Examples:
The President said, "My fellow Americans, I am speaking to you about a matter of utmost importance."

Jennifer, can you help me study for my physics test?

Please be patient, boys and girls, because the show will begin very soon.

Exercise Six

Add or delete commas where necessary in the following sentences.

1. Laissez-faire the philosophy that government should not interfere with commerce, or trade, was promoted by eighteenth century economist Adam Smith.

2. All polar bears are as a matter of fact left-handed.

3. Sherlock Holmes Sir Arthur Conan Doyle's brilliant detective first appeared in *A Study in Scarlet* in 1887.

4. Michael are you sure we're headed in the right direction?

5. I think Thomas won first prize.

6. Alan Turing, the father of computer science chained his mug to a radiator to stop anyone else, at work, from using it.

7. It was a pretty good poker hand I guess.

8. The Great Wall of China which runs from northern China for 2,162 miles is the largest man-made structure in the world.

9. Okay we'll do it your way.

10. The tallest monument in the United States, the Gateway Arch in St. Louis is 630 feet tall.

11. Well I thought it was a good idea Leslie.

12. One of the biggest events in the World Wrestling Entertainment schedule is *Wrestle Mania* which decides the world champions.

13. George Eastman the founder of Kodak Corporation hated to have his picture taken.

14. As a matter of fact it would be a good time to apologize.

15. Bobby Leach the second man to go over Niagara Falls in a barrel survived the fall but later died as a result of slipping on a piece of orange peel.

Chapter Review Four

Add or delete commas where necessary in the following sentences.

1. Extended exposure to dark, gloomy days can result in seasonal affective disorder. ✓

2. The first modern calendar was put into use in 45 B.C., by Julius Caesar.

3. Well, the U.S. has more lawyers per capita than any country in the world and twice as many prisoners as lawyers.

4. Kristen, do you know the Web address?

5. Jupiter, the fifth planet from the sun, is the largest planet, in our solar system.

6. The "black box", that houses an airplane's voice recorder, is actually orange so that it can be detected more easily amid the debris of a plane crash.

7. Animals, who eat other animals, are called carnivores.

8. People with high self-esteem have longer, more successful relationships.

9. Battle Creek, Michigan is the home of two of America's biggest brand names in cereals, Post and Kellogg's.

10. Jill has long, straight, dark, brown hair.

11. Honey, I'm home!

12. About 1,000 movies a year are produced in India, about twice the output of Hollywood.

13. The essence of citing expert opinion is to stay with reputable sources, such as those found in respected newspapers, magazines and academic journals.

14. Lisa, normally quite sensible, came up with a really, crazy, idea.

15. In China, clocks handkerchiefs straw sandals and flowers of any kind are all associated with death and funerals, and these items are considered too morbid to give to anyone as a gift.

16. No, I wasn't aware that white cats with blue eyes, are usually deaf.

17. The world's smallest butterfly, the dwarf blue from Africa, has a wingspan of only one-half inch.

18. A 30-year-old woman, in Des Moines, Iowa was arrested in an arson attack on the home of her former best friend, who had quarreled with her and un-friended her, on Facebook.

19. Claude Monet, the French painter, completed his famous water lily paintings when he was 84 years old.

20. Propylene Glycol, commonly used as an anti-freeze, can also be found in salad dressings as a thickening agent.

Use Commas to Set Off Introductory Clauses and Phrases.

Put a comma after an introductory adverb clause, a participial phrase, or two or more adjoining prepositional phrases.

Examples:

    A) Even though Alex set the alarm, it didn't go off.
    B) Thinking the alarm was set, he didn't worry.
    C) At nine o'clock in the morning, he was sleeping peacefully.
    D) To see more clearly, Annette stood on a chair.

When a phrase or clause is short, no comma is needed.

Examples:

    A) Whatever he says annoys our teacher.
    B) At times the class is enjoyable.

Use Commas Before *And, But, For, Or, Nor,* and *Yet* When They Separate Two Independent Clauses.

Examples:

    A) Dr. Frazier was tired, yet she still had four more hours on her shift.
    B) A 2009 search for the Loch Ness monster came up empty, but scientists recovered over 100,000 golf balls.

Do Not Use Commas Between Parts of a Compound Predicate.

Examples:

    A) Kristi was bored and drew butterflies on the margins of her paper.
    B) The gorilla was nervous and beat his chest.

Check very carefully to decide whether a sentence is *compound* or if it is a *simple sentence with a compound predicate.* Usually the difference between the two is a single word.

Compound predicate (no comma)
The International Space Station is as roomy as a five-bedroom house and travels at 17,500 mph.

Compound sentence (comma required)
The International Space Station is as roomy as a five-bedroom house, and *it* travels at 17,500 mph.

Exercise Seven

Add commas where they are needed.

1. The hostages in the bank robbery were released unharmed and police were able to persuade the bank robbers to give themselves up.

2. It takes most people 48 to 100 tries to solve a Rubik's Cube puzzle, but if done perfectly any cube combination can be solved in seventeen turns.

3. To reduce tiredness while driving long distances keep your back as straight as possible.

4. New Mexico State's first graduating class in 1893 had only one student and he was shot and killed before graduation.

5. Alligator meat is considered healthier than domestic chicken for cholesterol and fat content are lower.

6. In a war of wits you're an unarmed soldier.

7. Bruce Dickinson is not only the lead singer of *Iron Maiden* but he is also a world-class fencer author and licensed Boeing 757 pilot.

8. Saudi women have won the right to vote but not the right to drive to the polling station.

9. Men named Kent have a 69% chance of being Republicans while women named Annie have an 89% chance of being Democrats.

10. It is the female lion that does more than 90% of the hunting while the male is either afraid to risk his life or simply prefers to rest.

11. By the end of elementary school the average American child has witnessed more than 8,000 murders on television.

12. Since pumpkin pulp doesn't grind up thoroughly plumbers recommend that pumpkin pulp never be put into drains or garbage disposers.

13. A rectangle has four right angles while a rhombus has four equal sides and a square is both a rectangle and a rhombus.

14. Just as my friend told me someone had died in the fire we saw the hearse drive up.

15. Drivers tend to drive faster when other cars are around them and it doesn't matter if the other cars are in front beside or behind them.

16. After the union leader and the president of the company made the announcement that the strike had been settled reporters began shouting questions.

17. Alexander Hamilton and Aaron Burr fought a duel on July 11 1804 and Hamilton was mortally wounded and died the next day.

18. Italy is famous for its fine leather goods but Italian shoes are expensive.

19. Marco Polo was an Italian traveler and author of *The Travels of Marco Polo* and he gave 14th century Europeans the first accurate information about China and Asia.

20. When doing business in Turkey it's the custom for the host to pay for the meal and requests to split the bill won't be accepted.

Use a Comma to Separate Contrasting Elements.

Examples:

Throw your dirty socks in the hamper, not on the floor.

The harder we tried to paint neatly, the messier it looked.

Do not use a comma without a reason.

Many sentences do not require any commas.

Examples:

People who have no credit history or a poor credit history have difficulty getting a loan because lenders view these people as high-risk customers who might default on a loan.

A Michigan State University study found that workers who smiled as a result of cultivating positive thoughts exhibited improved mood and less social withdrawal.

Chapter Review Five

Add or delete commas where necessary in the following sentences.

1. Give the job to Halle not me.

2. During National Clean Your Closet Week in March the Dress for Success organization asks businesswomen to donate a suit to a woman who is trying to enter the job market.

3. A northern California couple out walking their dog on their property stumbled across a modern-day bonanza: $10 million in rare mint-condition gold coins buried in the shadow of an old tree.

4. Mrs. Hong should be promoted not fired.

5. Since it takes glass a million years to decompose it never wears out and can be recycled an infinite number of times.

6. Triggered by a landslide that buried the mountain town of Yungay Peru an estimated 50,000 people were killed.

7. Intelligent men and women are easily annoyed by people in general but they tend to say nothing in an attempt to avoid meaningless arguments.

8. After Washington state road crews removed three large dams built by the same beaver they decided to spend $15.000 to hire a beaver trapper.

9. Michelangelo was 26 when he began sculpting his celebrated *David* statue and he finished it seventeen months later in January 1504.

10. All of the roles in Shakespeare's plays were originally acted by men and boys since it wasn't proper for females to appear on stage in England at that time.

11. Carter get lost.

12. To be sure the package would arrive on time I sent it Federal Express.

13. The world's largest gothic cathedral the Cathedral of St. John the Divine is located on Amsterdam Avenue at 112th Street in New York City.

14. Americans eat more than 20 pounds of candy annually but the Dutch eat three times as much.

15. President Woodrow Wilson kept a flock of sheep on the White House lawn and he sold the wool and gave the money to the Red Cross.

16. The world's first face transplant was performed in 2005 on Isabelle Dinoire of Valenciennes, France, after her nose lips and chin had been seriously injured when she was attacked by her dog.

17. Japanese children cover their tummies when they hear thunder to keep the Thunder Oni demon from stealing their belly buttons.

18. Horatio Alger inspired many readers with his stories about poor boys who became rich but Alger himself died poor.

19. According to a recent study removing allergens such as dust from homes could reduce the chance of a child developing asthma by about 40%.

20. It is estimated that six year olds laugh 300 times a day but adults laugh only 15 to 100 times a day.

21. For people who have trouble sleeping, researchers say that one week of camping without electronics resets a person's biological clock and synchronizes melatonin hormones with sunrise and sunset.

22. Hollywood celebrities are boycotting the Beverly Hills Hotel, owned by the Sultan of Brunei, to protest Brunei's harsh Islamic criminal laws.

23. In Natoma, Kansas, it's illegal to throw knives at men wearing striped suits.

24. Amid an epidemic of overdose deaths from prescription drugs medical boards across the country are revising their recommendations for doctors when it comes to prescribing painkillers.

25. Scientists have found that during a good laugh three parts of the brain light up: a thinking part that helps you get the joke a movement area that tells your muscles to move and an emotional region that elicits the happy feeling.

Final Chapter Review

Add or delete commas where necessary in the following sentences. Four sentences are already correct.

1. *Of Human Bondage* is the title of British novelist's Somerset Maugham's most famous novel.

2. Whales are mammals not fish.

3. According to a recent poll most Americans believe that clothing made in the U.S. is higher in quality than clothes made in China Vietnam or Bangladesh.

4. On a raised platform, at the front of the ballroom, the wedding party posed for photographs.

5. In order to be able to see a rainbow you must have your back to the sun.

6. Pluto was once considered the ninth planet in our solar system but it was downgraded to the status of a dwarf planet.

7. I'm sure I need a period here not a comma.

8. They live at 2804 Washington Street San Jose California 97433.

9. People who own dogs tend to be more outgoing and more likely to start conversations with others.

10. Taylor would you give me a ride downtown tomorrow morning?

11. Denmark's largest power company Dong Energy plans to build thousands of charging poles in towns cities and service stations along highways in Denmark where depleted batteries can be exchanged for fresh ones on long trips.

12. HBO hired hip-hop and Latin music artists to create songs that would appeal to people who otherwise might not watch the medieval fantasy show *Game of Thrones*.

13. King George I of England who was born and raised in Germany never learned to speak English properly and relied on his government ministers to run the country for him.

14. As a precaution in the event of a crash Prince Charles and Prince William never travel on the same airplane.

15. A mythical creature the griffin had the body of a lion the wings of a bird and the head of an eagle.

16. Park your car in the parking lot not on the street.

17. The average child in the United States, spends approximately 28 hours a week watching television more time than in the classroom.

18. On May 25 2011 20 days after a tornado struck Joplin Missouri an Indiana couple discovered a receipt that had blown 525 miles from Joplin to their porch the longest recorded journey of debris from a tornado.

19. Forcing back his anger Jeffrey apologized to Latisha.

20. In most parts of the world brides wear vibrant colorful wedding dresses.

21. Fortune cookies were invented in the United States not China.

22. Jessica Alba's charity work includes working with Clothes Off Our Backs Habitat for Humanity the National Center for Missing and Exploited Children and Project HOME.

23. Keith is looking forward to his internship this summer but he can't decide whether he wants to work at a technology company or at an investment firm.

24. A Kansas basketball jersey adorned with a heart and Taylor Swift's autograph was sold as a collector's item for $1,005 on March 2 2011.

25. A cow that avoided slaughter by jumping a slaughterhouse gate and swimming in the Missouri River has been placed in the New Dawn Montana Farm Animal Sanctuary.

Irregular Verbs

Regular verbs pose no problems. A regular verb is one that forms its past and past participle by adding *-d* or *-ed* to the base form.

Examples:
Past: We ***volunteered*** to hand out leaflets for Senator Sheldon's campaign.
Past Participle: We ***have volunteered*** to hand out leaflets for Senator Sheldon's campaign.

Some irregular verbs are formed by changing the spelling.

Examples:
Who ***did*** this?
Who ***has done*** this?

Some irregular verbs are formed by adding *en.*

Examples:
Rufus ***hid*** the bone around here somewhere.
Rufus ***has hidden*** that bone around here somewhere.

Some of the most common irregular verbs are:

Base	Past	Past Participle
begin	began	(has, have) begun
break	broke	(has, have) broken
come	came	(has, have) come
do	did	(has, have) done
drink	drank	(has, have) drunk
fall	fell	(has, have) fallen
freeze	froze	(has, have) frozen
run	ran	(has, have) run
see	saw	(has, have) seen
speak	spoke	(has, have) spoken
steal	stole	(has, have) stolen
swim	swam	(has, have) swum
tear	tore	(has, have) torn
wear	wore	(has, have) worn
write	wrote	(has, have) written

Use the expression *worn out* to express exhaustion or to describe something that is too old or too damaged to be used any more.

Example: President Obama in his inaugural speech stated: "On this day, we come to proclaim an end to the petty grievances and false promises, the recriminations and *worn-out* dogmas that for far too long have strangled our politics."

You must use the *past participle* when there is a *helping verb* in a sentence.

Examples:
Incorrect: We have broke the glass.
Correct: We have *broken* the glass.

Never use freezed for *froze* or *frozen.*

Examples:
Incorrect: The mountain climbers would have froze to death if rescuers hadn't found them quickly.
Incorrect: The mountain climbers would have freezed to death if rescuers hadn't found them quickly.
Correct: The mountain climbers would have *frozen* to death if rescuers hadn't found them quickly.

Exercise One

Circle the correct verb form.

1. The prized NFL football uniform was **tore/torn** in several places.

2. Branding animals **began/begun** in Connecticut in the mid 19th century when farmers were required by law to mark all their pigs.

3. We **saw/seen** Jay Z and asked for his autograph.

4. I think they **did/done** the best they could, under the circumstances.

5. The term Indian summer **came/come** into existence from the celebrations American Indians held to honor the blessings of warm days for additional harvests.

6. After the Smiths had **spoke/spoken** to a landscape specialist, they decided to use native plants to conserve water and use less fertilizer.

7. Oh, I **drank/drunk** the last of the orange juice this morning.

8. If Lady Gaga **ran/run** for president, would you vote for her?

9. The Coast Guard **did/done** an outstanding job in saving their lives.

10. The *Guinness World Records* is the book most often **stole/stolen** from public libraries.

11. I've **wrote/written** an e-mail to Leah to tell her I tried to talk to her friends at the zoo, but they were all behind bars.

12. You should have been there and **saw/seen** the look on his face.

13. In the 1930s Texas **began/begun** a program for oil conservation.

14. Queen Latifah said, "I know things that are **broke/broken** can be fixed."

15. The Consumer Product Safety Commission has issued a warning that used, **wore/worn** out baby bibs pose a potential threat of lead exposure.

16. Katie **came/come** around that corner too fast and lost control of the car.

17. Edna Scott Parker had **broke/broken** the record as the oldest living person when she celebrated her 115th birthday in 2008.

18. Millions of people have **drove/driven** Volkswagen Beetles since they were first produced in Germany in 1937.

19. When the Cape Hatteras lighthouse **came/come** into view through the fog, we were very relieved.

20. Many people have successfully **swam/swum** the English Channel.

21. We **saw/seen** that Abraham Lincoln's presidential salary in 1861 was $25,000 a year.

22. Ted Williams, legendary left fielder for the Boston Red Sox, was **freezed/froze/frozen** cryogenically after his death in accordance with a "family pact" between two of his children.

23. Norwegian brides have traditionally **wore/worn** a silver crown with dangling chains to ward off evil spirits.

24. Some boxing fans believe that on June 9, 2012, Manny Pacquiao had a boxing victory **stole/stolen** when judges scored a controversial split decision in favor of Tim Bradley.

25. Prom Vannak **swam/swum** to freedom from a Thai fishing boat where he was held as a modern day slave, an unpaid, tortured laborer.

Other common irregular verbs are:

Base	Past	Past Participle
am/is/are	was/were	(has, have) been
beat	beat	(has, have) beaten
become	became	(has, have) become
choose	chose	(has, have) chosen
draw	drew	(has, have) drawn
drive	drove	(has, have) driven
eat	ate	(has, have) eaten
fly	flew	(has, have) flown
forbid	forbade	(has, have) forbidden
get	got	(has, have) gotten
give	gave	(has, have) given
go	went	(has, have) gone
grow	grew	(has, have) grown
hide	hid	(has, have) hidden
know	knew	(has, have) known
ride	rode	(has, have) ridden
ring	rang	(has, have) rung
show	showed	(has, have) showed, shown
spring	sprang	(has, have) sprung
take	took	(has, have) taken

Exercise Two

Circle the correct verb form.

1. I **was/been** trying to find the prize in my Cracker Jack's box.

2. Rocco had **ate/eaten** a healthy breakfast of scrambled eggs and black beans stuffed into a whole grain tortilla.

3. They should have **knew/known** that the Roman emperor Caligula made his horse a senator.

4. Jake's parents have **forbade/forbidden** him to get a tattoo.

5. The reporter should have **got/gotten** permission before he reported the story.

6. The jatropha bush, which is **grew/grown** in Haiti, shows great potential as a biofuel.

7. Melting ice caps have **became/become** a particular problem for Venice, Italy, because rising waters pose a great danger to the survival of Venice.

8. Gordon frequently claimed to have **rode/ridden** a bull in a rodeo.

9. No type of penguin has ever actually **flew/flown**.

10. By the final stroke of midnight on New Year's Eve, the Spanish couple had quickly **ate/eaten** twelve grapes, which was supposed to ensure them a prosperous new year.

11. You should have **took/taken** a map with you.

12. For years workers at Matsushita Electric Company in Japan have **beat/beaten** dummies of their foremen with bamboo sticks to let off steam and keep morale high.

13. Turkeys weren't **ate/eaten** by Native Americans because they believed killing such a timid bird indicated laziness.

14. She **sprang/sprung** into action as soon as she saw the rattlesnake.

15. We **were/been** reading that it's illegal to hunt camels in Arizona.

16. According to the notes I had **took/taken**, kids in Brazil do not have sleepovers.

17. Pictographs are pictures or symbols that have been **drew/drawn** on the walls of caves for thousands of years.

18. In Taiwan eating or drinking in the streets is **took/taken** as being extremely crude.

19. One of Murphy's laws that has **become/became** famous is, "If anything can go wrong, it will."

20. She shouldn't have **ate/eaten** so many jalapeño peppers.

21. Before signing the trade embargo against Cuba, John F. Kennedy had **got/gotten** his press secretary to buy him 1,000 Cuban cigars.

22. In Beijing, China we should have **gave/given** out our business cards with two hands.

23. By the end of the novel, the hero had **drove/driven** a stake into the vampire's heart.

24. A Powerball ticket worth $16 million **become/became** worthless because no winner claimed the prize money before the six-month deadline.

25. By the mid-1930s Hoovervilles, named after President Hoover, who was blamed for the Great Depression, had **sprang/sprung** up throughout the United States.

Here are a few additional irregular verbs:

Base	Past	Past Participle
bite	bit	(has, have) bitten
blow	blew	(has, have) blown
catch	caught	(has, have) caught
forget	forgot	(has, have) forgotten
forgive	forgave	(has, have) forgiven
shake	shook	(has, have) shaken
sing	sang	(has, have) sung
sink	sank	(has, have) sunk
swear	swore	(has, have) sworn
throw	threw	(has, have) thrown

Both *hanged* and *hung* are the past and past participle forms of *hang*. People are *hanged,* not hung, when they are executed.

Examples:

John Brown was *hanged* in 1859 for his attack on Harper's Ferry, Virginia.
A large mirror was *hung* above the fireplace.

Don't Use:
blowed for *blew*
busted for *burst*
catched for *caught*
drug for *dragged*
shaked for *shook*
throwed for *threw*
wringed for *wrung*
drownded for *drowned*

Examples:
Not correct: He drug the heavy container across the room.
    Correct: He *dragged* the heavy container across the room.

Not correct: The escape failed when the convict drownded in the water surrounding
              Alcatraz Island.
    Correct: The escape failed when the convict *drowned* in the water surrounding
              Alcatraz Island.
Not correct: The pipe busted.
    Correct: The pipe *burst.*

Exercise Three

Circle the correct verb choice.

1. I would have **swore/sworn** I left my books here, but I can't find them anywhere.

2. Throughout history, more ships have been **sank/sunk** by hurricanes than by war.

3. The medic **dragged/drug** the unconscious soldier to safety.

4. I had **forgot/forgotten** that in Michigan it's illegal to put a skunk in your boss's desk.

5. Before the game started, the fans rose and **sang/sung** the national anthem.

6. My confidence **sank/sunk** quickly when I began to read the test questions.

7. Long ago, the people of Nicaragua believed that if they **throwed/threw** beautiful young women into a volcano it would stop erupting.

8. Carla's little brother came inside crying because his tricycle **drowned/drownded** in the pool.

9. No one was injured when the house down the street from us **blowed/blew** up after a spark ignited an oxygen tank.

10. Beyonce has **sang/sung** on television many times.

11. Kaylee said that in some ways we've already **catched/caught** up with the predictions made by science fiction writers.

12. It's estimated that millions of trees are planted by squirrels who have **forgot/forgotten** where they hid their nuts and seeds.

13. The lender has **forgave/forgiven** some of the interest on the loan.

14. Second-born children have often **went/gone** in the opposite direction from the firstborn in their families.

15. Nicole Kidman described herself as "**shook/shaken** up" after a bicycle-riding paparazzo crashed into her on a sidewalk in New York City.

16. Workmen shut off the water after the pipe **busted/burst**.

17. In England Oliver Cromwell was **hanged/hung** and decapitated two years after his death.

18. Tyrone **throwed/threw** Patrick out at second base.

19. Lisa **brought/brung** the gifts in a shopping bag.

20. His parents haven't **forgave/forgiven** him for dropping out of college and joining a band.

Chapter Review One

Choose the correct verb in each of the following sentences.

1. The arrested man insisted he **did/done** nothing wrong.

2. Some members of Congress have **swore/sworn** off earmarks, which are specific pet projects of House members, paid for by taxpayers.

3. I should have **got/gotten** the I.O.U. in writing.

4. An estimated $8.9 million was **stole/stolen** in an armed robbery at the Dunbar armored facility in Los Angeles, California, on September 13, 1997.

5. An ancient virus that was dormant for at least 30,000 years has **sprang/sprung** back to life in a French scientific laboratory.

6. We **were/been** thinking about naming our dog Benito.

7. Lamont has **drew/drawn** the shortest straw, so he gets to start first.

8. The severe storm had **tore/torn** the main sail and forced the sailboat crew to rescue a man washed overboard.

9. The Liberty Bell was **rang/rung** for the last time when its repaired crack split while tolling in honor of George Washington's birthday on February 22, 1846.

10. Mateo **busted/burst** into the meeting and announced that we would have to evacuate the building because of a bomb threat.

11. Diana Nyad has successfully **swam/swum** from Havana to Key West without the aid of a shark cage.

12. About 230 no-hitters have been **threw/thrown** in major league history.

13. Nicole has **catched/caught** the flu and can't go with us.

14. Bedford Springs Resort, located in the Allegheny Mountains of Pennsylvania, has **sprang/sprung** back to life since undergoing a $120 million renovation to restore it to its former glory.

15. On December 5, 2008, $108 million worth of jewelry was **stole/stolen** from the Harry Winston jewelry boutique in Paris, France, by six robbers, including four men who were dressed as women.

16. Each of the 765 people in the auditorium who were **swear/sworn** in as new U.S. citizens was excited and happy.

17. The hopes of the Confederacy were **sank/sunk** when General Lee surrendered to General Grant at Appomattox Courthouse at the end of the Civil War.

18. Paula and I had never **rode/ridden** in a parade before.

19. A wind gust may have **blew/blown** a Bronx Zoo tram car partially off its tracks, but there were no injuries.

20. Apple's newest iPhone has **broke/broken** sales records set by the company's previous iPhone.

21. Evidence has **grew/grown** that Himalayan ice fields have shrunk drastically in the last 50 years.

22. In five days Jane Yatman had **rode/ridden** 675 miles on her bicycle.

23. If a caveman had **threw/thrown** out a glass bottle a million years ago, it might still be there today, because it takes that long for a bottle to decompose.

24. Have you **gave/given** blood today?

25. We **saw/seen** the article that Elvis Presley failed his music class.

Chapter Review Two

Correct each of the following sentences.

1. Even if I had saw the movie review, I'd have gone anyway.

2. Michael Phelps could have won 31,000 gold coins ($5.7 million) if he had swam for Turkey because Turkish regulations reward sportsmen who earn awards in international competitions.

3. I wish I had spoke up when Anthony unfairly criticized Willa.

4. Blues legend B.B. King had flew his own plane to concerts until he turned 75, when his manager and insurance company objected.

5. Doctors in London have gave a woman a new windpipe with tissue from her own stem cells, eliminating the threat of rejection.

6. Someone had threw a garbage bag by the side of the road.

7. Parasites such as roundworms, hookworms, flukes, and tapeworms, which have grew as long as 32 feet, can live inside our bodies.

8. We drunk the apple cider and ate hot dogs around the fire.

9. Avian or bird flu has sprang up in many parts of the world, potentially threatening humans if the virus mutates.

10. We been reading that the Arial Sea has shrunk from more than 24,000 square miles to about 10,000 square miles in the last 40 years because feeder rivers have been diverted for irrigation.

11. During a typical lifetime of a lead pencil, it has wrote 50,000 English words.

12. The roar of laughter during the play *Our American Cousin* drownded out the sound of gunshots fired by John Wilkes Booth during the assassination of Abraham Lincoln.

13. We drug the heavy chest up to the attic.

14. The all-time one day record for the most books sold was broke in 2007 by J.K. Rowling's *Harry Potter and the Deathly Hollows,* when 2,652,656 copies were sold in a single day in England.

15. The Russian nuclear submarine Kursk sunk in the Barents Sea on August 12, 2000, with a loss of all 118 crewmembers.

16. The irrigation pipe busted, flooding the field.

17. Shelly has been forbid to play her electric guitar in her apartment.

18. The Tesla, an electric car developed in California, has drawn favorable responses from people who have rode in it.

19. The *Mona Lisa*, which was painted in 1503, was stole from the Louvre in Paris on August 21, 1911.

20. We should have knew that in Texas it is illegal to put graffiti on someone else's cow.

21. Consumers have ran out of confidence in the economy.

22. Showing tolerance for other's mistakes and weaknesses is one sign that a person has grew up.

23. The hikers would have freezed to death if they hadn't found the shelter in time.

24. Residents of Corona, California, have ran out of patience with their city leaders because since the 1930s the city has lost all seventeen of the time capsules it originally buried.

25. No white man had saw the Grand Canyon until after the Civil War.

Chapter Review Three

Correct each of the following sentences.

1. A date that is well-planned is often more successful than one that is threw together at the last minute.

2. How safe are wore out tires?

3. At a shopping mall in Abbotsford, British Columbia, we seen the largest water clock in North America.

4. A car is stole every 30 seconds in the United States.

5. The practice of exchanging presents at Christmas begun with the Romans.

6. Ben Franklin impersonator Ralph Archbold had his heart stole by Linda Wilde, a Betsy Ross impersonator, and the two married in 2008.

7. Frank Oresnik has drove his 1991 Chevy pickup more than a million miles.

8. The hikers were hid from view in the rain forest.

9. Tracy must have forgot that in Minnesota it is illegal for women to be dressed as Santa Claus on city streets.

10. The ice cream tastes better when it's thawed and not froze.

11. We seen that the odds of being killed by a tornado are one in two million.

12. The football players come together in a quick huddle.

13. We have ate all the M & M's.

14. At a full gallop the giraffe run about 30 miles an hour.

15. Jasmine had swam in two other relay races besides this one.

16. Hundreds of thousands of people were drownded on December 26, 2004, when a tsunami caused catastrophic floods in Southeast Asia.

17. If you started with one cent and doubled your money every day, you would have became a millionaire in 27 days.

18. In seven years the price of American Apparel stock had fell from $27 to 68 cents.

19. The oldest known love song was wrote 4,000 years ago and comes from an area between the Tigris and Euphrates Rivers.

20. Clever bioengineers in the U.S. come up with Starlight Avatar, a glowing plant that can be used as a lamp, but it's not on the market yet.

Lie and *Lay*

Two verbs cause special confusion. These are:

lie	(is) lying	lay	(has) lain
lay	(is) laying	laid	(has) laid

The verb *to lie* means *to rest* or *remain in place*.

Examples:
The *Titanic* **lies** at the bottom of the ocean.
The *Titanic* **is lying** at the bottom of the ocean.
The *Titanic* **lay** at the bottom of the ocean after it sank.
The *Titanic* **has lain** at the bottom of the ocean since it sank in 1912.

Remember that *lay* is the past tense of *lie*.

Example:
Yesterday I **lay** in bed all day.

The verb to *lay* means *to put* or *to place*.

Example:
Please **lay** the tile carefully.
The workman **is laying** the tile carefully.
The workman **laid** the tile carefully.
The workman **has laid** the tile carefully.

Always remember: *laying* means *putting*.
                           ***laid* means *put*.**

If it doesn't make sense to substitute *put* for *laid* in a sentence, you can't use it. If it doesn't make sense to substitute *putting* for *laying* in a sentence, you can't use it either.

Examples:
Tony is carefully *laying (putting)* the engine parts on the shelf.

Tony carefully *laid (put)* the engine parts on the shelf.

Exercise Four

Circle the correct verb.

1. I **lay/laid** awake most of the night, worrying about giving my speech.

2. The crisp five dollar bills were **lying/laying** on the counter.

3. The building's foundation wasn't **lain/laid** properly.

4. Prince William and Prince Harry have **lain/laid** a wreath at England's Tomb of the Unknown Warrior.

5. The archeologists are discovering pottery that has **lain/laid** in the ground for centuries.

6. The ambulance attendant is **laying/lying** the injured worker on a stretcher.

7. The equator is an imaginary circle that **lies/lays** exactly between the North and South Poles and goes around the middle of the earth for 24,902 miles.

8. Frenchy is **lying/laying** down for a rest.

9. The ancient country of Greece **lies/lays** in an important position between Europe, Asia, and Africa.

10. If we **lie/lay** the umbrellas here, they'll dry off before we have to use them again.

Rise and Raise

Two other verbs are sometimes confused. These are:

rise	is rising	rose	(has) risen
raise	is raising	raised	(has) raised

The verb to *rise* means to *go up* or *get up*.

Examples:
The sun *will rise* at 6:04 tomorrow morning.
The sun *is rising*.
The sun *rose* at 6:03 yesterday morning.
By 6:10 the sun *had* fully *risen*.

The verb *raise* means to *lift*.

Examples:
We *will raise* the flag at sunrise.
We *are raising* the flag at sunrise.
We *raised* the flag at sunrise.
We *have raised* the flag at sunrise each day this week.

Exercise Five

Circle the correct verb.

1. The Mississippi River is **rising/raising** very quickly.

2. There was no reason to spend the money to **rise/raise** the ship, since there was very little valuable cargo left on board.

3. A full moon always **rises/raises** at sunset.

4. They **rose/raised** the hopes of conservationists with the purchase of the forest land to be put aside for a park.

5. We were nervous about performing until the curtain **raised/rose**.

6. Don't **rise/raise** your voice because the baby is taking a nap.

7. Table salt is the only commodity that hasn't **raised/risen** dramatically in price in the last one hundred-fifty years.

8. We are expected to **rise/raise** for the national anthem.

9. The marina **lies/lays** on the south side of the lake.

10. A treasure hunter from Los Angeles is in Texas looking for a sunken treasure ship that has **lain/laid** undisturbed for hundreds of years.

11. High barometric air pressure is characterized by clear skies with high pressure **rising/raising** air up.

12. Experts warn that as the climate warms, Neanderthal or even smallpox viruses that have **laid/lain** dormant for thousands of years could be released.

13. Some state legislators want to **rise/raise** the speed limit to 75 m.p.h.

14. It's estimated that 80% of items **laying/lying** in landfills could be recycled.

15. A flag with a symbol of a **rising/raising** sun is the Japanese military flag.

16. All U.S. Presidents have **wore/worn** glasses, although some didn't like being seen wearing them in public.

17. If this company has a plan for growth, it's well **hid/hidden** from those of us who work here.

18. Jennifer Figge, an endurance athlete, has **swam/swum** across the Atlantic Ocean from the Cape Verde Islands to Trinidad.

19. People are **forbid/forbidden** to serve on a jury if they have been convicted in a state or federal court of a crime punishable by more than one year of imprisonment, and that person's civil rights have not been restored.

20. The prosecutor **lay/laid** the crime scene photos on a table where jurors could see them.

Final Chapter Review

Correct each of the following sentences.

1. President Barack Obama was swore in as president on January 20, 2009.

2. Caleb don't believe acorns were used as a coffee substitute during the Civil War.

3. Actually, cheetahs have ran as fast as forty-five miles an hour.

4. You should have took my advice.

5. Stevie Wonder said he wasn't nervous when he sung at the White House.

6. Marcus hasn't ate much local food since he arrived in Scotland because he heard Mike Myers say, "My theory is that all of Scottish cuisine is based on a dare."

7. Robert "Hoot" Gibson has flew more than 110 different kinds of airplanes.

8. Before Calvin Coolidge become president of the United States in 1923, he was governor of Massachusetts.

9. Amy has chose not to believe that hard-rock music makes termites chew through wood at twice their usual speed.

10. We watched as the beavers drug big sticks through the water to build their dam.

11. Belgrade, Serbia, has rose from the destruction of its civil war in the 1990s to become a blossoming tourist city.

12. We seen that the original name of Scrabble was Lexico.

13. The abandoned boat was believed to have sank on February 13, 2014.

14. Dorothy Parker said, "This is not a novel to be tossed aside lightly. It should be threw down with great force."

15. An extremely rare mega mouth shark was accidentally caught and then later butchered and ate by Philippine fishermen.

16. Sofia said, "If you forget me, I will have already forgot you."

17. We sprung a great surprise party for Marco at the Thompson Hotel in Chicago.

18. The Aflac duck has rang the New York Stock Exchange closing bell.

19. Jose Reyes has stole 40 bases a season for the fifth time in his career.

20. NASA has discovered evidence of a sea on the planet Saturn that was previously hid from view.

21. Residents of three Oklahoma towns—Langston, Spencer, and Jones—have recently been shook by earthquakes, and Oklahoma has now surpassed California in the number of yearly quakes.

22. "Sugar can act like poison in high doses, and the amount in American diets has went beyond toxic," said Robert Lustig, M.D. a neuro-endocrinologist.

23. Smart Shops' profits have grew 5 percent a year for the past four years.

24. One survey reports that one-third of dog owners admit they have spoke to their dogs on the phone or left messages on answering machines while they were away.

25. Surfer Garrett McNamara has rode a 90-foot wave off the coast of Nazare, Portugal.

Usage Glossary

Homonyms that are often misused:

capital - a) a city or town that is the official seat of government of a state or nation
b) something punishable by death as a "capital offense"
c) an upper case (capital) letter
d) money used in an investment to make more money
capitol - the building where a legislature meets

Examples:

Tallahassee is the ***capital*** of Florida.
You need a ***capital*** letter here.
The company went bankrupt because it didn't have enough ***capital*** to pay its creditors.
The U.S. ***Capitol*** Visitor Center was opened in December 2008.

counsel - a) advice
b) a lawyer
council - a committee

Examples:

The governor's advisors provided good ***counsel.***
The ***council*** members engaged in a heated argument.

peak - highest level, top of a mountain
peek - look quickly

Examples:

Computers can't operate at ***peak*** performance if they're infected with viruses.
Take a ***peek*** and tell me what is going on.

compliment - praise
complement - to complete or make perfect
complimentary - given free of charge

Examples:

Purdue University sophomores Cameron Brown and Brett Westcott handed out **compliments** to fellow students on a crusade to make people happy.

Chopsticks may be the perfect **complement** to a Chinese meal.
More and more hotels are offering **complimentary** breakfasts.

stationary - not moving
stationery - paper used for writing

Examples:

My dog barks only at **stationary** objects, never at people or other dogs.
It was expensive **stationery**.

principle - accepted rule of action or conduct
principal - a) highest in rank or importance; foremost
             b) the amount of money that is invested or loaned

Examples:

We believe in the **principle** of fair play.
He is the **principal** investor in the company.
Being a school **principal** can be a difficult job.

sight - vision
site - location
cite - a) to quote
        b) refer to an example

Examples:

In 2008 some partygoers at an outdoor rave near Moscow, Russia, lost partial **sight** after a laser show burned their retinas.
The Veterans Administration has chosen the **site** for the new hospital.
I'm using the *MLA Handbook for Writers of Research Papers* to properly **cite** my sources.

Exercise One

Circle the correct word choice.

1. Former basketball star Manute Bol has provided the **capitol/capital** to build a school in the African village in the Sudan where he was raised.

2. The first word in every sentence begins with a **capital/capitol** letter.

3. In a U.S. courtroom the attorney or lawyer who represents the defendant is the defense **council/counsel**.

4. The U.N. Security **Counsel/Council** met recently in New York City.

5. Karen and Paul's baby learned to play **peak/peek**-a-boo.

6. Do you believe in the **principle/principal** of equal pay for equal work?

7. Members of the President's cabinet provide **council/counsel** and advice to the President.

8. The **peak/peek** decibel level of rock music concerts at 16 feet from a speaker is 150 decibels.

9. There's a resort in Japan located on a mountain **peak/peek** where one can observe a sea of clouds floating below.

10. Scientists **cite/site/sight** research to support the belief that the 1905 San Francisco earthquake, one of the most destructive on record, was probably an 8.25 on the Richter scale.

11. Most mobile homes are actually **stationary/stationery**.

12. The website said, "Finding the right personalized **stationary/stationery** can be the difference between sending the same boring thing as everyone else, and making an unforgettable first impression."

13. For most people around the world, their **principal/principle** Internet search engine is Google.

14. Mr. Sanchez, our old school **principal/principle**, is going to retire at the end of this year.

15. The state **capital/capitol** building is lit at night.

16. Bill Gates said, "In the long run, a country's human **capital/capitol** is its main base of competition."

17. In deep space nothing is **stationary/stationery**.

18. The sign said, "**Complementary/Complimentary** valet parking."

19. The Army Corps of Engineers' expert **council/counsel** was to rebuild the damaged levees two feet higher.

20. Most people have lost **cite/site/sight** of the fact that fresh fruits and vegetables are not more nutritious than frozen ones.

21. The Grand Canyon is the **sight/site** of many varieties of coyotes, foxes, bobcats, chipmunks, squirrels, and kangaroo rats.

22. Many doctors advise that sports drinks do not help an athlete achieve **peek/peak** performance.

23. The city **council/counsel** met until 6:45 p.m.

24. I think Jeremy was actually embarrassed by all the **complements/compliments** he received.

25. **Complimentary/Complementary** colors in paint, such as yellow and purple, are located directly opposite each other on the color wheel.

Similar Words that are Often Misused

a - Use 'a' before words that begin with a consonant.
an - Use 'an' before words that begin with a vowel or vowel sound.

Examples:

Apaches are *a* tribe of Native Americans who live in the southwestern United States.
I'll meet you in *an* hour.
Geronimo was *an* Apache.

accept - to agree or receive willingly
except - exclude; but

Examples:

Abdul Fakir, the lone surviving member of the Four Tops was present to *accept* a Grammy Award for the group.

Pumpkin meat was once recommended for removing freckles, *except* this advice didn't work.

advice - recommendation
advise - to give advice to

Examples:

The defense attorney's **_advice_** to his client was to take the plea agreement.
My sister refused to **_advise_** me one way or another about changing my major.

affect - to influence
effect - a) to accomplish
        b) the result of an action

Examples:

Some researchers believe the "Do Not Call" list might **_affect_** survey research results.
Losing his job seemed to have no **_effect_** on Kelton's behavior.

all ready - completely ready
already - before or by this time

Examples:

We are **_all ready_** to get started.
She has **_already_** made her speech about academic freedom.

anxious - uneasy
eager - excited, enthusiastic

Examples:

She's always **_anxious_** about getting to the airport on time.
People who are overly **_eager_** to please too often end up as doormats, taking whatever they are given instead of asking for what they want.

among – use among with three or more items
between – use with two items

Examples:

Among the alternative sources of generating electricity are solar, wind, and biofuels.
Individuals sometimes must decide **between** doing what is convenient and doing what is right.

amount - use for things that can't be counted
number - use for things that can be counted

Examples:

The magnitude 8.9 earthquake and subsequent tsunami in Japan on March 11, 2011, did a vast *amount* of damage.
There are a *number* of things we still haven't discussed.

Exercise Two

Circle the correct word choice.

1. Researchers have **all ready/already** studied more than 200,000 ostriches for over 80 years and never seen a single bird burying its head.

2. To experience greater happiness, psychologists **advice/advise** people to spend money on experiences as opposed to material possessions.

3. People who suffer from *agoraphobia* feel **anxious/eager** in situations where they perceive certain environments as dangerous or uncomfortable, and this feeling can be a reaction to either vast openness or crowded conditions.

4. Widespread drought is often called the costliest disaster **accept/except** for war.

5. The Ryder Cup is a men's golf competition **between/among** a team from Europe and a team from the United States.

6. Most people realize that the **affects/effects** of parental favoritism can be long-lasting.

7. Matt filled his notebooks with a large **number/amount** of trivial facts.

8. We were **eager/anxious** to discover that Orlando, Florida, has more to offer visitors than theme parks, gator farms, and citrus groves.

9. Positive text messages from people you care about positively **affect/effect** both your body and your mind.

10. It's hard to **accept/except** the fact that Elvis Presley was a natural blond.

11. Albert Einstein offered the **advice/advise**, "Learn from yesterday, live for today, and hope for tomorrow."

12. Starfishes, dolphins, and sea urchins are **among/between** the most common marine animals.

13. The rescue team took over **a/an** hour to reach the capsized sailboat.

14. We were **all ready/already** for our professor to finish her lecture.

15. The **amount/number** of money invested or borrowed is called the *principal*.

bad - use before nouns and after linking verbs
badly - use to modify action verbs

Examples:
It was a ***bad*** idea to pick the Rosetta Stone as a research paper topic.
Food additives may make children behave ***badly***.

can - the ability to do something
may - a) permission to do something
       b) the possibility of something happening

Examples:

Andy Roddick ***can*** serve a tennis ball faster than anyone else.
You ***may*** come with me.
Weather forecasters say that it ***may*** rain tomorrow.

conscience - inner sense of what is right or wrong.
conscious - aware of one's own existence, thoughts, surroundings, etc.

Examples:

His ***conscience*** was relieved after he returned the extra change he mistakenly received.
Natural foods are on the rise in an increasingly health-***conscious*** Europe.

bring - use *bring* when an object is being carried toward you.
take – use *take* when an object is being carried away.

Examples:

You could ***bring*** me a nice glass of lemonade.
A *New Yorker* magazine cartoon depicted two aliens telling a horse, "Kindly ***take*** us to your President."

152

desert - a) dry, arid land
         b) abandon someone or something
dessert - sweet treat eaten after a meal

Examples:

The Sahara in North Africa is the largest ***desert*** in the world, measuring approximately 3.5 million square miles.
It's cowardly to ***desert*** a friend in his or her time of need.
We all chose tiramisu for ***dessert.***

figuratively - not actually true, resembling in a symbolic way
literally - true, actual

Examples:

We had a blast, ***figuratively*** speaking.
Vice-President Biden has used the word ***literally*** when he was actually speaking figuratively.

irregardless - there is no such word
regardless - this word does exist

lead - when it rhymes with "deed" it means a) first place in a race
                                 b) an example
                                 c) a clue
                                 d) the main role in a play
lead - when it rhymes with "head" it means the metal
led - past tense of lead, the one that rhymes with "deed"

Examples:

Near the end of the marathon, Sterling took the ***lead.***
Men are expected to ***lead*** in ballroom dancing.
The detectives have few ***leads*** to follow.
Julia Roberts played the ***lead*** in the movie.
Workers installed the ***lead*** pipe.
Joseph ***led*** in the class rank.

Exercise Three

Circle the correct word choice.

1. Shabazz Napier **led/lead** his University of Connecticut team to a 60-54 victory over the University of Kentucky in the 2014 NCAA tournament final.

2. Don't feel **bad/badly** if you experience a failure early in your career because Walt Disney, Thomas Edison, and Oprah Winfrey weathered multiple failures before they found success.

3. Budget **conscious/conscience** tourists can enjoy a variety of free or low cost excursions in New York City including the Staten Island Ferry, The Metropolitan Museum of Art, and the Sony Wonder Technology Lab.

4. While it's impossible to be certain how many soldiers **deserted/desserted** during the Civil War, estimates are that one Union soldier in five left the army without permission, and estimates for Confederate soldiers are even higher.

5. You might need to **lead/led** a group discussion as part of your job.

6. "Juliet is the sun," is an example of **figurative/literal** language from *Romeo and Juliet.*

7. Brazilian prisoners **can/may** reduce their sentence by four days for every book they read and write a report on—up to 48 days a year.

8. Mark Twain said, "A clear **conscious/conscience** is a sure sign of a bad memory."

9. The *Huffington Post* rates a baked Alaska as the most difficult-to-make **desert/dessert**.

10. I'll help you **bring/take** the dogs to the vet.

11. Indian twins Shivanath and Shivram Sahu are living life fully, despite being **literally/figuratively** joined at the hip.

12. Narcissistic people don't have a **conscience/conscious** because they lack the ability to feel empathy for others.

13. Please **bring/take** a writing sample with you so that we can review it after your interview.

14. The player fumbled **bad/badly** when he bounced the ball off his knee.

15. One of the main advantages of refinancing a home loan—**regardless/irregardless** of equity—is reducing an interest rate.

16. During World War I Major General John J. Pershing **led/lead** the American Expeditionary Forces in Europe.

17. The Great Basin, the largest **desert/dessert** area of North America, covers most of Nevada, the western third of Utah, and parts of Idaho and Oregon.

18. Handheld cameras without flash or tripod **may/can** be used in the permanent collection of the Philadelphia Museum of Art.

19. On Facebook there are over 17,000 'likes' for images of **bad/badly** stuffed animals.

20. Bring/Take a sweatshirt or sweater with you on the hike in case it gets chilly.

Official U.S. Postal Abbreviations:

Alabama	AL	Montana	MT
Alaska	AK	Nebraska	NE
Arizona	AZ	Nevada	NV
Arkansas	AR	New Hampshire	NH
California	CA	New Jersey	NJ
Colorado	CO	New Mexico	NM
Connecticut	CT	New York	NY
Delaware	DE	North Carolina	NC
District of Columbia	DC	North Dakota	ND
Florida	FL	Ohio	OH
Georgia	GA	Oklahoma	OK
Hawaii	HI	Oregon	OR
Idaho	ID	Pennsylvania	PA
Illinois	IL	Rhode Island	RI
Indiana	IN	South Carolina	SC
Iowa	IA	South Dakota	SD
Kansas	KS	Tennessee	TN
Kentucky	KY	Texas	TX
Louisiana	LA	Utah	UT
Maine	ME	Vermont	VT
Maryland	MD	Virginia	VA
Massachusetts	MA	Washington	WA
Michigan	MI	West Virginia	WV
Minnesota	MN	Wisconsin	WI
Mississippi	MS	Wyoming	WY
Missouri	MO		

Chapter Review One

Circle the correct word choice.

1. The **number/amount** of people in the world who are infected with hookworms is estimated at between 500-700 million.

2. Kyle Wiens, CEO of iFixit, argues that it is important to take into account job applicants' grammatical abilities, **regardless/irregardless** of the job they are applying for.

3. If a manager reacts **bad/badly** to a resignation, it can have a profound impact on the remaining employees.

4. Freshman writing instructors **advice/advise** students that passing off someone else's writing as their own is an academic felony.

5. If you've ever had an instinctive sensation that things aren't going quite right, even if on the surface everything seems fine, then you're picking up subconscious clues that you're not **conscious/conscience** of.

6. Trader Joe's opened Friday, fulfilling a longtime dream of many locals **eager/anxious** to have the gourmet grocery closer to home.

7. The greatest similarity **among/between** the many tribes that inhabited North America at the dawn of European colonization was their distinct cultures had developed as adaptations to their local natural environments.

8. Although everyone knows that seawater is salty, few know that even small variations in ocean surface salinity can have dramatic **affects/effects** of ocean circulation.

9. Weather forecasters predict that there **may/can** be a drop in temperature tomorrow.

10. On New Year's Day in Russia, Father Frost **brings/takes** presents to the children's homes.

11. Historians **sight/site/cite** the unusual example of Gerald Ford, the only person to be President and Vice-president, but not elected to either.

12. The human brain is heavier than any other animal **accept/except** the elephant and whale.

13. The Malaysian Space Agency convened a conference of 150 Islamic scholars for **advice/advise** on how a Muslim astronaut on the Space Station should pray facing Mecca.

14. The Great Smoky Mountains Railroad **takes/brings** passengers through the beautiful countryside of western North Carolina.

15. Newman's Own food has **already/all ready** donated more than $400 million dollars to various charities.

16. Rihanna plays the first black **lead/led** character in the 3D animated film *Home*.

17. Dogs feel **bad/badly** when their owners admonish them, but not for what the dogs did, but rather for their owners' display of anger.

18. The **amount/number** of matter contained in an object is its *mass*.

19. The Carolina Abecedarian Project which was instituted to improve children's intellect also **lead/led** to much better health for these children when they became adults.

20. Dogs and cats **can/may** watch TV, especially the newer models, and TV producers have started special TV channels for dogs.

21. A fever, injury, anemia, or infection can **affect/effect** a person's heart rate.

22. Apple pie is not the most popular **desert/dessert** in America; fudge is.

23. General George S. Patton said, "**Accept/Except** the challenges so that you feel the exhilaration of victory."

24. A recent war of words **between/among** Russia and the United States raised tensions to one of the highest points since the Cold War.

25. The mayor said that city offices were **already/all ready** for the expected harsh weather later today.

26. Sedatives can be used for those people who are extremely **eager/anxious** in everyday life.

27. Previous **capitals/capitols** of the United States include Philadelphia, Pennsylvania, and New York, New York.

28. According to psychologists, if you have celebrated your 21st birthday, most likely you have **already/ all ready** met the man or woman that you will marry.

29. Some parents and teachers are urging school boards to **bring/take** back recess to get kids out on the playground for some much-needed exercise.

30. Scientists say that it's rare but possible for someone to **figuratively/literally** be scared to death as a result of a severe fright or traumatic event.

31. A sociopath is a person who has no **conscious/conscience** but who has effectively learned how to manage his or her way through life where few people can detect how different this person is.

32. People who try to suppress their thoughts discover this has an ironic rebound **affect/effect**: the thought comes back stronger than before.

33. The **Council/Counsel** of Economic Advisors is an agency within the Executive Office of the President that advises the President on economic policy.

34. Should we **accept/except** the theory that people are more productive in blue rooms?

35. The National Highway Traffic Safety Administration **advices/advises** that people not drive when they are tired, because being tired accounts for the highest number of fatal, single-car crashes, even more than alcohol.

36. **Regardless/Irregardless** of the fact that one marriage counselor noted that the most competitive, most volatile, and most discouraging marriage combinations are where both spouses are firstborns or, worse, only children, we are still engaged.

37. Nearly half of Iran has an arid **desert/dessert** climate, with less than four inches of rain a year.

38. Glitches in a new computer system in Dallas, Texas, **lead/led** authorities to mistakenly release more than 20 inmates from the county jail.

39. Similes are a type of **figurative/literal** language.

40. Patrick Henry, famous in history for his "Give me liberty or give me death" speech, was risking his life for his **principles/principals**, since to speak against the king of England was treason.

41. **Capital/Capitol** expenditures, by definition, are the business expenditures on assets that will last more than a year.

42. After seven weeks of climbing, New Zealander Edmund Hillary and Nepalese Tensig Norgay were the first climbers to reach the **peak/peek** of Mt. Everest on May 29, 1953.

43. Windmills always turn counter-clockwise, **accept/except** for windmills in Ireland.

44. At the retrial, the new defense attorney said that the previous ineffective assistance by defense **council/counsel** prevented the jury from hearing most of the important evidence in the case.

45. **Complementary/Complimentary** guest WiFi Internet access is now available at Disneyland's Animal Kingdom.

46. A **stationary/stationery** bike is a great way to burn calories, and there's no worry about bad weather because it's used indoors.

47. According to a pharmaceutical company study, accountants have the highest **amount/number** of on-the-job headaches followed by librarians and bus drivers.

48. Gloria Steinem said, "I have yet to hear a man ask for **advise/advice** on how to combine marriage and a career."

49. The U.S. Constitution states that a trial by jury is guaranteed **accept/except** in cases of impeachment.

50. After the accident Sabrina was barely **conscious/conscience**.

imply - to suggest
infer - to draw a conclusion

Examples:
I didn't mean to *imply* that I thought you were being rude.

If workers are asked to do their jobs differently, some employees will *infer* that the real message is that they aren't doing their jobs well.

later -coming after the usual time
latter - a) the second mentioned of two
   b) more advanced in time

Examples:
Write an essay before its due date so you can proofread it at a *later* time.

Although e-mails and text messaging are both widely used, people often prefer the *latter*.
The meeting is scheduled for the *latter* part of the day.

loose - not tight
lose - a) unable to find
   b) getting rid of
   c) defeated

Examples:
The United States formed a *loose* confederation of states under the Articles of Confederation.

I'm trying to think of putting my keys someplace where I won't *lose* them.
Sometimes in an argument you win the battle but *lose* the war.

moral - concerned with the principles of right and wrong
morale - emotional or mental condition

Examples:

Harvard professor Benjamin Friedman argues that there are *moral* benefits as well as material benefits to economic growth.

Poor worker *morale* negatively impacts production efficiency and product quality.

passed - past tense of pass

past - a) at a former time

b) proceed by

Examples:

Robert was disappointed that he was ***passed*** over for a promotion.

We shouldn't worry about what happened in the ***past***.

Tonia drove ***past*** their house, but there were no lights on.

quiet - silent, or nearly so

quit - to stop, give up, or resign

quite - very or completely

Examples:

The library was not really very ***quiet.***

He ***quit*** his job before he found another one.

I'm ***quite*** happy with the grade I got on this assignment.

thorough - a) extremely attentive to accuracy and detail

b) complete

threw - past tense of throw

through - a) in at one end and out at the other

b) during the whole period

Examples:

This book provides a ***thorough*** look at the use of robots around the world.

He ***threw*** a strikeout to win the game.

We lost radio reception as we drove ***through*** the tunnel.

uninterested - not interested, not enthusiastic, indifferent

disinterested - impartial and unbiased

Examples:

He was ***uninterested*** in studying parasites.

The county commissioner needs to be a ***disinterested*** party in making the decision.

Exercise Four

Circle the correct word choice.

1. Computer games have had a powerful **affect/effect** on films because several popular games such as *Lara Croft: Tomb Raider* and *Mortal Kombat* have been made into movies.

2. The army recruits received **thorough/through** instructions.

3. The **moral/morale** in the company was low after all raises were cancelled.

4. Governor John Kitzhaber, in stating that Oregon ranks high in "the happiness index," did not mean to **imply/infer** that a successful economy is unimportant.

5. Of the two earthquakes, the **later/latter** was far stronger.

6. When somebody asked me if I knew you, a million memories flashed **thorough/through/threw** my mind, but I just smiled and said, "I used to."

7. The **later/latter** Crusades were generally only expeditions to assist those who were already in the Holy Land and to defend lands they had captured.

8. It's up to the President's cabinet to **advice/advise** the President.

9. A U.S. nursing home specialist **cited/sited/sighted** the example of a Dusseldorf, Germany, nursing home with many Alzheimer patients that installed fake bus stops outside the facility to detain patients who wandered away.

10. Kevin Spacey was present to **accept/except** the 2009 Pell Award from the Trinity Repertory Company in Providence, Rhode Island.

11. In the Serengeti National Park in Tanzania, tourists can enjoy the spectacular **cite/site/sight** of gazelles, zebras, lions, elephants, and other animals in the wild.

12. Brit felt a **moral/morale** obligation to find the owner of the wallet.

13. During World War II the saying, "**Loose/Lose** lips sink ships," meant that people needed to be careful not to repeat any military information they might have heard.

14. Kaylee is a junk food addict, so she can't **lose/loose** weight.

15. On his Texas ranch, President Lyndon Johnson would often **bring/take** guests for a ride in his amphibious car and scare them by driving into his lake, while yelling that there was a brake failure.

16. "Sometimes I think what I write is funny in its **quiet/quit/quite** way," said Doris Lessing.

17. According to a medical study, it's common for a patient to forget half of his or her doctor's recommendations, often because a doctor failed to repeat the **advice/advise** or summarize it.

18. One child out of every 150 is **affected/effected** in some degree by autism.

19. From last week's report on consumer spending, we can **imply/infer** that Americans are saving a greater portion of their incomes.

20. **Literally/Figuratively** speaking, an Amazon is a large, strong, aggressive woman.

21. When people say, "Chickens have come home to roost," it means that **passed/past** actions are making themselves felt.

22. We were **all ready/already** to see if the groundhog will see its shadow on February 2.

23. Extended sleeplessness has **led/lead** people into mood swings, hallucinations, and in extreme cases, death.

24. In classical mythology, when Jason **deserted/desserted** Medea to marry another woman, Medea murdered his young bride as well as the children she had borne him.

25. At first the general had doubts about the proposed plan, but eventually he became **anxious/eager** to implement it.

26. Roadrunners, ostriches, meerkats, lizards, and poisonous spiders inhabit U.S. **desserts/deserts**.

27. The Dalai Lama has **lead/led** his people for more than 68 years, longer than Queen Elizabeth II.

28. The municipal judge needs to be a **disinterested/uninterested** observer to fairly pass judgment.

29. Robert Mugabe, once a prisoner of **conscious/conscience**, has become a brutal dictator of Zimbabwe.

30. Mariano Rivera, in his 19 seasons as a relief pitcher for the New York Yankees, **threw/through** the best slider in major league baseball and was the career leader in saves with 652.

31. "The Capitol twinkles like a vast swarm of fireflies," is an example of **literal/figurative** language.

32. In accounting, the formal process of choosing **between/among** three or more alternatives is known as a decision model.

33. On May 31, 2013, a large asteroid **passed/past** relatively close to earth, coming within 6 million kilometers, or about 15 times the distance to the moon.

34. Emotional pain is more clearly remembered than physical pain and has more **affect/effect** on a person's behavior.

35. U.S. businesses **lose/loose** more than $1 billion a year in productivity due to chronic illness.

Fewer versus *Less*

Fewer is used only with plural nouns that can be counted.

Examples:

The airline promised *fewer* delays in the future.

Less is used only with singular nouns that can't be counted.

Examples:

The poet Lawrence Ferlinghetti said, "Paintings may communicate better because people are lazy, and they can look at a painting with *less* effort than they can read a poem."

Farther versus *Further*

Farther usually refers to a physical distance.

Example:

If humans are going to travel *farther* into space than the moon, it will likely take a partnership of government and private industry.

Further refers to a greater amount, degree, or extent.

Example:

We need to examine these issues *further* before we make any decision.

Writing Abbreviations

Useful Abbreviations:

Mr.   Mister
Mrs.   Missus
Ms.   (No written out form)
Dr.   Doctor
A.D.   in the year of the Lord (anno domini)
A.M.   before noon (ante meridiem)
P.M.   after noon (post meridiem)
Ph.D.   Doctor of Philosophy
RSVP   please reply (repondez s'il vous plait)
w/o   without

In formal writing do not abbreviate the word Miss or the days of the week or the months of the year.

Use Adjectives and Adverbs Correctly

Use adjectives to modify nouns and after linking verbs.

Examples:

After Hurricane Katrina, Matthew McConaughey helped rescue ***lost*** pets.

This kale tastes ***awful.***

Use adverbs to modify verbs, adjectives, and other adverbs.

Examples:

Maria sat ***quietly*** at the back of the lecture hall.

Casey Stengel said, "All right everyone, line up ***alphabetically*** according to your height."

The rescue was completed ***surprisingly*** quickly.

Frequently misused adjective/adverb pairs: *real/really, slow/slowly, bad/badly, easy/easily, simple/simply, careful/carefully, excellent/excellently, beautiful/beautifully, loud/loudly, quick/quickly, poor/poorly, tight/tightly, perfect/perfectly,*

Exercise Five

Circle the correct word choice.

1. The pilots of Asiana Flight 214 were flying too **slow/slowly** as they approached the airport, triggering an onboard stall warning, but it was too late for the pilots to abort the landing.

2. After the devastating typhoon, relief supplies to the 150,000 residents of Tacloban City trickled in very **slow/slowly**.

3 The *Voyager* spacecraft is now 125 times **farther/further** from the sun than we are on earth.

4. Drivers should not pass bicyclists so **close/closely** that cyclists are pushed to the edge of the road.

5. Physiotherapist Maureen Dwight of the Orthopedic Therapy Clinic, Inc. said, "People have changed relatively **quick/quickly** from being hunters and gatherers to becoming techno-sedentary beings."

6. Radio waves travel more **easy/easily** through space than through water.

7. Germany's Bundersbank has completely exhausted its stock of private assets and has sunk **farther/further** into debt in an attempt to prop up the European financial system.

8. The Navy is stuck with a number of **poor/poorly** performing ships that can't be fixed because Congress hasn't resolved its budget stalemate.

9. A South Carolina mother was arrested for cheering too **loud/loudly** at her daughter's high school graduation.

10. The U.S. Forest Service study provides **farther/further** evidence of the key role forests play in flood control and reducing sediment flow from agricultural lands into our watersheds.

11. After Continental and United Air Lines merged, the two computer systems integrated very **smooth/smoothly.**

12. There are now **fewer/less** restrictions for religious, academic, and cultural groups who want to travel to Cuba.

13. Nina answered **correct/correctly** that St. Patrick's Day was first celebrated in Boston before the American Revolution.

14. The consensus of opinion among the U.S. delegation is that the world is now **farther/further** away from a financial crises.

15. After cleaning the chimney masonry, Landon used a crack and joint sealant to reseal the chimney **tight/tightly**.

16. Herbie Hancock said, "My father always wanted to be a doctor, but he came from a **real/really** poor family in Georgia, and there was no way he was going to be a doctor."

17. A recent survey shows that there are now **fewer/less** cars per person in U.S. cities than there were five years ago.

18. Yahoo CEO Marissa Mayer was widely criticized when she banned her 12,000 employees from working from home, but a company spokesperson now insists returning everyone to the workplace is working out **perfect/perfectly.**

19. Don't drown yourself in sorrow just because you performed **poor/poorly** on a test.

20. After a mother tiger lost her **premature/prematurely** born cubs and was diagnosed as depressed, zoologists wrapped newborn piglets in tiger-print cloth, and the tiger treated those piglets as if they were her own.

21. Grammatically correct signs at grocery store checkout lanes read, "Twelve items or **fewer/less**."

22. An island in Italy that was a dumping ground for plague victims and the insane is considered so **dangerous/dangerously** haunted that the Italian government doesn't allow public access.

23. **Less/Fewer** than 60% of Americans can read well enough to understand the label on their prescription medicine.

24. A study conducted by the University of Southern California found that people who switched from eating snacks with their dominant hand to their non-dominant hand ate **less/fewer** snacks.

25. Because Stockton, California, is in bankruptcy, there are **fewer/less** police officers to patrol the city streets.

Exercise Six

Circle the correct word choice.

1. We saw a strange face **peeking/peaking** at us through the window.

2. The U.S. Congress meets at the **Capital/Capitol** Building in Washington, D.C.

3. We went **threw/through/thorough** two bags of potato chips last night.

4. The **moral/morale** of journalists covering China has improved since the Chinese government lifted many restrictions on what journalists could report.

5. Nelson Mandela's monument is at the **cite/site/sight** in South Africa where he was arrested 50 years ago.

6. People have greater success when they can **accept/except** criticism gracefully.

7. The fact that primary care doctors earn far less, on average, than specialists has **affected/effected** the number of new doctors who are willing to become primary care physicians.

8. The historian **cited/sited/sighted** statistics to prove that more American soldiers died of yellow fever during the Spanish-American War than in combat.

9. Many investors lost **capital/capitol** when the value of their mutual funds fell.

10. After a **through/thorough** investigation, scientists now realize that food cravings are driven by emotions and psychology, not because people are deficient in a specific nutrient.

11. Hurry, it's **later/latter** than you think.

12. Nicholas is so unpredictable that several of his friends call him "a **loose/lose** cannon."

13. **Through/Thorough** the years there has been a great deal of speculation about what caused the *H.L. Hunley* to mysteriously disappear after becoming the first submarine in history to sink an enemy warship during the Civil War in 1864.

14. The detectives made a **through/thorough** investigation of the crime scene.

15. During the early years of a home mortgage, very little of the payment goes to reduce the **principle/principal** of the loan; instead most of the payment goes to repay the interest.

16. A **through/thorough** investigation of decaffeinated coffee has resulted in the discovery that most of these coffees actually contain between 8 and 32 milligrams of caffeine, compared to 100-150 grams in regular coffee.

17. Chain gangs, in which prisoners were chained together as they did heavy labor, were discontinued in the U.S. in 1955 when such punishment was no longer considered **moral/morale**.

18. The Icelandic volcanic eruptions had very little **affect/effect** on the air quality in Europe.

19. One **affect/effect** of the hurricane was reduced oil supplies throughout the nation.

20. A recent study found that workers' **moral/morale** is hurt most by failure in communication.

21. Beijing, China, was the **cite/site/sight** of the 2008 Summer Olympics.

22. Randall has decided to **accept/except** the Rhodes scholarship to study at Oxford.

23. The banker seemed to **imply/infer** that I hadn't been completely honest on my loan application.

24. I've **already/all ready** made my decision.

25. Aging male monkeys **loose/lose** the hair on their heads the same way human males do.

Latin Abbreviations

e.g.	for example (exempli gratia)
et. al.	and others (et alia)
etc.	and so on (et cetera)
i.e.	in other words or that is (id est)
viz	namely
vs.	versus

Use Latin abbreviations sparingly, always making sure your readers clearly understand what you are saying.

Chapter Review Two

Circle the correct word choice.

1. One hundred dollars of his mortgage payment went toward the payment of his **principle/ principal**.

2. In Taiwan belching after a meal is considered a **complement/compliment** to the cook.

3. The **site/cite/sight** of a white flag on a battlefield signifies a surrender.

4. Very few criminals seem to suffer from a guilty **conscience/conscious**.

5. The sound **affects/effects** in the movie were incredible.

6. According to one experiment, starting high school one hour **later/latter** may reduce teen traffic accidents because students get more sleep and are less tired drivers.

7. Harvard professor Marc Hauser said, "**Moral/Morale** judgment is pretty consistent from person to person."

8. The Peter **Principle/Principal** states that people will be promoted to their highest level of incompetence.

9. Denzel shops online for cards and **stationary/stationery**.

10. The National Safety **Counsel/Council** is an organization that educates and influences people to prevent accidental injury and death.

11. A company's working **capital/capitol** is made up of a company's current financial assets minus its current financial liabilities (debts).

12. Advocates insist that some of the Medicare changes **complement/compliment** recent health care reform.

13. New Jersey officials plan to look at ways to nudge residents to lower electric use during **peek/peak** demand periods during the day.

14. The official J.K. Rowling Web **sight/site/cite** contains information in six languages about the Harry Potter books.

15. President Bush mourned the 2008 death of ABC New correspondent Tim Russert, calling him a "**thorough/through**, decent man."

16. Cost **conscience/conscious** consumers can save a lot of money on everything they buy.

17. The sense of **site/cite/sight** is one of the five senses which also include the sense of touch, smell, hearing, and taste.

18. A suburban Atlanta, Georgia, **principle/principal** was arrested in connection with an investigation into whether student scores were altered to improve school performance.

19. Why does it sometimes appear that **stationary/stationery** objects are moving?

20. Some low carb diets have been shown to negatively **affect/effect** dieters' memory skills.

21. Students need to **sight/site/cite** all the sources they use in research papers, including books, periodicals, and online information.

22. The Colorado State **Capitol/Capital** Building was built in the 1890s in Denver, Colorado.

23. A surprising number of people don't know how to accept a **complement/compliment** gracefully.

24. Signs advised drivers to turn on their headlights as they drove **thorough/through** the tunnel.

25. Of the two speakers, the **later/latter** was far more interesting.

Final Chapter Review

Correct each of the following sentences by crossing out the incorrect word and writing the correction above it.
One sentence is already correct.

1. In baseball a *walk off* home run is a run that gives the home team the led (and consequently the win) in the bottom of the final inning, and thus the home team can *walk off* the field immediately afterward.

2. In 2007 Microsoft CEO Steve Ballmer counciled fellow executives that there was "no chance the iPhone is going to get any significant market share."

3. The Children's Museum of Indianapolis is building a $25 million, 8,000 square foot "Dinosphere" featuring misty ponds, greenery, and a state-of-the-art sound system to compliment a dinosaur named Bucky which will be displayed there.

4. Desserts cover about one fifth of the earth's surface and occur where rainfall is less than 20 inches a year.

5. You should read the article "13 Big-Time Business Leaders Share the Best Advise They Ever Got" by Nina Zipkin.

6. One way to boost employees' moral is to always recognize people when they do a good job, either by praising them in a staff meeting or taking the time to thank them in a handwritten note.

7. Experts in Idaho Falls, Idaho, said a dinosaur fossil bed containing some 200 specimens could be the most important such sight in the state.

8. Mark Twain said, "Nothing is quiet so annoying as to have two people go right on talking when you're interrupting."

9. There is actually no danger in swimming right after you eat, though it may feel uncomfortable.

10. For the passed twenty years, consumers have ranked McDonalds last in customer satisfaction in a national survey of the most popular fast-food chains.

11. In York, England, it's perfectly legal to shoot a Scotsman with a bow and arrow, accept on Sundays.

12. Who knows what the recent record corporate profits infer about future stock market prices?

13. Our neighbor damaged his house bad when he used a can of spray paint and a lighter as a makeshift blowtorch to kill a spider in his laundry room, starting a blaze that caused $60,000 worth of damage.

14. Workers in Greece clock an average 2,034 hours a year versus an average of 1,302 hours in Germany, but the productivity of the later is 70 percent higher.

15. We've had more successful fishing results further up the coast.

16. Hugh Laurie said, "I am terribly conscience of the fact that the world doesn't need any more actors."

17. Express your style and sophistication with embossed, personalized stationary, notes, and invitations.

18. Irregardless of the fact that she was his wife, Nora Barnacle once asked James Joyce, "Why don't you write books people can read?"

19. Sports' psychology demonstrates that any skill must be mastered in practice before an athlete can experience peek performance in competition.

20. A report by the U.S. Product Safety Commission indicated that between 1978 and 1995 no less than 37 deaths in the U.S. resulted from falling vending machines.

Writing Numbers

Most people write out numbers that can be expressed in one or two words. Also, always write out a number if it begins a sentence.

Examples:

I only needed ten minutes to pick up a few things at the grocery store.

Three girls were riding bicycles through Central Park.

However, if spelling out the number would require three or more words, do not spell it out, but rearrange the sentence so that the number does not come first.

There were only 13,500 votes separating the winning candidate from the losing candidate.

When you use more than one number to modify a noun, spell out the first number or the shorter of the two numbers to avoid confusion.

Examples: four 6X10 feet of plywood, 14 three-inch nails, 20 five-gallon containers.

Use numerals for addresses, dates, exact times of day, exact amounts of money, exact measurements such as miles per hour, scores of games, and page numbers.

Examples:

Their address is 2930 Laramie Street.
My brother was born on May 11, 1989.
My alarm went off at 6:30 on Saturday morning.
This bread is $4.29 a loaf.

You can use numerals or write out simple fractions.

Examples:
A centimeter is two-fifths of an inch.
A centimeter is 2/5 of an inch.

The most important consideration in writing numbers is to be consistent within each category. For example if you choose numerals because one of the numbers is more than two syllables, then everything else in the category should also be written in numerals.

Example:

The exterior measurements of the house are 68 feet by 30 feet. The room sizes range from 12X15 feet to 22X28 feet.

Double Negatives

Generally, don't use two negative words together in the same sentence.

A negative word is a word that means *no* or *not*.

List of Negative Words

Some negative words are:

no	no one	scarcely	nowhere
not	never	neither	barely
none	hardly	rarely	nothing

Words that end in *n't* are also negative.

isn't	haven't	doesn't	weren't
hasn't	aren't	don't	shouldn't
won't	wouldn't	couldn't	can't

Correcting Double Negatives

Notice that double negatives can usually be corrected two ways.

Not correct: I haven't done nothing.
Correct: I haven't done anything.
Correct: I have done nothing.

Not Correct: We don't have nothing to do.
Correct: We don't have anything to do.
Correct: We have nothing to do.

Do not use ain't, which is non-standard, in place of *am not, is not, are not, has not, have not,* and their contractions.

Not correct: We ain't never seen such a good game.
Correct: We haven't ever seen such a good game.
Correct: We have never seen such a good game.

Exercise One

Circle the correct word choice.

1. It wasn't **any/no** surprise that workers at a Las Vegas hospital were suspended because they bet on when mortally ill patients would die.

2. There **was/wasn't** hardly enough time to eat our egg rolls.

3. When we got back from Australia, we looked up information on spiders there and didn't find **anything/nothing** about the ones we saw that were big enough to eat snakes.

4. We looked all over for that sign and couldn't find it **anywhere/nowhere**.

5. There **is/isn't** nothing for me to do here.

6. There haven't been **any/no** prisoners on Alcatraz Island since 1963.

7. Ice cream was served to new arrivals at Ellis Island, but since most people hadn't **ever/never** encountered it before, they thought it was butter and spread it on their toast.

8. Jefferson **could/couldn't** hardly keep from laughing when he told us what happened.

9. I **can/can't** hardly believe Coca-Cola was originally green.

10. We hadn't heard **anything/nothing** about the hacker group that took down the Papa John's website because their pizza was two hours late.

11. We were disappointed that there weren't **any/no** tickets left for the concert.

12. I **can/can't** hardly wait for those juicy steaks to come off the grill.

13. We didn't have **any/no** idea that scorpions can hold their breath for up to 6 days.

14. Harry S. Truman, who was president of the United States from 1945-1953, didn't have **any/no** college degree.

15. There **was/wasn't** no one who could figure out how to put it together.

16. No one **ever/never** told me that lab mice can run five miles a night on their treadmills.

17. We don't have **any/no** turkey for Thanksgiving.

18. The music was so soft we **could/couldn't** hardly hear it.

19. In Japan and Korea it isn't **ever/never** polite to leave a tip in a restaurant for good service.

20. That isn't **any/no** way for you to act.

Exercise Two

Circle the correct word choice.

1. Can't **anything/nothing** be done about this situation?

2. Therapists who specialize in treating couples say that partners that don't **ever/never** fight are keeping an emotional distance and don't really know each other.

3. There **is/isn't** hardly enough work here to keep us busy.

4. They **were/weren't** nowhere in sight.

5. Although Danny was in Boston at the time, he doesn't know **anything/nothing** about the hundreds of people who tossed rubber chickens in an attempt to break the chicken throwing world record.

6. Cory **could/couldn't** hardly get the heavy door open.

7. We didn't know **anything/nothing** about the website Split the Rent, which helps roommates pro-rate rent by the square foot while also taking into account different bedrooms' perks and faults such as variations in street noise and closet size.

8. I **can/can't** hardly believe that fingernails grow four times faster than toenails.

9. The U.S. retail industry makes $6.8 billion a year from gift cards that no one **ever/never** redeems.

10. We hadn't **ever/never** heard about the Harvard University study that suggested easily distracted people are more creative.

11. Morgan couldn't find the word in the dictionary **anywhere/nowhere**.

12. Nobody mentioned that to me **either/neither**.

13. We were surprised that there wasn't **anyone/no one** to tell us that forest fires move faster uphill than downhill.

14. We've been reading Walt Whitman's *Song of Myself* in English class, and I **can/can't** barely understand what it's all about.

15. Lara won't **ever/never** believe that forty percent of McDonald's profits come from the sale of Happy Meals.

Exercise Three

Correct each of the following sentences by crossing out the incorrect word or words and writing the correction above it.

1. Kevin ain't got money to go with us.

2. We couldn't never have predicted that the hat Princess Beatrice wore to the wedding of Prince William and Catherine Middleton would sell at a charity auction for $131,000.

3. I couldn't have no dessert until I ate my green beans first.

4. Since I don't know nothing about French painting, I'm the wrong person to ask.

5. I couldn't hardly have guessed that it takes food twelve hours to completely digest.

6. Eight-year-old Cayden Tarpalus raised money to pay off all the overdue lunch accounts at his school after he saw his friend didn't have no money for a hot lunch.

7. We don't want no more criticism.

8. You ain't seen nothing yet.

9. There isn't never a good time to be pulled over for speeding.

10. Mr. Wong hasn't never given us a compliment about our work, but I'm not sure there is anything to compliment us about.

11. We wouldn't never have guessed that the U.S. consumes 25% of all the earth's energy.

12. Daniel isn't never going to believe that right-handed people live, on average, nine years longer than left-handed people.

13. Shannon said, "I guess there ain't nothing more I can say to make you change your mind."

14. I didn't know there weren't no poisonous snakes in Maine.

15. Sam said, "We didn't see nobody famous."

Chapter Review One

Correct each of the following sentences by crossing out the incorrect word or words and writing the correction above it.

1. It ain't easy to remove that fake anti-spyware program.

2. There shouldn't be no more bugs in this building because the exterminators were here last week.

3. The doctor said Susan didn't get no booster shot.

4. The National Weather Service didn't issue no storm warning in time for people to take shelter.

5. The Hubble Space Telescope wasn't worth no $2.1 billion dollars.

6. Kate and Jackie couldn't do nothing other than apologize for being late.

7. Rachel didn't have no idea that the thyroid cartilage is another name for Adam's apple.

8. We didn't have no Internet connection for twelve hours.

9. Isabella didn't have no interest in the fact that a tree planted in Los Angeles to honor former Beatle George Harrison has been killed by actual beetles.

10. They couldn't hardly have procrastinated much longer and still been able to get their passport in time for their vacation.

11. Thomas doesn't look like no poet to me, and he couldn't have come up with the line, "Hers was a face that could launch a thousand ships," on his own.

12. Chris said that he couldn't see nothing special about the Jonas Brothers.

13. We hadn't hardly sat down before the waitress came over to take our order.

14. I can't hardly believe that North Dakota is the only state that has never had an earthquake.

15. It wasn't no poison leaf that I could recognize.

Final Chapter Review

Correct each of the following sentences by crossing out the incorrect word or words and writing the correction above it.

1. Two hundred strangers showed kindness when they responded to a Facebook invitation to attend the funeral of a veteran without no friends or family.

2. Brandon hasn't done none of the things I asked him to do.

3. I didn't have no idea that opening that e-mail would damage my computer.

4. Her apartment building doesn't have no elevators, so we had to walk up three flights of stairs.

5. We couldn't hardly believe secondhand smoke contains more than four thousand chemicals, including more than forty cancer-causing compounds.

6. Jada hasn't done nothing about getting her dog vaccinated for rabies.

7. We hadn't never realized that diabetes is one of the fastest growing health problems in industrialized nations today.

8. Clark wouldn't have no idea whether it was a diamond or cubic zirconium.

9. We couldn't find no crater in the picture, and we looked carefully.

10. Most people can't hardly understand the concept of globalization.

11. Gus wouldn't never believe that two dogs were hanged for witchcraft during the Salem witch trials.

12. Most people haven't never realized that fruits and vegetables, after being harvested, can spend days being sorted, packaged, and shipped, and during this time nutrients are lost.

13. They couldn't hardly believe that President Bill Clinton sent only two e-mails during his entire eight years in office.

14. It wasn't no surprise that David Letterman was voted "Class Smart Aleck" at his high school.

15. We aren't never going to believe that fingernails are made from the same substance as a bird's beak.

Successful Writing Strategies

Unlike acquiring grammar and vocabulary competency, learning to write effectively is more of an art than a science. The following exercises are likely to be challenging, but if you put effort into them, your writing will show real improvement.

Part One: Write Concisely: Eliminate Wordiness

Most unsophisticated writers use too many words to say what they mean. **Eliminate all wordiness.**

Whenever possible, eliminate duplicate information. Often it's possible to combine two weak sentences into one strong sentence.

Examples:

Two sentences: When Scott's parents bought an old house they were not pleased to find a huge swarm of bees in the siding. They were not happy to find termites in the foundation.

One sentence: When Scott's parents bought an old house they were not pleased to find a huge swarm of bees in the siding and termites in the foundation.

Two sentences: Kyla will be a model in the fashion show. The show will take place on March 8th.

One sentence: Kyla will be a model in the fashion show on March 8th.

Two sentences: Adam plays the banjo. It is a five string banjo.
One sentence: Adam plays a five string banjo.

Exercise One

Reduce duplicate information by combining each of the following pairs of sentences into one clear sentence.

1. Neil Armstrong and Edwin Aldrin Jr. were the first two men to walk on the moon. They walked on the moon on July 20, 1969.

2. The car seemed to be in perfect condition when I bought it. I bought it from my friend Garrett.

3. Anne Bradstreet was a Puritan poet. She was a poet during Colonial times.

4. Queen Elizabeth II became queen of England after the death of her father. He died in 1952.

5. The Great Smoky Mountains are located in western North Carolina. They are also in eastern Tennessee.

6. George Washington was born in 1732. He was born in Virginia.

7. It was a black and white movie. The movie was old.

8. My father insisted that I clean up the yard. He also told me to pull the weeds.

9. We moved the bed from my brother's room. We moved it to the basement.

10. We boarded the Cog Railroad at Manitou Springs, Colorado. We rode it to the top of Pike's Peak.

11. The A&P was the first chain store business to be established. It began in 1842.

12. Lonny and I listened to the radio. We listened to KLOL.

13. King Ferdinand and Queen Isabella were Spanish monarchs who had faith in Christopher Columbus. They agreed to fund his exploration.

14. I have to rewrite my resumé. I also have to rewrite my cover letter.

15. Ketchup is excellent for cleaning brass. It is especially good at cleaning tarnished or corroded brass.

Eliminate All Unnecessary Words and Phrases

Substitute *"although"* for "regardless of the fact" or "in spite of the fact."
Substitute *"since"* for "because of the fact."

Examples:
Regardless of the fact that twenty craftsmen worked 10 hours a day, seven days a week, it still took six months to finish the torch-holding hand of the Statue of Liberty.

Although twenty craftsmen worked 10 hours a day, seven days a week, it still took six months to finish the torch-holding hand of the Statue of Liberty.

Because of the fact that the High Line Railway in New York City had been abandoned, the city turned it into a $170 million park.

Since the High Line Railway in New York City had been abandoned, the city turned it into a $170 million park.

Most sentences that begin "There is" or "There are" or "The reason why... is" are unnecessarily wordy and should be rewritten.

Examples:
The reason why many tourists visit the Smoky Mountains in the fall is to see the brilliantly colored trees.

Many tourists visit the Smoky Mountains in the fall to see the brilliantly colored trees.

There are good reasons why I won't take up skate boarding.

I won't take up skate boarding for good reasons.

Sometimes "to be" and "that" can be omitted.

Examples:
Hakeem Olajuwon and David Robinson were considered to be outstanding basketball centers.

Hakeem Olajuwon and David Robinson were considered outstanding basketball centers.

In the fall there are many songbirds that migrate to Mexico.

In the fall many songbirds migrate to Mexico.

Instead of "at about" just use "about."

Example:
The lecture ended at about three.
The lecture ended about three.

A number of other phrases are **meaningless sentence extenders** and should be eliminated. These include:

in my opinion	**the fact is**
obviously	**all things considered**
I feel	**without a doubt**
it seems to me	**in conclusion**
for the purpose of (to)	**at this point in time (now)**
make contact with (contact)	**give consideration to (consider)**
has the capacity for (can)	**in the event that (if)**
aware of the fact (know)	**sufficient amount of (enough)**

In general, remove nonessential words or phrases whenever possible.

Examples
City residents suffer from a rate of depression that's 39% greater than the rate of depression of rural residents.
City residents suffer from a 39% greater rate of depression than rural residents.

People who are looking for bargains often shop at outlet malls or discount warehouses.
People looking for bargains often shop at outlet malls or discount warehouses.

Where's the meeting at?
Where's the meeting?

Exercise Two

Eliminate unnecessary words in each of the following sentences.

1. The fact is that Maine is the only state in the U.S. that has just one syllable.

2. In spite of the fact that most people picture the Tower of London as a single tower, it is a group of buildings covering 13 acres along the north bank of the Thames River.

3. Regardless of the fact that Emily Dickinson wrote more than 1,700 poems, only four were published in her lifetime.

4. Because of the fact that there are so many smokers in the country, China must import tobacco.

5. The fact is, Jacob is the best guitar player.

6. There are many factors that influenced Jimmy to major in theater.

7. Shigeru Miyamoto is considered to be the father of modern video games for his successful Nintendo franchises.

8. Regardless of the fact that most people believe the story of the little Dutch boy who placed his finger in the dike to save a town from a flood, it is actually an American fabrication.

9. Where will the class be offered at?

10. The reason that gasoline prices rose after the hurricane was that the demand increased while production decreased.

11. Her mother seemed to be angry that we stayed out so late.

12. The reason that there are so many bicycles on the island of Bermuda is that private automobiles were forbidden until 1948.

13. Regardless of the fact that a suntan is considered attractive, a moderately severe sunburn damages blood vessels to the point that it takes four to fifteen months to return to normal.

14. In my opinion, most people think fall is the most beautiful season of the year.

15. Motorists who are trying to conserve gas should not drive above the speed limit.

Eliminate the phrases "He is a man who" and "in terms of."

Examples:
He is a man who is hard to get to know.

He is hard to get to know.

The employee was undependable in terms of often coming to work late.

By often coming to work late, the employee was undependable.

This ficus plant was not a good choice in terms of requiring too much care.

This ficus plant was not a good choice because it required too much care.

Exercise Three

Eliminate all unnecessary words in each of the following sentences.

1. The reason why a kangaroo can't jump if its tail is off the ground is because it needs its tail for pushing off.

2. It's a fact that the earth rotates on its axis more slowly in March than in September.

3. The mayor seemed to be angry that the sanitation workers had gone on strike.

4. Regardless of the fact that Jamie had plenty of time to study for her history test, she didn't do it.

5. In the spring there are many people who suffer from allergies from pollen.

6. She wasn't a good singer in terms of singing off-key.

7. In spite of the fact that young people are generally considered healthier than older people, teenagers are 50% more susceptible to colds than people over 50.

8. Without a doubt, learning to write well is a necessary skill.

9. Because of the fact that a diamond is exceptionally hard, it will not dissolve in acid.

10. I have given up looking for a job, for all intents and purposes.

11. All things considered, I would rather be on vacation than working.

12. Victoria is a girl who has a great personality.

13. Without a doubt, classified ads in Tokyo are among the most expensive in the world.

14. It was a fact that in Puritan times to be born on a Sunday was interpreted as a sign of great sin.

15. The resort was poorly rated in terms of the lack of good restaurants.

Chapter Review One

Eliminate wordiness in each of the following sentences. When there are two sentences, combine them into one.

1. Shoppers spend an average of eight minutes waiting in line at the grocery store. Most people waiting in line would rather be doing something else.

2. Because of the fact that ostriches can run faster than horses and the males can roar like lions, they are one of the most unusual creatures on the planet.

3. It's a fact that approximately 55 percent of people yawn within five minutes of seeing someone else yawn.

4. David will take us to the concert on Saturday night. He will take us to the concert if he doesn't have to work.

5. Mr. Lewis is a man who is well liked by all his employees.

6. During a serious recession most retail businesses lose revenue. Movie theatres often increase revenue during a serious recession, however.

7. The fire broke out at about three in the morning, but no one was injured and in terms of damage there wasn't that much.

8. A person uses more than seventy muscles to say one word. A person uses three hundred muscles to balance himself or herself when standing still.

9. The Minnesota Vikings' player crossed the goal line. The player did a little dance.

10. The reason why Texas prisons are saving six million dollars a year is that they are reducing the number of daily calories served to prisoners.

11. The house has a beautiful mountain view. We rented the house.

12. The Japanese keep birds as pets. They also keep crickets as pets.

13. Harry Houdini, the world famous magician, died of a ruptured appendix. He died on Halloween.

14. Zeke is clever. He is also ingenious.

15. Because Venice is built on water, large motor boats are used as buses. Venice also has small motor boats used for taxis.

Part Two: Write Clearly

Avoid Unclear Pronoun References

Pronouns are pointing words. When you speak, a nod can show which of two people or things you mean. When you write, there is no nod to identify exactly which person or thing you mean. Often, if the pronoun reference isn't clear, a reader can't tell who did what.

Example:

Confusing: Kip told Ben that he'd landed on Park Place and owed $200 rent. (Who owed rent?")

Clear: When Ben landed on Park Place, Kip told him, "You owe $200 rent."

If there are two people or things for the pronoun to point to, try shifting one of them to a different part of the sentence.

Example:

Confusing: Joseph talked to Travis about his recent bout with pneumonia. (Who had pneumonia?)

Clear: Joseph talked about his recent bout with pneumonia to Travis.

If necessary, drop the pronoun and substitute the noun you are pointing to.

Example:

Confusing: Since the student exhibit was scheduled for the same night as the election, it had to be postponed.

Clear: Since the student exhibit was scheduled for the same night as the election, the exhibit had to be postponed.

Avoid the use of the mysterious "they."

Example:

Mysterious: They said that there will be rain by Thursday.

Clear: The weather forecaster said there will be rain by Thursday.

Avoid using vague pronouns. One problem occurs when there is more than one noun that the pronoun could refer to.

Example:

Confusing: When the car hit the house, it burst into flames. (What burst into flames?)

Clear: When the car hit the house, the car burst into flames.

Another problem occurs when a pronoun used refers to a word that is implied but not specifically stated. Rewrite the sentence with an explanation, if necessary.

Confusing: I have given up gymnastics. This bothered my mother. (Was the mother bothered by the sport or giving up the sport?"

Clear: I have given up gymnastics, a sport which bothered my mother because she thought it was too dangerous.

Exercise Four

Each of the following sentences is written two different ways. Pick the sentence that is clearer.

1. A) I knew about the change of plans, but Nicholas didn't realize I knew.
   B) I knew about the change of plans, but Nicholas didn't realize this.

2. A) Kayla and Victoria went backstage to congratulate Josh and Ryan on their outstanding performance, which impressed them.
   B) Kayla and Victoria, impressed by Josh and Ryan's outstanding performance, went backstage to congratulate them.

3. A) In major Italian cities, we found that they often speak English.
   B) In major Italian cities, we found that many people speak English.

4. A) She sent me an invitation to her wedding, which surprised me.
   B) I was surprised that she sent me an invitation to her wedding.

5. A) Ella had an e-mail from her friend and told Lilly.
   B) Ella told Lilly that she had an e-mail from her friend.

Exercise Five

Rewrite each of the following sentences so that the meaning is clearer.

1. When the Smashing Pumpkins' concert was announced, they sold out all the tickets in less than one day.

2. Brandon told James that he couldn't be an astronaut because he was over six feet tall and that is too tall for NASA's height requirements.

3. On television it said that there is a serious flu epidemic sweeping the country.

4. In *To Kill a Mockingbird* it has a theme of racial injustice.

5. After Sophia and Tyler carefully wrapped the presents, Mrs. Saunders quickly delivered them next door.

6. Alyssa smiled at Tanna when she introduced her to the group.

7. Some of the eyewitnesses to the robbery described the getaway car as gray and others said it was blue, and this confused the police investigators.

8. We were upset by the messy apartment, but this will change.

9. They were opposed to gun control because they felt every citizen should have one for protection.

10. When our cat crept into Mrs. Lock's house, she created such an uproar I thought our friendship was damaged forever.

11. Over 50 million tourists a year visit Italy, and this provides nearly 63% of Italy's national income.

12. Noah locked his laptop in his car, and then it was stolen.

13. A person's nose is connected to the memory center of the brain, which is why it can trigger powerful memories.

14. They approved a ballot initiative in San Francisco that allowed police officer Bob Geary to take his ventriloquist's dummy, Brenden O'Smarty, on foot patrol.

15. Jackson told Liam that he didn't have enough money to visit Peru this year.

Use Parallel Constructions

Keeping sentence elements parallel in construction demonstrates good organization. Therefore, match verbs with verbs, nouns with other nouns, infinitives with infinitives, connectives with other connectives, etc.

Not parallel: Noah is an avid skateboarder, jogger, and loves to wrestle.

Parallel: Noah is an avid skateboarder, jogger, and *wrestler.* (series of nouns)

Not parallel: Since all things are not equal, since consequences are often unknown, and life always includes some risk, take a chance now and then.

Parallel: Since all things are not equal, since consequences are often unknown, and *since* life always includes some risk, take a chance now and then. (series of (prepositions)

Not parallel: Ella said there was a danger of getting malaria in the jungle or we might be bitten by snakes.

Parallel: Ella said there was a danger of getting malaria in the jungle or *getting* bitten by snakes. (series of verbals)

Exercise Six

Rewrite all of the following sentences so they are parallel in construction.

1. Reduce the amount of water you use by fixing leaking plumbing fixtures, use less water in toilets, and turning off the water while you brush your teeth.

2. Prescription medications are expensive because the pharmaceutical companies spend hundreds of millions of dollars developing them, testing them, and marketing the medications.

3. The book explains how to build a safe, diversified investment portfolio and saving for college tuition costs.

4. At the craft fair artists demonstrated glass blowing, pottery making, and how to weave.

5. To lose weight, eat foods with fewer calories, eat smaller portions, and you should exercise regularly.

6. Electronic switches, computerized ticketing for passenger trains, and the introduction of electronic signaling equipment have eliminated the need for cabooses on many trains.

7. To become an elite figure skater requires more than $130,000 a year to cover the cost of private lessons, ice time, custom made boots, blades, and making specially designed costumes.

8. The committee is not only working to preserve historical buildings, but also is interested in developing a local museum.

9. The tennis coach patiently taught her students how to serve, rush the net, and winning the point.

10. Zachery was healthy, wealthy, and an athlete.

11. NASCAR driver Brian Vickers said, "You'll never win unless you're willing to push everyone around you to their limit, to push your car to the limit, and try pushing yourself to your limit."

12. IKEA founder Ingvar Kamprad lives in a small home, eats at IKEA, takes the bus, and flew coach, despite being the 5th richest man in the world.

13. Standing while doing work increases productivity and does keep people focused.

14. Modern homing pigeons find it more convenient to follow highways and beltways and turn left and right at junctions rather than using their built-in navigational abilities.

15. On the day of the high school final exam in Korea, government workers can arrive one hour late to reduce traffic congestion, motorists can't honk their horns near exam venues, and taxis are offering free rides to students who need them.

Exercise Seven

Rewrite all of the sentences so they are parallel in construction.

Example:

Not parallel: Contented workers work more efficiently, have fewer absences, and fellow workers like them better.

Parallel: Contented workers work more efficiently, have fewer absences, and **are** better *liked* by fellow employees. (series of verbs)

1. A nanometer is to a meter what the diameter of a hazelnut is relating to the diameter of earth.

2. Advertising is used to make consumers aware of a product, feel positive about a product, and make consumers remember the product when they go shopping.

3. Creating recycled paper uses significantly less energy than the creation of new paper from wood.

4. Societies around the world expect parents to pass on the shared values, the role expectations, and teach the rules of each society.

5. Leah loves to read, dance, and talking.

6. Helicopters are unique flying machines because they can hover over a single spot, fly slowly, and are capable of flying backward.

7. People often judge others at first sight using stereotypes based on clothing, personal attractiveness, and how a person behaves.

8. During recycling, plastics are collected, sorted, chopped, melted, and then undergo remolding.

9. More than one billion people worldwide use the Internet to send e-mails, search for information, listen to music, or for shopping online.

10. Political leaders try to increase employment, grow the economy, and do so while controlling inflation.

Use an Active, not a Passive Voice

Using an active voice is usually more energetic and concise than a passive voice. The voice of the verb indicates whether the subject performs (is active in) or receives (is passive to) the action of the verb.

Examples:
Passive: The game was won by Maryland.
Active: Maryland won the game.

Passive: The new policy was described by Ms. Shaw.
Active: Ms. Shaw described the new policy.

Exercise Eight

Rewrite **all** of the passive sentences into active sentences.

1. Menus were distributed by the waiter.

2. *The Kite Runner* was written by Khaled Hosseini.

3. The part of the Cowardly Lion was played by Ben.

4. The Massachusetts Minutemen were warned by Paul Revere of the approach of the British.

5. About seven quarts of oxygen are consumed by a runner while running a hundred-yard dash.

6. An amazing 816 million pounds of sugar are used by the cereal industry each year.

7. Half of the world's black pepper is produced in Vietnam.

8. Reproductions of these great paintings are sold in the gift shop.

9. The only U.S. president to have been unanimously elected was George Washington.

10. Ice cream specifically for dogs is being produced by a Belgian company.

11. Many pictures of George Washington were painted by Charles Wilson Peale.

12. The growth in power of the Roman Empire was reflected in the Roman architectural grandeur.

13. More eggs are laid by chickens when pop music is played.

14. Apricot pies are sold in a McDonald's in New Zealand.

15. A small-sized dog can be killed by eating a few ounces of chocolate.

16. Knots have been used as symbols of eternal love by many cultures.

17. The Pringles' can was invented by Frederic Baur, and when he died his ashes were buried in one.

18. The first bulletproof vest and windshield wiper blades were both invented by women.

19. Lincoln Logs were invented by Frank Lloyd Wright's son.

20. Two billion You Tube videos a day are watched by people around the world.

Mastering Comparatives and Superlatives

Many adjectives and adverbs express three levels or degrees of comparison:

The **positive** form describes a person or thing without drawing a comparison:
Driving a few hundred miles can be an *easy* method of traveling.

The **comparative** form compares one person or thing with another:
Driving a few hundred miles is often *easier* than flying

The **superlative** compares one person or thing with all others in a group of three or more.
Driving a few hundred miles is often the *easiest* method of traveling.

To form comparatives of longer adjectives use *more/most* or *less/least*.

Examples:

Jimmie Johnson is one of the ***most talented*** NASCAR drivers.

Rosanna's speech was ***less effective*** than it could have been.

Modifiers with Irregular Forms of Comparison

Positive	Comparative	Superlative
good/well	better	best
bad/badly/ill	worse	worst
careful	more careful	most careful
far (distance)	farther	farthest
far (degree, time)	further	furthest
little	less	least
many/much	more	most

Include the word *other* or *else* when comparing one member of a group with the rest of the group.

Examples:

Not correct: The U.S. Navy has more aircraft carriers than all the navies in the world combined. (The U.S. Navy is a part of this class and cannot have more aircraft carriers than itself.)

Correct: The U.S. Navy has more aircraft carriers than all the ***other*** navies in the world combined.

Avoid using double comparisons.

Examples:

Not Correct: The Burj Khalifa in Dubai, United Arab Emirates, is the most tallest skyscraper in the world.

Correct: The Burj Kahalifa in Dubai, United Arab Emirates, is the ***tallest*** skyscraper in the world.

Exercise Nine

Correct each of the following sentences. Add words that were incorrectly omitted, cross out any incorrect word or words, and write corrections where they are needed.

Example:
Not Correct: Of the three alternatives, I consider the first the less viable.
Correct: Of the three alternatives, I consider the first the *least* viable.

1. Of all the items at the auction of *Star Wars* memorabilia, which do you think was more expensive?

2. Liechtenstein, the world's sixth-smallest country, is the world's most largest exporter of false teeth.

3. You're more likelier to be killed by a champagne cork than by a poisonous spider.

4. The continent of Australia, with just 5% of the earth's land area, is smaller than any continent.

5. Some psychologists believe that the person who tries to keep everyone happy often ends up feeling the loneliest.

6. Of all the complaints about Internet dating sites, misrepresentation by both men and women is more frequent.

7. Both men and women are most likely to be attracted to someone wearing the color red than any other color.

8. Illinois has the greatest number of license plates than any state.

9. Blind people smile despite never having seen someone smile because it's a natural human reaction.

10. Researchers have discovered that people who regularly help others are usually significantly more happier and less likely to become depressed as they get older.

Part Three: Write Varied Sentences

Vary Sentence Length

There is no one best kind of sentence. Short sentences are better than long ones for emphasizing a particular point. On the other hand, you don't want to write a long string of short, choppy sentences. A balance of short and long sentences is best. Sentences can often be combined to streamline meaning or eliminate duplicate information.

Use transition words and phrases to create sentence variety. Transition words improve connections between thoughts and link one sentence or paragraph with another.

To acknowledge or concede a point:
although
of course
granted

To show a result or consequence:
therefore
consequently
because

To show an additional idea:
also
in addition
again
furthermore
besides

To show a comparison or contrast:
instead
rather
however
nevertheless
on the other hand

To conclude or clarify:
therefore
finally
in conclusion
in other words

To signal time:
when
now
afterward
later

Put limiting modifiers in front of the words they modify.

Examples of limiting modifiers are: *even, only, almost, hardly, nearly, just, simply*, and *merely*. To avoid confusion, place modifiers as closely as possible to the word or phrase being modified.

Where you place modifiers can change the meaning of the sentence.

Examples:

Alyssa lost her only set of directions. (She only had one.)
Alyssa lost only her set of directions. (She didn't lose anything else.)
Only Alyssa lost her set of directions. (All the others had their directions.)

Place modifying words, phrases and clauses correctly

Words, phrases, and clauses provide important information in sentences. When a writer places a word, a phrase, or a clause too far from the word it describes, the sentence will not convey the intended meaning or even become unintentionally funny.

Not clear: The defense attorney described the testimony of a handful of prison inmates angling for early release doubtful. (Is the early release or testimony doubtful?)

Rewritten: The defense attorney described the testimony of a handful of prison inmates doubtful because they were angling for early release.

Not clear: At the age of eight, a sheep mauled Bill Clinton.

Rewritten: At the age of eight, Bill Clinton was mauled by a sheep.

Exercise Ten

Each sentence in the following exercise is written two different ways. Put an X next to the version that places the modifying word or phrase in the better position.

1. _____ a. Jerome found a UPS package on his front porch that did not belong to him.

   _____ b. Jerome found a UPS package that did not belong to him on his front porch.

2. _____ a. We need to install the new window shades that arrived yesterday in the second floor conference room.

   _____ b. We need to install the new window shades in the second floor conference room that arrived yesterday.

3. _____ a. After years of denial, Lance Armstrong finally admitted he used performance enhancing drugs in an interview with Oprah.

   _____ b. In an interview with Oprah, after years of denial, Lance Armstrong finally admitted he used performance enhancing drugs.

4. _____ a. We observed ants nodding to each other with the aid of a magnifying glass.

   _____ b. With the aid of a magnifying glass, we observed ants nodding to each other.

5. _____ a. If you feel the need to print the class schedule, please print only the pages you need.

   _____ b. If you feel the need to print the class schedule, please only print the pages you need.

6. _____ a. The President just seems to relax on weekends.

_____ b. The President seems to relax just on weekends.

7. _____ a. New houses are being built in our neighborhood with solar heating.

_____ b. New houses with solar heating are being built in our neighborhood.

8 _____ a. We drove nearly four miles past our intended exit.

_____ b. We nearly drove four miles past our intended exit

9 _____ a. Good table manners require that both hands should be kept in sight, preferably on the table in France.

_____ b. In France good table manners require that both hands should be kept in sight, preferably on the table

10. _____ a. Cancer death rates have nearly remained unchanged over the last 80 years.

_____ b. Cancer death rates have remained nearly unchanged over the last 80 years.

Being a good writer requires more than simply following grammatical rules. Good writers produce sentences in which ideas are expressed clearly, logically, and eloquently.

Examples:

Unclear: A Child's Feeding Fund helps impoverished families in Arizona and northern Mexico by collecting nutritious fruits and vegetables rescued from landfills.

Rewritten: A Child's Feeding Fund helps impoverished families in Arizona and northern Mexico by collecting nutritious fruits and vegetables that would otherwise be destined for landfills.

Unclear: Stunt performers in Hollywood are becoming less of a commodity because they are being replaced by special effects that are advanced and relatively inexpensive.

Rewritten: Stunt performers in Hollywood are becoming less of a commodity because they are being replaced by advanced and relatively inexpensive special effects.

Unclear: Looking outside dejectedly, the rain picked up again.

Rewritten: Looking outside dejectedly, Courtney saw that the rain had picked up again.

Exercise Eleven

Rewrite the following sentences, placing modifying words, phrases, and clauses correctly.

1. Although Orcas live longer in the wild, in captivity Orcas just live, on average, 20 years.

2. Even if you do not drink it, in Egypt it's considered rude not to accept tea or coffee if it is offered.

3. Wealthy Russians hire fake ambulances with couches and flat screen TVs inside to beat city traffic.

4. Adults dream for about one and a half to three hours a night off and on.

5. A carrier pigeon can deliver a message faster than a fax machine over a distance of about a mile.

6. It's an act of treason to place a postage stamp of the Queen upside down in England.

7. Officials stated that a central Florida woman was just attacked by one bear, not five.

8. It's considered rude to stand with your hands in your pockets in Russia.

9. More than 8,000 pieces of space debris are orbiting around earth left over from previous space missions.

10. Cockroaches are now able to survive New York City's brutal winters that were originally native to Asia.

11. President Warren G. Harding once gambled away a box of priceless presidential china playing poker with friends at the White House.

12. Security guards spotted a suspicious device with wires connected to a battery at a southwest Wyoming power plant and called a bomb squad, but the device turned out to be a mosquito trap.

13. Emma was just rushed by three sororities, not seven.

14. We could see the city's amazing fireworks display from our backyard.

15. Alison and I were able to spot the bacteria looking through a microscope.

Maintain consistency in verb tenses

A verb tense establishes the time of action in writing. Do not change needlessly from one tense to another.

When describing events that occur at the same time, use verbs in the same tense. Examples:

Not correct: In Taiwan a giant 40 foot rubber duck nicknamed "Duckzilla," which **was** on display in front of hundreds of onlookers, **deflates** after a power failure from a 6.3 magnitude earthquake **caused** the duck's air pump to fail.

(Verb tenses shift from past to present and back to past.)

Correct: In Taiwan a giant 40 foot rubber duck nicknamed "Duckzilla," which **was** on display in front of hundreds of onlookers, **deflated** after a power failure from a 6.3 magnitude earthquake **caused** the duck's air pump to fail.

(Verb tenses are all past tense.)

When describing events that occur at different times, use different verb tenses to reflect the changes in time.

Example:

Sting **makes** an average of $2,000 a day in royalties for his song "Every Breath You Take," which **was released** in 1986.

(The verb tenses correctly shift from present to past.)

Exercise Twelve

Correct unnecessary verb tense shifts in the following sentences by making the verb tenses consistent. Four sentences are already correct.

1. The motion-activated singing fish "Big Mouth Billy Bass" apparently scared off a would-be burglar who breaks into a bait and tackle ship, but left without stealing anything, including cash that had been left in a visible spot.

2. It is illegal to lock car doors in downtown Churchill, Manitoba, in case someone needed to escape from a polar bear.

3. In 2000 the KKK adopted a stretch of highway near St. Louis, but the Missouri government responds by renaming the road the "Rosa Parks Highway."

4. Because sophisticated consumers now regard sugar and fat as unhealthy, they are not buying as much high-end gourmet chocolate as they did a year ago.

5. When *Jurassic Park* author Michael Creighton was a student at Harvard, he feels his literature professor isn't grading him fairly, and to prove it Creighton submitted a paper written by *1984* author George Orwell and got a B- on it.

6. Flamboyant ex-NBA star Dennis Rodman visited North Korea in 2013 and calls the ruthless dictator Kim Jong-un a "friend for life."

7. When "Elephant Whisperer" Lawrence Anthony died, a whole herd of elephants arrives at his house to mourn his death.

8. People all over the world are walking 10% faster than they did a decade ago.

9. Guided by a few clues from Twitter, Stephanie hailed a cab to Central Park and starts searching for money planted there by Hidden Cash, the scavenger hunt craze that recently made its way from California to New York.

10. At the Lizzie Borden Bed and Breakfast in Fall River, Massachusetts, guests sleep in the very rooms where Lizzie's father and stepmother were murdered.

11. The Strait of Dover separates France from England, and on the English side near the town of Dover, white chalk cliffs lined the coast.

12. Gypsies were originally from India, and these nomadic people are found in various parts of Asia, Europe, and North America.

13. Two-thirds of people report they fell in love with someone they have known for some time rather than someone they just met.

14. American schoolchildren rank 25th in math and 21st in science out of 30 developed countries, but they ranked first in confidence that they out-perform everyone else.

15. William Whipple frees his slaves when he signed the Declaration of Independence because he believed he could not fight for freedom and own slaves.

Exercise Thirteen

Correct unnecessary verb tense shifts in following sentences by making the verb tenses consistent. Four sentences are already correct.

1. Before becoming a popular talk show host, Montel Williams attends the U.S. Naval Academy in Annapolis, Maryland, where he studied Mandarin Chinese.

2. During his second campaign for the presidency, Teddy Roosevelt was shot by a would-be assassin while giving a speech in Milwaukee, but he continues to deliver his speech with the bullet in his chest.

3. Cats are one of the few animals to domesticate themselves and approached humans on their own terms.

4. On New Year's Eve in Ecuador, people dress and fill scarecrows with paper and pieces of wood to burn at midnight, and people believe this tradition scares off bad luck and destroys all the bad things that took place in the past twelve months.

5. A study of more than 38,000 people in the U.S. and thirteen European countries finds that Americans were more prone to developing depression if they became unemployed, compared to their European counterparts.

6. The business concept of "doing well by doing good works" is a practice that pre-dates the Revolutionary War, such as Josiah Wedgewood's porcelain factory, which provided housing for its workers.

7. A Connecticut woman became concerned when she heard someone repeatedly calling "Daddy," but when she starts looking for a child, she found a large green parrot in a tree, which had escaped from its home less than a mile away.

8. Both the players and owners finally resolved the contract dispute when they reach a compromise on players' salaries.

9. A man received the transplanted heart of a suicide victim, married the donor's widow, and kills himself exactly the same way the donor died.

10. Partygoers attending a bachelor party at Elephant Butte State Park in New Mexico find a fossil mastodon skull with tusks that was more than 10 million years old.

11. Studies have shown that being in the center of a room makes a person more likely to meet someone new than being positioned anywhere else.

12. Residents of Erie, Pennsylvania, hear a cat in a tree crying for two days, and 21-year-old Tara Dennis decided to rescue it, but she ended up needing to be rescued by firefighters herself, when she couldn't get down from the tree either.

13. Researchers have proven that a "50% off" sign results in increased sales, even if shoppers don't know the original price or what a reasonable price for the product would be.

14. A physically fit felon in a detention facility in Arizona climbs a 10-foot-tall basketball hoop and used it as a platform to leap over a high fence and escape.

15. Adele Laurie Blue Adkins is an English singer-songwriter who was offered a recording contract after a friend posts her demo on Myspace in 2006.

Combine Sentences Using Appositives

An appositive is a word or phrase that identifies or restates an immediately preceding noun or pronoun. Remember to set off an appositive with a comma or commas as necessary.

Examples:

Two sentences: Robert Todd Lincoln was the son of Abraham Lincoln. He witnessed the assassination of three presidents: his father's, President Garfield's, and President McKinley's.

One sentence: Robert Todd Lincoln, *the son of Abraham Lincoln*, witnessed the assassination of three presidents: his father's, President Garfield's, and President McKinley's.

Two sentences: Justine gave me a Mr. Goodbar. It is my favorite candy bar.

One sentence: Justine gave me a Mr. Goodbar, *my favorite candy bar*.

Exercise Fourteen

Identify the appositive in each of the following sentences by drawing a line under each one.

1. Arthur Conan Doyle, the author of the Sherlock Holmes stories, was also an eye doctor.

2. The first plastic ever invented, celluloid, is still used in billiard balls.

3. Sir Christopher Wren, a mathematician and an astronomer, designed St. Paul's Cathedral in London.

4. The ring-tailed lemur, a primate found only on the island of Madagascar, meows like a cat.

5. Anna Mary Roberson "Grandma" Moses, the famous American artist, didn't start painting full time until she was in her seventies.

6. Noah Webster's greatest work, the *American Dictionary*, took thirty-six years for him to write.

7. Rome was ruled by patricians, the upper class descendants of its original citizens.

8. Charles Carroll, a signer of the Declaration of Independence, died in 1832 at the age of 95.

9. Babe Ruth, one of the greatest hitters in baseball history, began his career as a pitcher.

10. John Reid, a balloon artist from New York, spent 42 hours building a 50-foot Transformer robot using over 4,000 different balloons.

11. A third Apple founder, Ronald Wayne, sold his 10% stake for $800 in 1976.

12. Euclid, a Greek mathematician born around 300 B.C., is considered the father of geometry.

13. Scrabble fans have voted to add *geocache* to the players' dictionary, the first new addition in nine years.

14. The *Titanic*, a British luxury ship, hit an iceberg and sank in less than three hours on April 14, 1912.

15. Esmeralda, a 70 pound chocolate Labrador, was almost too friendly toward children.

Exercise Fifteen

Combine each of the following sentences using an *appositive phrase*.

1. Paul Revere was a famous American patriot. He was once court-martialed for cowardice.

2. The strongest bone in the human body is the thigh bone. It is hollow.

3. The first macaroni factory in the United States was started by Antoine Zegera in Brooklyn, New York. It was established in 1848.

4. The Sahara Desert is as large a land area as Europe. Its total land mass is 3,565,565 square miles.

5. The first ferryboat route in America was established in 1630 between Boston and Charleston across the Charles River. The ferryboat charged riders one cent for every 100 pounds of goods transported.

6. The mosquito is one of the hardiest of the world's insects. It can live comfortably at the North Pole and is at home in equatorial jungles.

7. Salt is the most widely used seasoning in the world. It was given as monthly wages to Roman legionnaires.

8. Michelangelo was the greatest painter and sculptor of his time. He was also considered a great poet by his contemporaries.

9. The shortest intercontinental commercial flight in the world is from Gibraltar in Europe to Tangier in Africa. It is a distance of thirty-four miles and a flight time of twenty minutes.

10. The world's fastest dog is the greyhound. It can reach speeds of up to forty-five miles an hour.

11. The border between Canada and the U.S. is the world's longest frontier. It is a distance of 3,987 miles.

12. Sue is the world's largest, most complete, and best preserved Tyrannosaurus Rex. She made her grand debut to the public on May 17, 2000, at the Field Museum in Chicago, Illinois.

13. Health insurance for pets is a rapidly growing industry. Health insurance guarantees people can afford expensive veterinary care for their pets.

14. The shortest British monarch was Charles I. He was four feet, nine inches.

15. The largest employer in the world is the Indian railway system. It employs more than a million people.

16. Dexter is a six-month-old pit bull. He was rescued from the rubble of an apartment building nine days after a tornado struck Washington, Illinois.

17. The wreckage of *The Keystone State* has been found by a crew of shipwreck explorers. The ship was a wooden steamship that sank in a storm on Lake Huron in 1861.

18. Heath Ledger was a famous actor who died young. He won western Australia's junior chess championship at age 10.

19. Air pressure is the weight of the atmosphere pressing down on the earth. It is measured by a barometer in units called *millibars*.

20. The custom at weddings of throwing rice goes back to the time when people thought rice would appease evil spirits, so they would not bother the wedding couple. Rice is a symbol of health and prosperity.

Combine Sentences Using Adjective Clauses

Use an adjective clause to combine sentences.

The relative pronouns **who, which,** and **that** are frequently used to introduce an adjective clause.

Examples:

Two sentences: Queen Elizabeth I was completely bald. She always wore a wig in public.

One sentence: Queen Elizabeth I, **who was completely bald**, always wore a wig in public.

Two sentences: The parking meter was invented by Carl Magee. The first meter appeared in 1935 in Oklahoma City, Oklahoma.

One sentence: The parking meter, **which was invented by Carl Magee**, first appeared in 1935 in Oklahoma City, Oklahoma.

Exercise Sixteen

Identify the *adjective clause* in each of the following sentences by drawing a line under each one.

1. The earth, which is estimated to be 4.5 billion years old, travels through space at 660,000 miles an hour.

2. The King Ranch in Texas, which is larger than the state of Rhode Island, currently consists of 825,000 acres.

3. John Bunyan, who was jailed in London for twelve years for preaching without a license, wrote *Pilgrim's Progress* in jail.

4. The young man who made the offending remark is my brother.

5. Gin and canasta are both descended from the ancient Chinese game of mah-jongg, which is more than a thousand years old.

6. Jayden quickly identified the man who had tried to sell him the fake Rolex watch.

7. The famous "Constable Tree," which was an orange tree brought to France in 1421, lived and bore fruit for 473 years.

8. Alaska, which is the largest state in land mass, is the only state without a motto.

9. My uniform is inside my locker, which I can't get open.

10. Citrus fruits, which are important sources of vitamin C, also contain important minerals.

Combine each of the following sentences using an *adjective clause*.

1. The girl borrowed my cell phone. She disappeared.

2. Owls have huge eyes. Owls have the best night vision of all creatures.

3. Leonardo DiCaprio first became famous as the star of *Titanic*. He is passionately interested in reversing global warming.

4. The short-term memory capacity for most people is between five and nine items or digits. This is one reason that phone numbers are seven digits long.

5. Fingerprints were not accepted as evidence in U.S. courtrooms before 1941. They are now considered an infallible method of personal identification.

6. *Gone With the Wind* was the longest film (238 minutes) to win the best picture Oscar. It was also the first color film to win best picture.

7. Samuel got a job with UPS. It is a good company to work for, because it offers generous reimbursement for education costs.

8. The immigration bill was passed by the U.S. House of Representatives. It did not pass the Senate.

9. The presidential one-dollar coins are plated in brass. This is what gives them their golden tone.

10. The deadliest natural disaster in U.S. history was the Galveston, Texas, hurricane of 1900. It killed between 8,000-10,000 people.

11. Methane gas can often be seen bubbling up from the bottom of ponds. It is produced by the decomposition of dead plants and animals in the mud.

12. Lucy and Linus have another little brother named Rerun. He sometimes plays left field on Charlie Brown's baseball team.

13. The Slinky toy was invented by an airplane mechanic. He was playing with engine parts and recognized the possible secondary use of one of the springs.

14. Mark Twain thought fasting was a cure for illness. He would cure his colds and fevers by not eating for one or two days.

15. Howard Schultz is the high-profile chief executive officer of Starbucks. He was not one of the original founders.

Combine Sentences Using Participial Phrases

Use a participial phrase to combine sentences.

A participle begins with a **verb** plus **ing** (present tense) or a **verb** plus **ed** (past tense).

Examples:

Two sentences: The first telephone book ever issued contained only fifty names. It was published in New Haven, Connecticut, in 1878.

One sentence: The first telephone book, ***containing only fifty names***, was published in New Haven, Connecticut, in 1878.

Two sentences: China has the largest population of any country on earth. The total population is estimated to be more than 1.3 billion.

One sentence: China has the largest population of any country on earth, ***estimated to be more than 1.3 billion.***

You may need to move the subject of the first sentence into a later position in the combined sentence.

Example:

Two sentences: Isabella found all the gas stations closed. She drove to the next town.

One sentence: ***Finding all the gas stations closed***, Isabella drove on to the next town.

Exercise Eighteen

Combine each of the following sentences with a *participial phrase*. In several sentences it will be necessary to move the subject.

1. George Custer was the youngest American officer ever to become a general in the United States Army. He made his rank at the age of twenty-three.

2. My grandfather doesn't know how to send e-mails. He prefers to send postcards instead.

3. The President recognized the need for immediate action. He declared the entire state a disaster area.

4. Jacob was tired from loading and moving his friend's furniture. He was eager to finish and go home.

5. The Appalachian Trail winds through 14 states. It is 2,175 miles long.

6. The Golden Gate Bridge is an internationally recognized symbol of San Francisco. It connects the northern tip of the San Francisco Peninsula to Marin County.

7. Richard Gere was dressed in a tight T-shirt and fitted jeans. He was being interviewed about his new movie.

8. *An American in Paris* is filled with lavish sets and exciting dance numbers. It is the story of a struggling American painter who falls for a French girl.

9. Shel Silverstein was a talented poet, playwright, screenwriter, and songwriter. He is best known for his popular children's books including *The Giving Tree, Falling Up,* and *A Light in the Attic.*

10. The biggest natural crystals in the world are found in a silver mine in Mexico called the Cave of Crystals. They are made of gypsum.

11. Costa Rica is located on the Central American isthmus. It is a middle-income, developing country with a strong democratic tradition.

12. Some engineering students have come up with a device designed to prevent small planes from colliding on runways. It uses ultrasonic sensors that set off warning sounds and lights if a plane is in danger of clipping the wings of another plane.

13. The bee hummingbird is the world's smallest bird. It weighs about as much as a teabag.

14. A Georgia man spent 15 hours in jail on charges of misdemeanor theft for plugging his electric car into an outlet at a school. This drew about five cents worth of energy.

15. One of Italy's biggest businesses is the Mafia. It earns over $178 billion a year and accounts for 7% of Italy's GDP.

Combine Sentences Using Adverb Clauses

Use an adverb clause to combine sentences.

Adverb clauses begin with a subordinating conjunction such as *after, although, because, if, since, so, that, when,* or *while.*

Examples:

Two sentences: We were in Mexico City recently. My favorite attractions were the Zocalo and the Frida Kahlo Museum.

One sentence: ***When we were in Mexico City recently***, my favorite attractions were the Zocalo and the Frida Kahlo Museum.

Two sentences: The big M on McDonald's signs in Paris is the only one in the world that is white rather than yellow. Parisians thought yellow was too tacky.

One sentence: The big M on McDonald's signs in Paris is the only one in the world that is white rather than yellow ***since Parisians thought yellow was too tacky.***

Exercise Nineteen

Combine each of the following sentences with an *adverb clause* beginning with a subordinating conjunction such as *after, although, because, if, since, so, that, when,* or *while.* In some sentences you will need to begin the sentence with a conjunction.

Example:

Two sentences: Venice is a city with streets of water. Its only traffic is boats on the canals.
One sentence: Since Venice is a city with streets of water, its only traffic is boats on the canals.

1. The human attention span maxes out at about 10 minutes. People will revert to daydreaming after that.

2. Mexico City has sunk several feet during the 20th century. The water table underneath the city is being drained for human consumption.

3. To study faster, read the first and last paragraphs of the material. This is about as effective as reading everything.

4. Harvard uses Yale brand locks on their buildings. Yale uses Best brand.

5. The United States dominates film, television, pop music, the Internet, and business. This has increased the importance of the English language in recent decades.

6. Leap year occurs every four years. This is when all the extra hours, minutes, and seconds of the solar year are added up to make an extra day.

7. In the 20ᵗʰ century thousands of new, disposable goods were invented and fewer people had open fires to get rid of these items. As a result, more garbage was thrown away.

8. Pigs are generally thought of as being as intelligent as most dogs. Pigs can be taught to accomplish almost any task a dog can perform.

9. Used car buyers are sometimes at a disadvantage. Sometimes sellers don't give complete information about the cars they are selling.

10. Radio and TV serials about everyday life in the U.S. have been sponsored by soap manufacturers since the 1930s. These serials have been called soap operas or just soaps.

11. Lucretia Mott, Elizabeth Cady Stanton, and Susan B. Anthony were all abolitionists. They were more famous as pioneers for women's rights.

12. Bullies in the workplace harm not only the targeted person, but also the company as well. This is because it can lead to absences, decreased productivity, and even the loss of an employee.

13. The first regular phone service was established in 1878. People answering the phone said "Ahoy."

14. Introverted people prefer to express differences of opinion by e-mail. Extroverts generally seek out face-to-face conversations.

15. College baseball players are allowed to use aluminum baseball bats. Professional players are not.

16. A Hard Rock Casino security employee asked Ben Affleck to stop playing blackjack because he was "too good at it." He is allowed to play other games there.

17. The 2013 government shutdown threatened to close a national program that gave medical attention and meals to children. John D. Arnold donated $10 million to keep it afloat.

18. Most airlines have adjusted their flight arrival times. They wanted to have a better record of on-time arrivals.

19. Albert Einstein couldn't speak fluently until after his ninth birthday. His parents thought he was mentally retarded.

20. Under Chairman Mao, every Chinese family was required to kill a sparrow a week to stop them from eating all the rice. The project was ineffective because sparrows don't eat rice.

Chapter Review Two

Combine each of the following sentences using an *appositive*.

Example of an *appositive:*

Two sentences: Many Muslim nations have problems finding jobs for young people.
Even wealthy oil producers have these problems.

One sentence: Many Muslim nations, ***even wealthy oil producers***, have problems
finding jobs for young people.

1. The Concorde was the only passenger aircraft ever to fly faster than the speed of sound. It made its last flight on October 24, 2004.

2. Thousands of extravagantly dressed fans of punk, Goth, Romanticism, and Victoriana celebrate the annual Goth Weekend in the English seaside town of Whitby. Whitby is the fictional home of Bram Stoker's *Dracula*.

3. An important book about the Holocaust is *The Diary of Anne Frank*. This book describes a Jewish family's life in hiding until they were discovered and sent to a concentration camp, where Anne later died.

4. Robert Frost was famous for his poems about New England. He was born in San Francisco.

5. President McKinley was the twenty-fifth president of the U.S. He died of gangrene, after being shot by an assassin, and his wounds were not properly treated.

6. The besenji is an African dog. It is the only dog breed that doesn't bark.

7. The U.S. has the world's largest geothermal resource. It is the Geysers, 72 miles north of San Francisco.

8. Ernest Hemingway was one of 20th century America's most respected writers. He lived in Cuba for many years.

9. One of the largest beds in the world is the Great Bed of Ware. It measures over 10 feet wide and over 11 feet long.

10. Katia and Maurice Draft were two of the world's most famous volcano investigators. They were killed in the eruption of the Japanese volcano Unzenin in 1991.

Chapter Review Three

Combine sentences using an *adjective clause*.

Example of an adjective clause:

Two sentences: Ragweed is an allergy culprit for many people.
It can cause sneezing, itching eyes, and runny noses.

One sentence: Ragweed, ***which is an allergy culprit for many people***, can cause
sneezing, itching eyes, and runny noses.

1. Jesse Owens was an American track star. He outran a racehorse in 1936 over a 100 yard
course, even through the horse had a head start.

2. The Passenger Rail Investment and Improvement Act will allocate more than $10 billion for
Amtrak over the next several years. The bill was passed by both the House and Senate.

3. The Maglev train is named from combining the words magnetic and levitation. This
train does not run on a track, but floats above it by means of magnetic repulsion.

4. One of the most famous Mongol emperors was Genghis Khan. He started out as a
goat herder.

5. Snow is important in the wheat growing regions of America's Western states. It
provides moisture and protects crops from the intense winter cold.

6. The Australian koala looks like a toy teddy bear. It is actually a marsupial, a mammal
with a pouch for carrying its young.

7. Johnny Appleseed earned his name by planting apple seedlings over a large area of the
Midwest. He was really named John Chapman.

8. We crept cautiously around the deserted Warfield Mansion. It was rumored to be haunted.

9. Nearly 1.4 billion people live in China. This is over one-fifth of the world's population.

10. The Golden Raspberries were initiated in 1980. They are joke awards presented to the worst films
and actors, such as Sandra Bullock, who won in 2010, and the entire cast of *Sex and the City #2*,
who won in 2011.

Final Chapter Review

Combine sentences using a _participial phrase_. In some sentences, you may need to move the subject of the first sentence into the second part of the sentence.

Examples of a _participial phrase_:

Two sentences: The wooly mammoth has been extinct since the ice age. It had tusks about 16 feet long.

One sentence: Extinct since the ice age, the wooly mammoth had tusks about 16 feet long.

Two sentences: In geothermal power capacity the Philippines ranks number two in the world. The Philippines narrowly trails the U.S., which has far more geothermal potential.

One sentence: In geothermal power capacity the Philippines ranks number two in the world, narrowly trailing the U.S., which has far more geothermal potential.

1. The first real motion picture theater was called a nickelodeon. It opened in McKeesport, Pennsylvania, on June 19, 1905.

2. A series of financial crises brought the Lehman Brothers firm to bankruptcy. The crises were caused by mismanagement in the company.

3. The test used to measure a newborn's health is known as the Apgar Score. It was named after its inventor Dr. Virginia Apgar.

4. Cliff found Botswana on the map. He impressed all of us.

5. Twelve American astronauts have walked on the moon. They explored highlands and craters, took photographs, and gathered soil and rocks for study.

6. Water expands as it freezes and contracts as it melts. It displaces the exact same amount of fluid in either state.

7. The historic district of Williamsburg in Virginia has some of the most famous colonial buildings in America. These date from before the American Revolution.

8. During the storm, power outages were frequent. They were annoying to utility customers.

9. Dinosaurs were among the most sophisticated animals that ever lived on earth. They survived for nearly 150 million years.

10. Sheepdogs have 220 million olfactory cells. This enables them to smell 44 times better than humans.

Part Four: Writing Essays

Pre-write if you have difficulty getting started on a writing project.

For students who are so self-critical that to begin writing an essay is torture, spending half an hour pre-writing is an excellent idea. In pre-writing, write rapidly and freely, producing a flow of ideas and useful information relating to the assigned essay. At this stage of writing, don't try for perfect grammar usage, word choice, or sentence structure, just write. For assignments relating to literature, answering pertinent questions from the following list may be helpful.

1. What was the basic situation at the beginning of the story/novel/play? What was the resolution?

2. For each main character, describe the actions or behavior that reveals how he or she feels about another character. Does any character change the way he or she feels?

3. What problems do the main characters have and how do they deal with them?

4. List details of each character's physical appearance. Do the physical characteristics provide clues to the character's behavior? Are the characters sophisticated, complex, mysterious, or simple people?

5. Describe specific, unique, or unexpected actions that make a character memorable.

6. Write down dialog that seemed striking to you, even if you can't remember the words precisely. (If you include any of these quotations in your paper, you will, of course, quote *exactly* from the piece of literature.)

7. What are the most important events in the plot? What are unexpected plot incidents?

8. How relevant is the setting to the story or novel?

9. What is the overall mood of the story? Is it depressing, suspenseful, or optimistic?

10. What unusual figurative language (similes, metaphors, and personification) does the author use?

Begin Writing Your Essay.

While most students begin by writing an introduction, it's not essential to begin this way. If you are unsure about what you want to say in your introduction, start with a body paragraph. However you start, write as rapidly and freely as if you were pre-writing.

Write an Introduction.

An introduction should: 1) arouse the reader's interest 2) present the subject by telling readers what the composition is about 3) establish the writer's tone, whether serious, humorous, straightforward, or angry. Since the introduction is the first thing your reader sees, it should make a strong impression.

There are a number of good ways to write an introduction.

Begin with an example or an anecdote (a short, interesting or humorous story).

Begin with a startling fact or stating a strongly held opinion on a particular topic.

Begin with a pertinent quotation or brief dialogue.

Begin with a direct statement of the thesis. (Sometimes being direct is best.)

When you are writing about a literary topic, be sure to include the title and author in the introduction.

Build an Essay Paragraph by Paragraph.

Write a topic sentence and then stick to it. Select vivid, relevant details to support your topic sentence. Remember to write first and revise later. When writing about novels, plays, or poetry include *exact* quotations to illustrate any general statements you make. Each paragraph should contain enough details to develop its idea fully. Be generous with details in your first draft because it's easier to later delete than have to hunt for enough details to illustrate the point you're trying to make. When you revise, deal with any piece of information that does not support your topic sentence by moving it elsewhere in the essay or by deleting it.

Write a Conclusion.

A conclusion should convey to the reader that you've finished, not just stopped writing. You can do this by 1) summarizing the main idea of the paper or 2) by repeating in different words the main idea in the introduction. Do not introduce new ideas in the conclusion.

Writing an Autobiography

For many people, writing an autobiography is difficult, but it shouldn't be. First, study the following list of questions which might get you started. Then, to jog your memory, look at photograph albums, talk to your parents, and take the time to look through your keepsakes.

Possible autobiographical topics:

1. Tell as much as you can about your grandparents. How did your paternal and maternal grandparents meet their spouses? What major historical events occurred during their lives? How many children did they have? Which grandparent was the most athletic or the greatest sports fan? What were your grandparents' greatest challenges? What were their pets, interests, or hobbies?

2. Tell as much as you can about your parents. How did they meet? What major historical events occurred during their lives? Which one enjoyed sports more? Which one enjoyed school more? What work do they do? What interests or hobbies do they have? Are there any family stories that are passed down through the generations or more recent stories that are told again and again?

3. Who came before you in your family? If you have older brothers or sisters, tell about them. Provide complete physical descriptions. What are their talents and weaknesses? What are their strongest interests? How do they feel about you? How do you feel about them?

4. When and where were you born? Do you know anything about your birth? Why was your name chosen? Do you like your given name or not? Do you have any nicknames?

5. What stories do family members tell about your early years? What were your favorite toys? What was your favorite book? What about your favorite movie? Did you have a favorite outfit or a favorite food? What was your most frightening or wonderful childhood experience?

6. Where have you lived? Did you ever have a favorite hiding place or a secret place? What do you like best about your current home? Have you moved? Describe your move.

7. What is the best thing about your life right now? What is the worst thing about it? Do you consider yourself a good friend? When have you made mature decisions? When have you not made mature decisions? Have you fallen in love? Did it last?

These are just a few ideas. . . .

Revise and Rewrite

The most serious mistake anyone can make in writing is turning in a first draft as a final draft. The results are disappointing to readers.

People who manage their time better, who prepare a first draft days ahead of its due date, and then revise, produce dramatically superior writing. They also subject themselves to less stress!

The rewrite is actually the easiest and most productive effort in the writing process. Most people are surprised by the errors they find in proofreading a paper several days after it was written. Also, it's common to discover that there are serious flaws in the arrangement of the paper. This is what the cut and paste function on the computer was made for. The minimal time spent on revising will produce a significantly improved manuscript.

When you rewrite:

Be sure your thesis is clearly stated.

Arrange your ideas in a logical order.

Check each sentence to be sure it states exactly the meaning you intend.

Do not overstate. As soon as you state that something is interesting, exciting, or wonderful, your reader is sure to disagree with you.

Use active verbs. Limit the use of *is, am, are, was, were,* etc.

Eliminate all unnecessary words and do not repeat yourself.

The single most frequent weakness in unsophisticated writing is unnecessary restatement. Whether this is done because the writer lacks enough illustrative details or because the writer wants to emphasize an important point, the result is tedious repetition.

Vary sentence patterns.

Examples:

Begin some sentences with prepositional phrases: Inside the test room no one spoke.
Begin some sentences with adverb clauses: When the door opened, the crowd rushed in.
Begin some sentences with participle phrases: Saying goodbye, she started to cry.

Vary sentence lengths.

Writing a Research Paper Requires Specific Strategies.

By far the most critical element in writing any research paper is gathering good sources.

1. A source must deal adequately with your subject. You must read several pages of each potential source to decide on its worthiness.

2. In order to be of any use, a source must be comprehensible. If you don't completely understand it, don't use it.

3. Sources should contain information that fascinates you, or you'll be awfully bored spending the time it takes to transform the information into a research paper. Your time will be best spent if you keep searching until you discover facts, data, and details that genuinely ignite your enthusiasm.

4. Eliminate sources that are either too general or too specific for your topic.

5. When you find a great source, start writing. Take notes that can be incorporated into your paper.

Writing a Research Paper on a Literary Topic is Different from Other Kinds of Research Papers.

A research paper on a literary topic is part comments from critics (your sources) and part you. Include critical comments only when you agree with them. Sometimes a critic may say something that triggers an insight on your part. Good! This is called thinking and evidence of this behavior should be included in your paper. In fact, while the majority of ideas should come from the various critics, all papers should include some student observations as well.

When you are writing about longer literary works such as novels or plays, be sure to organize the comments chronologically according to the action in the novel or play. Otherwise, both you and your reader will become hopelessly confused.

Part Five: Writing Letters

Writing to ask for a Letter of Reference

You might want to ask a current boss, someone you've worked for in the past, or a teacher, or professor for a letter of reference. Since good recommendations are often crucial for getting a job, earning a scholarship, or gaining admission to a university or a special program, you need to show extreme consideration when you ask someone for his or her recommendation.

First, choose your letter-writer carefully. The ideal letter-writer is knowledgeable about you, about the place you are applying to, and how to write letters of recommendation. You should only request letters from people who will write you a good letter.

When requesting a letter of reference, remind supervisors of any event that showed special dedication. ("I was happy I was able to let the plumber in after work hours." Or "I really appreciated the special raise you got for me.") Remind a professor of the classes you had with him/her, the semester and year, and the grade (if it was a good one). Offer to attach an example of your best work from his/her class, such as an especially strong paper. Also, you could briefly highlight some of the achievements in your academic career.

Second, request your letter of reference as soon as you know you'll need one, and write a brief description of what position or honor you are applying for. Include the deadline. Give letter-writers at least two weeks' notice, and more, if possible.

You may be asked on an application whether you waive your right to view the letters of recommendation. You should always agree to waive that right to protect the integrity of the recommendation.

You will need to follow up to be sure that the letter arrived at its destination. Some letters do get lost, and some people forget to write them. In this case, ask the writer (or the writer's secretary) to send another copy.

Once you've received a letter of reference, write a thank-you note to the writer. A brief hand-written note is preferred to e-mail, but since so few students are polite enough to do either, writers appreciate any follow-up gesture. Letter-writers care about you, and whether you got the job, scholarship, or admission. Writers want to know the outcome of the applications they have played a role in.

Writing a Cover Letter

Before you write a cover letter, research the company and the job you want.
- Cover letters are nearly always an e-mail with a resume attached.

- Start by stating clearly what job you're trying to get.

- In the second paragraph demonstrate that you've done your research on the company by concisely admiring specific things like statistics, recent research, latest technological advances, or newspaper/web comments about the company.

- Limit the letter to four short paragraphs.

- There's no need to state, "I've attached my resume for you to view." The recipient will see the attachment.

- When you are applying for an entry level job, it's fine to include volunteer experiences, internships, projects and extra-curricular activities, but only when they clearly relate to the job.

- Suggest what you can do for the company, not what it can do for you.

- Don't be presumptive by closing with, "I look forward to being interviewed for the position."

- It's better to close with the traditional, "I look forward to hearing from you."

Format of a Business Letter

Sender's Address: The sender's address is usually included in a letterhead. If there is no letterhead, include the sender's address, city, and zip code. Do not write the sender's name or title, since it is included in the letter's closing.

Date

Name of recipient
Recipient's title
Name of company, organization, or institution
Street address or post office box
City, state and zip code (No comma between the state and zip code)

Salutation: Use the same name as the inside address, including the personal title. If you don't know a reader's gender, use a nonsexist salutation such as the job title followed by the receiver's name. (It's also acceptable to use the full name in a salutation if you can't determine gender.)

Body of letter

Closing: The closing begins at the same vertical point as your date and one line after the last body paragraph. Leave four lines between the closing and the sender's name for a signature.

Your signature

Your name

Enclosure:

In all writing, including business writing, use the most direct and personal language you know.

Avoid trite phrases like *enclosed please find* and *first and foremost*. Phrases like this have become so over-worked that they're almost meaningless.

Avoid	**Use Instead**
Enclosed please find. . .	Here are. . .; Enclosed are . . .
First and foremost . . .	First . . .
As per your request . .	As you requested . . .
Due to the fact that . . .	Because . . .
Interface about this . . .	Talk about this . . .

Drop meaningless tack-on words such as *factor*, *aspect*, and *situation*.

Example:
The convenience factor of holding the meeting during the lunch hour can't be underestimated.
The convenience of holding the meeting during the lunch hour can't be underestimated.

Avoid adding *–ize* or *–wise* to verbs and adverbs.

Example:
Weatherwise, it was a great day for the company picnic.
The fair weather made it a great day for the company picnic.

Write effective e-mails.

Write a short, meaningful subject line.

Not: Program
Better: March 12 Internship Program

Keep your message brief. Generally compose no more than a single screen of reading.

Use Standard grammar and punctuation.

Check with the sender before forwarding any e-mail messages.

Use a signature that displays your title and contact information. It should look professional, not be too long, and provide recipients with a choice in how to contact you.

- Remember that everyone is very busy. Keep your letter to one page.

- When writing to a specific person, be sure to get the name right. To a person named Lynne, getting a letter addressed to "Lynn" is not amusing.

- Don't be presumptuous. Assume your reader has adequate intelligence to make a decision.

In a letter of complaint, it's important not to be too aggressive.
- Not: "I **know** you don't want to run your business this way."

- Instead: "I **don't believe** you want to run your business this way."

The Most Common Business Letter—Complaints

- In writing complaint letters, be sure you have the facts straight and that your complaint is legitimate.

- State the complaint clearly and concisely.

- State clearly what the reader can or should do to address your complaint.

- Keep your tone polite.

- Include copies of any documentation relating to your complaint.

- Keep a copy of your complaint letter for your records.

- If you don't get the results you were seeking, write another firmer letter or write to someone higher up the corporate ladder.

- Even if the issue is complex, work hard to keep the letter to one page.

- Don't send an e-mail, which is usually handled by low level "customer service" people who have little real authority to handle a serious complaint.

- Ask for a response by a certain set time.

Sample Complaint Letter

July 21, 2009

Mr. Kevin Simmons
Vice President, Customer Service
De Lovely Sporting Goods
788 De Lovely Avenue
Rochester, New York 14604

Dear Mr. Simmons:

I recently purchased one of your deluxe badminton sets for my family. While the rackets
were clearly new and wrapped in plastic, two of the birdies looked as if they had been used.
Also, the first time we attempted to set up the net, one of the main strings broke.

I am writing to request replacements for the two used birdies and defective net. If we do not
receive replacements in two weeks, I will return the badminton set to the store and expect a full refund.
I am inclosing a copy of my sales receipt and a photo of the deficient equipment.

My family and I have purchased a wide range of sporting equipment from your store in the
past, and we have always been pleased with the quality, selection, and service at your store.
We hope to continue to do business with your store in the future.

Sincerely,

Marty Hammond

Sometimes **you** have to respond to complaint letters.

- Always thank the writer for writing to you.
  "Thank you for your letter dated . . . regarding . . ."

- Apologize when it's appropriate and empathize with the inconvenience the problem has caused.
  "I appreciate how frustrating this must have been . . ."

- State what you have done to correct the situation or what you will do in the future.
  "We will take action immediately to refund your purchase price . . ."
  "As an apology we are sending discount coupons for you to use in the future . . ."

- Close by thanking the writer for bringing the problem to your attention.
  "I am always attempting to improve the quality of my lawn care service . . ."
  or
  "Thank you for taking the time to let me know when my service has not been what you expected."

- In your closing, state something positive.
  "I will work hard to meet your expectations in the future."

Answer Key

Chapter One - Subject-Verb Agreement

Exercise One - Complete verbs p 5

1. has been shown
2. was called
3. can be recycled
4. has caused
5. defended

6. do celebrate
7. has seen
8. was removed
9. can identify
10. is displayed

11. is haunted
12. are considered
13. are required
14. are reconstructed
15. will have

Exercise Two - Complete verbs p 6

1. has become
2. is remembered
3. is traveling
4. was created
5. appears

6. are created
7. served
8. has been published
9. should be used
10. was passed

11. has had
12. presented
13. get
14. receives
15. was writing

Exercise Three - Subject/Verb p 8

1. Mosquitoes/have
2. you/did know
3. Feelings and emotions/are stored
4. Boring, Oregon/has become
5. Recycling/can reduce, save

6. North Carolina/is nicknamed
7. Shakespeare/attended
8. rivers/are
9. foot/has
10. sketch/looked

11. section/is
12. Lightening/strikes
13. you/do have
14. human/loses
15. Justin Timberlake/is

Exercise Four - Prepositional Phrases p 10

1. (in the province) (of Quebec) (in French)
2. (by the Chemical Bank) (at Rockville Center) (in January)
3. (on international flights) (in English)
4. (over an attractive body) (for a long-term mate)
5. (During a sunstroke)
6. (of Henry VIII) (with six fingers) (on her right hand)
7. (By 2018) (of all new jobs) (with an education) (beyond high school)
8. (in the world) (in northwest Alaska) (to Chile)
9. (In many North African countries) (to school) (on donkeys)
10. (by F. Scott Fitzgerald) (of the top 100 American novels) (of the 20th century)
11. (Between 1895 and 1905) (on fossil collecting trips)
12. (around their eyes) (for beauty) (of the sun)
13. (under the sign) (of the dog) (in Chinese astrology)
14. (Throughout Europe) (with the fork) (in the left hand) (in the right)
15. (on January 25) (in 38 minutes)

Exercise Five - Prepositional Phrases p 11

1. (In Turkey) (of mourning)
2. (in Toronto, Ontario,) (of the largest electric guitar) (in North America)
3. (of the best values) (at a warehouse club)
4. (According to the Commerce Department) (of the U.S. economy) (in one way or another) (by the weather)
5. (In China) (for 68 different crimes)

Chapter One - Subject-Verb agreement

Exercise Five con't. p 11

6. (of snakes) (without eating) (of food)
7. (In California) (for anyone) (at any kind) (of game) (from a moving vehicle)
8. (of astronauts) (on the moon)
9. (from an unemployment form) (in England)
10. (by a Chinese cook) (in a California mining camp) (in the 1800s)
11. (of monkeys) (in Indonesia) (for the animal) (with a photo) (of the monkey)
12. (of people) (on earth) (of all the people)
13. (of a lion) (from five miles away)
14. (in a bottle) (at an average) (of four miles an hour)
15. (by John Henry Kellogg) (at the beginning) (of the 20th century)

Exercise Six - Correct Verbs p 13

1. was	8. is	15. were
2. are	9. was	16. is
3. makes	10. was	17. is
4. lives	11. makes	18. manages
5. was	12. is	19. reveals
6. predicts	13. is	20. were
7. were	14. was	

Exercise Seven - Correct Verbs p 15

1. was	8. was	15. are
2. is	9. deserve	16. earns
3. was	10. was	17. were
4. are	11. are	18. is
5. was	12. was	19. knows
6. have	13. have	20. have
7. is	14. increase	

Chapter Review One - Correct Verbs p 18

1. was	6. Here are	11. is
2. wants	7. is	12. Where are
3. indicates	8. was	13. have
4. There are	9. make	14. was
5. was	10. There are	15. needs

Chapter Review Two- Correct Verbs p 19

1. flavored milk/has	6. neither/has	11. name/is
2. One/is	7. parts/contain	12. Each/has
3. children/are	8. Christina Aguilera/doesn't	13. complaint/is
4. one third/were	9. Each/was	14. Neither/seems
5. periods/are	10. One/was	15. Either/carries

Chapter One - Subject-Verb agreement

Chapter Review Three p 20
Subject/Verb

1. fingerprints/are
2. report/was
3. job/is
4. One/is
5. one/was

6. one/is
7. one/is
8. Either/is
9. One/works
10. Research/has

11. Neither/seems
12. Miss Tennessee/is
13. value/improves
14. person/needs
15. experts/There are

Chapter Review Four p 21
Subject/Verb

1. one/survives
2. houses/are
3. quality/is
4. Each/has
5. brains/increase

6. one/Here's
7. One/has
8. size/looks
9. spread/is
10. demand/is

11. each/has
12. Neither/leads
13. attendant/was
14. number/is
15. Each/was

Chapter Review Five p 22

1. correct
2. is
3. There are
4. was
5. was

6. is
7. Here are
8. was
9. was
10. were

11. was
12. are
13. sells
14. expects
15. are

Final Chapter Review p 23

1. has
2. are
3. makes
4. correct
5. have

6. fails
7. make
8. is
9. believes
10. attends

11. makes
12. was
13. there are
14. was
15. uses

Chapter Two - Common Errors

Exercise One p 26

1. their
2. whose
3. There
4. Who's
5. Your

6. whose
7. its
8. Whose
9. your
10. their

11. your
12. It's
13. its
14. Who's
15. their

Exercise Two p 27 Correct answers will vary.

Exercise Three p 27

1. your
2. their
3. It's
4. they're
5. its

6. whose
7. its
8. their
9. whose
10. There

11. they're
12. Who's
13. its
14. you're
15. It's

Chapter Two - Common Errors

Exercise Four p 29

1. well
2. too
3. good
4. too
5. good

6. to
7. well
8. good
9. well
10. well

11. well
12. to
13. well
14. well
15. too

Exercise Five p 30 Correct answers will vary.

Exercise Six p 31

Incorrect/Correct

1. alright/all right
2. alot/a lot
3. Alot/A lot
4. would of/would've
5. them/those

6. should of/should've
7. Alot/A lot
8. alot/a lot
9. could of/could've
10. them/those

11. your/you're
12. Its/It's
13. them/those
14. must of/must've
15. there/their

Chapter Review One p 33

Incorrect/Correct

1. would of/would've
2. their/there
3. there/their
4. them/those
5. who's/whose

6. alright/all right
7. good/well
8. Its/It's
9. there/their
10. there/their

11. to/too
12. should of/should've
13. Them/Those
14. Whose/Who's
15. to/too

Chapter Review Two p 34

Incorrect/Correct

1. Its/It's
2. should of/should've
3. your/you're
4. There/Their
5. alot/a lot

6. Whose/Who's
7. good/well
8. there/their
9. them/those
10. it's/its

11. it's/its
12. alright/all right
13. good/well
14. should of/should've
15. there/their

Chapter Review Three p 35

Incorrect/Correct

1. their/there
2. it's/its
3. Your/You're
4. should of/should've
5. their/there

6. it's/its
7. alright/all right
8. you're/your
9. good/well
10. could of/could've

11. whose/who's
12. to/too
13. there/they're
14. good/well
15. would of/would've

Chapter Two - Common Errors

Final Chapter Review p 36

Incorrect/Correct

1. Correct
2. who's/whose
3. alot/a lot
4. Them/Those
5. Your/You're

6. should of/should've
7. who's/whose
8. to/too
9. Its/It's
10. They're/There

11. who's/whose
12. Your/You're
13. Its/It's
14. alright/all right
15. them/those

Chapter Three - Pronouns

Exercise One p 39

1. her
2. his or her
3. him or her
4. it
5. he or she

6. his or her
7. his or her
8. his
9. her
10. them

11. their
12. himself or herself
13. he or she
14. his or her
15. their

Exercise Two p 40

1. his or her
2. he or she
3. his or her
4. their
5. he or she

6. he or she
7. he or she
8. his or her
9. its
10. its

11. his
12. their
13. their
14. his or her
15. his or her

Exercise Three p 41

Incorrect/Correct

1. their/its
2. its/their
3. their/his
4. they/he or she
5. their/his or her

6. they/he or she
7. they/he or she
8. their/its
9. their/its
10. their/his or her

Exercise Four p 42

1. he or she
2. his or her
3. he or she
4. he or she
5. its

6. he or she
7. him or her
8. he or she
9. their
10. his

Chapter Three - Pronouns

Exercise Five p 43

1. he or she
2. his or her
3. its
4. he or she
5. her

6. he or she
7. his or her
8. its
9. he or she
10. his or her

11. his or her
12. his or her
13. his or her
14. its
15. his or her

Exercise Six p 44

Incorrect/Correct

1. they/he or she
2. you/he or she
3. their/its
4. their/his or her
5. your/his or her

6. their/his or her
7. your/his or her
8. their/his or her
9. their/his or her
10. their/his or her

11. their/her
12. your/their
13. his or her/their
14. Correct
15. their/his or her

Exercise Seven p 46

1. We
2. I
3. him
4. them
5. me

6. We
7. He/I
8. us
9. she
10. she

11. her
12. we
13. We
14. I
15. we

Exercise Eight p 47

1. me
2. I
3. he or she
4. me
5. me

6. us
7. them
8. us
9. she
10. us

11. they
12. them
13. us
14. He
15. I

Exercise Nine p 48

Incorrect/Correct

1. Me/I
2. I/me
3. us/we
4. Me/I
5. he/him

6. I/me
7. Us/We
8. me/I
9. him/he
10. me/I

11. correct
12. he/him
13. him/he
14. Us/We
15. Her and me/She and I

Chapter Review One p 49

1. who
2. whom
3. Whoever
4. that
5. who

6. Who
7. Whoever
8. whom
9. Whoever
10. that

Chapter Three - Pronouns

Chapter Review Two p 51

1. him
2. She/I
3. Whoever
4. his or her
5. who
6. me
7. me

8. whom
9. She
10. his
11. who
12. I
13. I
14. his or her

15. him
16. I
17. his or her
18. him
19. him
20. Whoever

Exercise Ten p 53

1. me
2. they
3. we
4. he
5. him

6. they
7. I
8. he
9. she
10. they

11. her
12. they
13. him
14. I
15. she

Exercise Eleven p 54

1. him
2. she
3. he
4. I
5. they

6. I
7. he
8. she
9. they
10. he

11. us
12. her
13. her
14. them
15. they

Chapter Review Three p 55

1. his or her
2. he
3. me
4. she
5. he
6. me
7. he or she
8. they
9. she

10. whom
11. him
12. he or she
13. I
14. who
15. him
16. him or her
17. me

18. he
19. its
20. I
21. who
22. she
23. its
24. who
25. their

Final Chapter Review p 56

1. she
2. me
3. its
4. she
5. He and I
6. me
7. she
8. them
9. me

10. her
11. that
12. he
13. I
14. he or she
15. we
16. he or she
17. his or her
18. that

19. its
20. he or she
21. his or her
22. he
23. themselves
24. which
25. they

Chapter Four - Capital Letters

Exercise One p 60

1. Count Dracula, Sighisoara, Transylvania, Romania
2. A.D., Ireland, Christianity, Romanized Briton, Patrick
3. Norway, Christmas Eve
4. Sandburg, American, Galesburg, Illinois, January
5. Forty-first Street
6. Athens, Greek, Zeus
7. Fourth of July
8. South
9. Medieval
10. War, White House, British
11. Forty-eighth Street, Wilson Avenue
12. The
13. March
14. Alexander Pope, A
15. State, Boone Pickens Stadium
16. Netherlands, Dutch
17. Bodie, California, Sierra Nevada Mountains
18. Golden Gate Bridge
19. Aztec, Mexico, Cortez
20. Point, Long Island

Exercise Two p 62

1. Golden Globe Awards, January, Hollywood Foreign Press Association
2. Girl Scout, Philadelphia, Pennsylvania
3. Maya Angelou, *On Pulse Morning,* President Clinton's
4. South
5. H. Prescott, *The History Conquest Mexico,* Aztec, Spaniards
6. Saxons, William Conqueror, Normans
7. Washington, D.C., Mount Vernon, George Washington
8. Native American, Alex, Meg, Heard Museum, Phoenix, Arizona.
9. Pacific Ocean
10. New England, Maine, New Hampshire, Vermont, Massachusetts, Rhode Island, Connecticut
11. John F. Kennedy, Nobel Prize, White House, The White House, Thomas Jefferson
12. United States, World War, Japanese, Pearl Harbor, December
13. *Newsweek,* Sony Corporation
14. Huntington Library, Geoffrey Chaucer's, *Canterbury Tales*
15. Labor Day, San Diego Zoo, Balboa Park
16. Navaho Indians
17. god, god, soldiers, worship
18. High School Football Stadium, Dallas, Texas
19. Forty-eighth Street, Buffalo, New York
20. Clark, Atlantic Ocean, Pacific Ocean

Exercise Three p 65

1. Petrified Forest, Desert, eastern, fossilized trees, Period
2. Avenue, Seventy-ninth Street
3. Plowshare, colonists, Captain, execution

Chapter Four - Capital Letters

Exercise Three con't p 65

4. South, Day
5. World War, pigeons
6. Takabisha Fuji-Highland Amusement Park, Japan
7. century painting, canvas
8. Burger King, Wendy's
9. Paris, Jews, Nazis, Muslim I.D.'s, World War
10. German measles
11. Corvettes, National Corvette Museum, Bowling Green, Kentucky
12. Rome, European, folklore, owl
13. fall, senior, State University
14. doctor, allergy
15. The Crusades

Exercise Four p 66

1. Elizabeth, Kenilworth Castle, Stratford, plays
2. biology, Vassar
3. Duran, Simon Le Bon, French, England, France, Catholics, Protestant beliefs.
4. tuna, Mrs. Baird's, Breyer's, Krogers
5. Declaration of Independence
6. Knowles', Crazy Love, England
7. Correct
8. Ukraine, English
9. Declaration, My, heart
10. pickup truck
11. Billy Bob Thornton, Los Angeles, pizza parlor
12. Room Store Corporation
13. National History Museum, London, England, "Darwin Day," February, Charles Darwin's
14. Tyler, physics
15. aunt, uncle, Automotive Hall Fame, Dearborn, Michigan

Chapter Review One p 67

1. Mexico, bridge, River
2. President U.S. Greek Latin
3. European, Calculus, English
4. Marching Band, Bowl
5. Irish, Day, patron saint
6. This, devil
7. west, south
8. architecture, Southwest, history
9. World War, Allies, Berlin, Berlin Zoo
10. Native American World War code
11. Uncle Ryan, Red Cross
12. Bible, King David
13. Mother (optional), Sony
14. Department Defense, D.C.
15. explorer, Thor, Peru, Islands, Kon-tiki

Chapter Four - Capital Letters

Chapter Review Two p 68

1. Buffalo, New York, Lake Erie
2. German
3. Chicago's O'Hare Airport
4. Emerald Isle, gemstones
5. Guam, Anderson Air Force Base
6. Baptist
7. Roman, Juno
8. Maytag
9. *Patriot-News* Harrisburg, Pennsylvania, Abraham Lincoln's Gettysburg Address
10. White Star Cleaners, Spruce Street
11. Boston Tea Party, Boston, Native, British, British
12. Governor (optional), campaign
13. Great Wall China
14. proposal
15. We're, hamburgers, French (optional) fries

Final Chapter Review p 69

1. First Continental Congress, British, colonial
2. Airport, New York's
3. Caverns National Park, Mountains, southeast, subterranean, caverns, world
4. Correct
5. salad, Caesar (optional) dressing, blue
6. Reed College Portland, Oregon
7. Empire State Building, Manhattan
8. aunt, uncle, Olive Garden Restaurant, birthday
9. Beth Israel Medical Center New York
10. Monticello
11. Italian, Varallo
12. University, New York City, Catholic Church
13. War, African-American, Battle Lake Erie
14. National Sleep Foundation
15. Coachella Valley Music Arts Festival, Indio, California

Chapter Five - Apostrophes

Exercise One p 71

1. miners'
2. President's
3. Fitzhenrys'
4. journalist's
5. doctors'
6. night's
7. children's
8. lawyers'
9. night's
10. employees'
11. owners'
12. women's
13. can't
14. band's
15. girl's

Exercise Two p 73

1. correct
2. officers'
3. correct
4. everyone's
5. weeks
6. writer's
7. Women's, men's
8. one's
9. weeks'
10. You're
11. lifetime's
12. inmates'
13. correct
14. sports'
15. '13

Chapter Five - Apostrophes

Exercise Three p 74

1. year's
2. yours
3. bears'
4. children's
5. correct
6. correct
7. minutes
8. its
9. Ben's

10. today's
11. driver's
12. women's
13. world's
14. dollars'
15. Piggy's
16. show's
17. pilots'

18. Children's
19. men's
20. people's
21. children's
22. England's
23. People's
24. correct
25. Adam and Melinda's

Chapter Review One p 76

1. consumers', its
2. Sherry's, everyone's
3. dictatorship's, States'
4. countries
5. its, weeks'

6. prisoners' cells
7. year's, year's
8. Diane's
9. husband's
10. correct

11. world's
12. father's
13. Earhart's, people's
14. minutes'
15. parents'

Chapter Review Two p 77

1. council's, its
2. dealer's
3. Samson's
4. It's, nobody's
5. farmers'

6. painter's
7. correct
8. people's
9. students' (lockers)
10. p.j.'s

11. England's, people's
12. Senate's
13. driver's
14. Armando's
15. Keisha's, everyone's

Chapter Review Three p 78

1. fans'
2. Pasteur's
3. men's
4. Scotland's
5. students

6. its
7. children's
8. Sheen's
9. Arthur's, day's
10. astronaut's

11. nation's
12. someone's
13. people's
14. customers'
15. correct

Final Chapter Review p 79

1. correct
2. parents'
3. people's
4. women's
5. everyone's

6. men's
7. reporters'
8. years'
9. nation's
10. parents'

11. everybody's
12. children's
13. hers
14. men's
15. customers'

Chapter Six - Complete Sentences

Exercise One p 80

1. F	6. F	11. C
2. F	7. C	12. F
3. C	8. F	13. F
4. F	9. C	14. C
5. C	10. C	15. F

Exercise Two p 81

1. F	6. C	11. F
2. F	7. F	12. F
3. F	8. F	13. F
4. F	9. C	14. F
5. F	10. F	15. F

Exercise Three p 83

1. F	6. C	11. F
2. C	7. F	12. F
3. F	8. C	13. F
4. F	9. F	14. F
5. F	10. F	15. F

Exercise Four p 84

1. F	6. F	11. F
2. F	7. F	12. F
3. F	8. C	13. F
4. C	9. C	14. C
5. F	10. F	15. F

Chapter Review One p 85

1. C	8. F	15. F
2. F	9. F	16. F
3. F	10. F	17. F
4. F	11. F	18. F
5. F	12. F	19. F
6. F	13. C	20. F
7. C	14. F	

Chapter Review Two p 86

1. F	8. C	15. F
2. F	9. F	16. F
3. F	10. C	17. F
4. F	11. F	18. F
5. C	12. F	19. C
6. F	13. F	20. F
7. F	14. F	

Chapter Six - Complete Sentences

Exercise Five p 88

1. R	6. C	11. R
2. R	7. R	12. R
3. R	8. R	13. R
4. R	9. R	14. C
5. C	10. R	15. R

Exercise Six p 90

1. R	6. C	11. R
2. R	7. R	12. R
3. R	8. R	13. C
4. R	9. R	14. R
5. R	10. C	15. R

Exercise Seven p 91

1. R	6. C	11. R
2. R	7. R	12. R
3. R	8. R	13. C
4. R	9. C	14. R
5. R	10.C	15. C

Chapter Review Three p 92

1. F	10. F	19. F
2. F	11. C	20. R
3. R	12. F	21. C
4. F	13. R	22. R
5. C	14. C	23. R
6. F	15. C	24. R
7. F	16. R	25. R
8. R	17. C	
9. R	18. C	

Final Chapter Review p 93

1. C	10. C	19. F
2. F	11. F	20. R
3. R	12. R	21. R
4. F	13. R	22. R
5. C	14. C	23. F
6. C	15. R	24. R
7. R	16. F	25. R
8. C	17. C	
9. R	18. F	

Chapter Seven - Punctuation

Exercise One p 97

1. . . .biologist said**,** **"G**lobal warming . . .coral reefs**."**
2. Correct
3. Mom said**,** **"T**urn . . .TV**."**
4. . . .teacher said, **"***Uncle Tom's* . . .copies**."**
5. Steven said, **"Ti**gers . . .fur**."**
6. Coffman said, **"D**id . . .minutes**?"**
7. Mason said**,** **"S**everal. . .communicate**."**
8. Correct
9. **"**Am I the only . . . who has boring dreams**?"** asked Sydney.
10. . . .report stated, **"A**bout . . .water**."**
11. Lily said, **"T**hings . . .better**."**
12. Holmes never said**,** **"E**lementary . . .Watson**."**
13. Correct
14. **"N**o eye gouging,**"** was . . .Rome.
15. Correct

Exercise Two p 98

1. Marley said**,** **"W**e . . .Nebraska**."**
2. Kyle shouted**,** **"B**ring . . .extinguisher**!"**
3. Correct
4. **"D**o . . .this**?"** **a**sked Mr. Statler.
5. **"Y**ou're out!**"** **y**elled the umpire.
6. Lenny asked, **"D**o . . .money**?"**
7. Adam said, **"I**s . . .do**?"**
8. Correct
9. Hunter said**,** **"S**leeping on. . .to their job**."**
10. Russell said**,** **"E**very . . .facts**."**
11. Correct
12. Chrissy yelled**,** **"C**hange the channel**!"**
13. Correct
14. **"L**et's . . . try,**"** **s**aid Monty.
15. Kate Winslet said**,** **"I** do . . .don't really look like that**"**

Exercise Three p 99 Correct answers will vary.

Exercise Four p 99

1. **"I**'m so sorry,**"** **s**aid Jenney**,** **"b**ut I really do have to leave**."**
2. **"I**f you . . .minute,**"** **s**aid Taylor**,** **"t**here's . . .time**."**
3. **"D**rinking black tea,**"** **s**aid Lisa**,** **"h**as. . .cortisol**."**
4. **"I** agree, **"** **s**aid Brandon. **"**Let's get started right away**."**
5. **"W**hen you see her,**"** **s**aid Jamie**,** **"t**ell . . .her**."**
6. **"I**. . . presentation,**"** **s**aid Lee Iacocca**,** **"b**ut I did**."**

Chapter Seven - Punctuation

Exercise Four con't p 99

7. "Let's talk somewhere else," said Makayla. "It's bedlam in here."
8. Our mechanic said, "If . . .bills."
9. "All hands on deck," said the captain. "I have an important announcement."
10. "Oh, I see," said Sally. "That's fantastic."
11. Dan said, "Some astronomers believe in the existence of living things on other planets."
12. Correct
13. Britney Spears said, "I'm rich, freakin' rich."
14. "Mountain goats are not goats, but small antelopes," said Ben.
15. Mr. Madison said, "The earth is turning to desert at a rate of 40 square miles a day."

Chapter Review One p 101

1. "Bring your umbrella," said Jared. "It's still raining."
2. Mrs. Riley said, "In. . .food."
3. "I love. . .Revere," said President Harding, "whether. . .not."
4. "Take all . . .you want," Maya said, "but don't. . .Facebook."
5. "Doing. . .problem," said President Lyndon Johnson. "It's. . .right."
6. Mark Twain said, "The difference . . .lightening."
7. "Everybody. . .weather," said Charles Dudley Warner, "but. . .it."
8. "Show. . .loser," said Knute Rockne, "and I'll show you a failure."
9. "England and America," said George Bernard Shaw, "are two countries . . .language."
10. "I have a doctor's appointment," said Sam, "so. . .rehearsal."
11. "Eleanor Rigby"
12. "Never. . .things," said General George S. Patton. "Tell. . .ingenuity."
13. Matt asked, "Was Jules Verne the first author to specialize in science-fiction books?"
14. "History," said Henry Ford, "is more or less bunk."
15. . . .Galbraith said, "More. . .little."

Chapter Review Two p 102

1. Travis said, "I still have a cold. . .anymore."
2. "Hey," said Paige, "you're walking so fast I can't keep up with you."
3. "By channeling my inner heiress, I created. . .heiresses," said Paris Hilton.
4. Mrs. Freeman said, "What we call soccer. . .world."
5. Correct
6. "Make yourself useful," said dad. "Wash the dishes."
7. The police officer said, "The. . . curve."
8. Gus said, "Thomas. . .summer."
9. The weather forecaster said, "These rains we've been having will end soon."
10. Rita Dove said, "If only sun-drenched. . . keeping society together."
11. "I. . .outline," said Rebecca.
12. "Attractive politicians," said Ms. Warning, "typically . . .politicians."
13. The banner read, "Everything on Sale!"
14. Correct
15. My brother said to me, "Don't . . .tank."

Chapter Seven - Punctuation

Exercise Five p 106

1. *Teenage Dream*
2. following:
3. *American Gothic*
4. *Othello*
5. "Dear Mayor White:"
6. anti-intellectual
7. Corn-rowing--styling hair in thin braids-- *or* Corn-rowing (styling hair in thin braids)
8. Cybersickness—cases. . .dizziness--
9. *Queen Mary*
10. statement:

Exercise Six p 107

1. *Mona Lisa*
2. semi-independent
3. Birmingham, England, *Titanic II*
4. financial literacy—from how. . .of a good credit report—
5. *The Happiness Advantage*
6. *Antiques Road Show*
7. home-cooked
8. . . .books and papers:
9. . . .he never got: love
10. time and money: ten years
11. Correct
12. The long-lost document
13. Maintaining good credit is important:
14. *Harry Potter and the Order of the Phoenix*
15. Every job . . .a job interview:

Final Chapter Review p 108

1. "Get up," said mother. "You'll be late for work."
2. "Get up," said mother, "or you'll be late for work."
3. Monet's *Water Lilies*
4. Robert Frost said, "Poetry. . .books."
5. "We all have flaws and mine is being wicked," said James Thurber.
6. Paul said, "Beethoven was totally deaf when he composed his *Ninth Symphony*."
7. Correct
8. Will said, "David Beckman got $150 million. . .team."
9. *Aida*
10. "Do you know how fast you were driving?" asked the policeman.
11. "You. . .speeding," said the policeman, "and I have to give you a ticket."
12. "You were speeding," said the policeman. "I have to give you a ticket."
13. Gabriella said, "The time spent . . .annually."
14. "Man is a complex being," said Gil Stern. "He makes deserts bloom and lakes die."
15. Kevin Bacon said, "There are two kind of actors: those. . .liars."

Chapter Eight - Commas

Exercise One p 109

1. I just talked to Alisha, and Jody got angry.
2. The day after, I leave on vacation to the Bahamas.
3. If Jaclyn had known, everything would have been different.
4. Dolly Parton said, "The funny thing is, that the poorer people are, the more generous they seem to be."
5. By the time we found out about it, it was too late.
6. The week before, she lost her keys.
7. Trent and I finally got a response from Rodney, and Meredith hasn't e-mailed us yet.
8. We're planning a party for Friday, and Saturday we're going to a hockey game.
9. I yelled for my cat, and my dog came running.
10. In this company, rules are very strictly enforced.

Exercise Two p 110

1. Research studies show . . .schools, colleges, coffee shops, and malls . . .
2. Ron cleared his throat, tried to speak, and started laughing.
3. In Hawaii. . .spring, summer, fall, and winter.
4. The entire month before, the candidates campaigned throughout the state.
5. Most people . . .by inheriting it, successfully investing in real estate, owning a profitable business,
6. Correct
7. Soon after, Paige apologized.
8. Four common . . .showing up late, about yourself too much, revealing too much about an ex,
9. At the conference . . .poised and regal, intelligent and intimidating, and steely and arrogant.
10. We cleaned the basement, vacuumed the rug, and swept . .to make a good impression.
11. Efficient people write down their goals, prioritize them, and spend . . .them.
12. I called Matt, a foolish thing to do.
13. People . . .willing to take chances, have a sense of perspective,
14. The week before, Frida lost her glasses.
15. If we had known, the rehearsal could have been rescheduled for another time.
16. Some . . .web-developer, medical secretary, insurance agent,
17. As you depart, the baggage area is on your right.
18. Correct
19. Pink said, " I work hard, I have talent, I'm funny, and . . .
20. We loaded the boat, hoisted the sails, and set off on our Caribbean adventure.

Exercise Three p 113

1. . . .110 Peacock Dr., Seattle, Washington, December 30, 2008.
2. To an. . .North and South Atlantic, the North and South Pacific, the Indian, the Arctic, and. . .
3. The meeting is scheduled for 2 p.m., Thursday, May 18th.
4. "All you need to grow healthy, vigorous grass . . .
5. Correct
6. The beautiful, simple furniture made by the Shakers . . .
7. In order . . .35 years-old, a natural-born citizen of the United States, . . .
8. Correct
9. The adoring supporters . . .funeral for his amputated leg on September 26, 1842, in Mexico City.
10. Correct
11. Steady, dependable Paul Revere. . .
12. At Sequoyah Hills . . .visitors can jog, walk, bike, or paddle.
13. The company . . .815 Broad Street, San Francisco, California 90477.
14. He . . .and ill at ease, tongue-tied and bumbling, and foolish . . .sophisticated, wealthy parents.
15. Minnie Munro . . .May 31, 1991.
16. Correct

Chapter Eight - Commas

Exercise Three con't. p 113

17. Correct
18. Cheryl's address is 2005 Winona Street, Pasadena, California 91103.
19. The big, smelly ogre made all the fairy tale creatures leave the swamp.
20. Superman . . "faster than a speeding bullet, more powerful than a locomotive, and able. . ."

Exercise Four p 115

1. Essential, no commas
2. Essential, no commas
3. Non-essential, add commas
4. Non-essential, add commas
5. Essential, no commas

6. Essential, no commas
7. Non-essential, add commas
8. Essential, no commas
9. Essential, no commas
10. Non-essential, add commas

11. Non-essential, add commas
12. Non-essential, add commas
13. Essential, no commas
14. Non-essential, add commas
15. Non-essential, add commas

Exercise Five p 116

1. Attila the Hun, who died on the night of his marriage, is thought. . .
2. Harriet Tubman, an escaped former slave, was . . .
3. The University of Dublin, opened by Queen Elizabeth I in 1592, is the oldest . . .
4. People who have poor vision need corrective lenses . . .
5. Food which is too spicy makes me very sick.
6. The Pony Expresss, which lasted only 18 months, began . . .
7. In Wisconsin, a leading milk producer, it's illegal . . .
8. The part of the fireplace behind the screen is called the firebox.
9. Correct
10. Correct
11. Savir Mirchandani, a 14-year-old student from Pittsburgh, Pennsylvania, . . .to Garamond, which would . . .
12. William, who's embarrassed because he's so skinny, just sent off . . .
13. The Taj Mahal, which was commissioned in 1630, was built by Shah Jehan. . .
14. Izaak Walton . . .most calm, quiet, innocent recreation in the world.
15. Correct
16. Krystal Smith, a 24 year-old Vermont grocery bagger, won. . .
17. Vanessa, who is from Martinique, speaks both French and English.
18. Soap, which is now universally accepted as a cleanser, was originally . . .
19. Manuel, who was tired from working all day, decided not to go with us.
20. The hand fan, the world's most basic air conditioner, . . .of years.

Chapter Review One p 117

1. The twins were born on July 29, 1995, in Sarasota, Florida.
2. The world's oldest musical instruments, laboriously carved . . .years ago, were . . .
3. In Florida a special law . . .Sunday, or they risk arrest, a fine, or a stay in jail.
4. Remove the comma.
5. The seven dwarfs are Bashful, Doc, Dopey, Grumpy, Happy, Sleepy, and Sneezy.
6. My best friend, Martin Andrew De Salvo, was the first to wish me good luck.
7. The heroes of American legends are generally tall, big-muscled men with fierce, undaunted courage.
8. I have had enough, that's all.
9. Pamela Anderson is Canada's Centennial Baby, the first baby born on the 100th anniversary. . .
10. Correct
11. Correct
12. Please mail the receipt to Janice Malley, 20801 Lansing Lane, Littleton, Colorado 80124.

Chapter Eight - Commas

Chapter Review One con't. p 117

13. Correct
14. Steve Jobs, the founder of Apple Corporation, acupuncture, dietary supplements, and juices
15. Adrian insists he doesn't believe in UFOs, aliens, or ghosts.
16. Our club met for the first time at 7 p.m. on January 21, 2009, in downtown Phoenix, Arizona.
17. Before Brad Pitt . . .chauffeur, a furniture mover, and . . .
18. Correct
19. Correct
20. The Declaration of Independence was signed on July 4, 1776, in Philadelphia, Pennsylvania.

Chapter Review Two p 118

1. Mr. Andrews, who teaches digital photography, is a professional photographer.
2. Remove the commas.
3. Jesse James, Billy the Kid, and Butch Cassidy are famous American outlaws.
4. Remove the commas.
5. Correct
6. Colin Marley, who is working this month as a fortune teller, always has unusual jobs.
7. Correct
8. Camel's milk, a popular drink in Arab countries, has ten times more iron than cow's milk.
9. Buddy, the first seeing-eye dog in America, was brought to the U.S. from Switzerland in 1928.
10. Shangri-La, the first name of the Presidential retreat in Maryland, was. . .grandson, David.
11. Remove the commas.
12. The novel, a book recommended by Oprah Winfrey, is tense, exciting, and difficult to put down.
13. The Henry Ford Museum, located in Dearborn, Michigan, is well worth seeing.
14. Since the 1940s the American Ad Council, a non-profit corporation, has been . .
15. Yu Youzhen, a Chinese millionaire, works . . .
16. Asia, the largest of the earth's continents, accounts for three fifths of the world's population.
17. Remove the commas.
18. Ulysses Grant, a Civil War hero of the Northern Army, became the 18th president. . .
19. The cheeta, found in southern Asia and southern Africa, can run 45-70 miles an hour . . .
20. Correct

Chapter Review Three p 120

1. A daily dose of aspirin, taken by many people to prevent heart attacks, may also reduce . . .
2. The Calvin Klein model was a slim, dark, dashing figure.
3. Remove the commas.
4. *Notes From a Small Island*, written by American author Bill Bryson, was recently . . .
5. Craigslist, which started in San Francisco in 1995, . . .
6. Victoria Woodhall, an American political reformer, ran for president in 1872.
7. The only two Southern state capitals not occupied by Northern troops during the Civil War were Austin, Texas, and Tallahassee, Florida.
8. The restaurant is located at 185 East Bay Street, Charleston, South Carolina 29401.
9. Patrick Dempsey began . . .juggling, unicycle-riding clown.
10. Remove the commas.
11. Halley's Comet, named for astronomer Edmund Halley, appears approximately every 76 years.
12. The term cop comes from constable on patrol, a term used in England.
13. Sheila ordered a dainty breakfast of scrambled eggs, bacon, wheat toast, hash browns, orange juice, and coffee.
14. Remove the commas.

Chapter Eight - Commas

Chapter Review Three con't. p 120

15. The Pentagon in Arlington, Virginia, has five sides and five stories and five acres of land.
16. Kristen carefully washed her shiny, new red convertible.
17. Maps, blueprints, and photographs were on the table.
18. Two log cabins . . .relax in an intimate, rustic space.
19. The letter . . .to Mr. Jack Watson, 111 Water Tower Place, Apt 806, Chicago, Illinois 60605.
20. Remove the commas.

Exercise Six p 122

1. Laissez-faire, the philosophy that government should not interfere with commerce or trade, was . . .
2. All polar bears are, as a matter of fact, left-handed.
3. Sherlock Holmes, Sir Arthur Conan Doyle's brilliant detective, first appeared . . .
4. Michael, are you sure we're headed in the right direction?
5. Remove the comma.
6. Alan Turing, the father of computer science, chained . . .to stop anyone else at work from using it.
7. It was a pretty good poker hand, I guess.
8. The Great Wall of China, which runs from northern China for 2,162 miles, is the largest . . .
9. Okay, we'll do it your way.
10. The tallest monument in the United States, the Gateway Arch in St. Louis, is 630 feet tall.
11. Well, I thought it was a good idea, Leslie.
12. One of the biggest events in . . .is *Wrestle Mania*, which decides the world champions.
13. George Eastman, the founder of Kodak Corporation, hated to have his picture taken.
14. As a matter of fact, it would be a good time to apologize.
15. Bobby Leach, the second man . . .in a barrel, survived the fall, bur later died . . .

Chapter Review Four p 123

1. Extended exposure to dark, gloomy days . . .
2. Remove the comma.
3. Well, the U.S. has more lawyers . . .
4. Kristen, do you know the Web address?
5. Jupiter, the fifth planet from the sun, is the largest planet in our solar system.
6. The "black box" . . .is actually orange, so that . . .
7. Remove the commas.
8. People with high self-esteem . . .longer, more successful relationships.
9. Battle Creek, Michigan, is the home of two of America's biggest brand names in cereals, Post and Kellogg's.
10. Jill has long, straight dark brown hair.
11. Honey, I'm home!
12. About 1,000 movies a year are produced in India, about twice the output of Hollywood.
13. The essence . . .found in respected newspapers, magazines, and academic journals.
14. Lisa, normally quite sensible, came up with a really crazy idea.
15. In China, (optional) clocks, handkerchiefs, straw sandals, and flowers . . .with death and funerals, and . . .
16. No, I wasn't aware . . .
17. The world's smallest butterfly, the dwarf blue from Africa, has a wingspan of only one-half inch.
18. A 30-year-old woman in Des Moines, Iowa, was arrested . . .former best friend, who . . .
19. Claude Monet, the French painter, completed his famous water lily paintings when he was 84 years old.
20. Propylene Glycol, commonly used as an anti-freeze, can . . .

Chapter Eight - Commas

Exercise Seven p 125

1. The hostages in the bank robbery were released unharmed, and police were able to persuade . . .
2. It takes most people 48 to 100 tries to solve a Rubik's Cube puzzle, but if done perfectly . . .
3. To reduce tiredness while driving long distances, keep your back as straight as possible.
4. New Mexico State's . . . one student, and he was shot . . .
5. Alligator meat is considered healthier than domestic chicken, for the cholesterol and fat content are lower.
6. In a war of wits, you're an unarmed soldier.
7. Bruce Dickinson . . .world-class fencer, author, and licensed Boeing 757 pilot.
8. Correct
9. Men named Kent have a 69% chance of being Republicans, while women named Annie . . .
10. It is the female lion that does more than 90% of the hunting, while the male is either . . .
11. By the end of elementary school, the average American child has witnessed . . .
12. Since pumpkin pulp doesn't grind up thoroughly, plumbers recommend that pumpkin pulp . . .
13. A rectangle has four right angles, while . . .four equal sides, and . . .
14. Just as my friend told me someone had died in the fire, we saw the hearse drive up.
15. Drivers tend . . .around them, and it doesn't matter if the other cars are in front, beside, or behind them.
16. After the union leader and the president of the company . . .settled, reporters began shouting questions.
17. Alexander Hamilton and Aaron Burr. . .on July 11, 1804, and Hamilton was mortally wounded and . . .
18. Italy is famous for its fine leather goods, but Italian shoes are expensive.
19. Marco Polo was . . .*The Travels of Marco Polo*, and he gave 14th century Europeans the first . . .
20. When doing business in Turkey, it's the custom . . .for the meal, and requests . . .

Chapter Review Five p 126

1. Give the job to Halle, not me.
2. During National Clean Your Closet Week in March, the Dress for Success organization . . .
3. A northern California couple . . .a modern-day bonanza: $10 million in rare, mint-condition . . .
4. Mrs. Hong should be promoted, not fired.
5. Since it takes glass a million years to decompose, it never wears out and can be recycled an infinite . . .
6. Triggered by a landslide that buried the mountain town of Yungay, Peru, an estimated . . .
7. Intelligent men and women . . .people in general, but they . . .
8. After Washington state road crews removed three large dams built by the same beaver, they decided to spend $15,000 to hire a beaver trapper.
9. Michelangelo was 26 when he began sculpting his celebrated *David* statue, and he finished it . . .
10. All of the roles in Shakespeare's plays were originally acted by men and boys, since it wasn't . . .
11. Carter, get lost.
12. To be sure the package would arrive on time, I sent it Federal Express.
13. The world's largest gothic cathedral, the Cathedral of St. John the Divine, is located on. . .
14. Americans eat over 20 pounds of candy annually, but the Dutch eat three times as much.
15. President Woodrow Wilson . . .White House lawn, and he
16. The world's first transplant . . . her nose, lips, and chin had been seriously injured when she . . .
17. Correct
18. Horatior Alger inspired . . .who became rich, but Alger himself died poor.
19. According to a recent study, removing allergens such as dust from homes could reduce the chance . . .
20. It is estimated that six year olds laugh 300 times a day, but adults laugh only 15 to 100 times a day.
21. For people who have trouble sleeping, researchers . . .
22. Hollywood celebrities . . .the Beverly Hills Hotel, owned by the Sultan of Brunei,
23. In Natoma, Kansas, it's illegal . . .
24. Amid an epidemic of overdose deaths from prescription drugs, medical boards. . .
25. Scientists . . .brain light up: a thinking part . . .get the joke, a movement area that tells your muscles to move, and . . .

Chapter Eight - Commas

Final Chapter Review p 128

1. Correct

2. Whales are mammals, not fish.

3. According to a recent poll, most Americans . . .China, Vietnam, or Bangladesh.

4. On a raised platform at the front of the ballroom, the wedding party posed for photographs.

5. In order to be able to see a rainbow, you must have your back to the sun.

6. Pluto was once considered the ninth planet in our solar system, but. . .

7. I'm sure I need a period here, not a comma.

8. They live at 2804 Washington Street, San Jose, California 97433.

9. Correct

10. Taylor, would you give me a ride downtown tomorrow morning?

11. Denmark's largest power company, Dong Energy, plans to build . . .in towns, cities, and. . .

12. Correct

13. King George I of England, who was born and raised in Germany, never learned . . .

14. As a precaution in the event of a crash, Prince Charles . . .

15. A mythical creature, the griffin, had the body of a lion, the wings of a bird, and the head of an eagle.

16. Park your car in the parking lot, not on the street.

17. The average child in the United States spends . . .watching television, more time than in the classroom.

18. On May 25, 2011, 20 days after a tornado struck Joplin, Missouri, an Indiana couple discovered a receipt that had blown 525 miles from Joplin to their porch, the longest recorded journey of debris from a tornado.

19. Forcing back his anger, Jeffrey apologized to Latisha.

20. In most parts of the world, brides wear vibrant, colorful wedding dresses.

21. Fortune cookies were invented in the United States, not China.

22. Jessica Alba's charity work includes working with Clothes Off Our Backs, Habitat for Humanity, the National Center for Missing and Exploited Children, and Project HOME.

23. Keith is looking forward to his internship this summer, but he can't decide whether he wants to work at a technology company or at an investment firm.

24. A Kansas basketball jersey adorned with a heart and Taylor Swift's autograph was sold as a collector's item for $1,005 on March 2, 2011.

25. Correct

Chapter Nine - Irregular Verbs

Exercise One p 131

1. torn	10. stolen	19. came
2. began	11. written	20. swum
3. saw	12. seen	21. saw
4. did	13. began	22. frozen
5. came	14. broken	23. worn
6. spoken	15. worn	24. stolen
7. drank	16. came	25. swam
8. ran	17. broken	
9. did	18. driven	

Chapter Nine - Irregular Verbs

Exercise Two p 133

1. was
2. eaten
3. known
4. forbidden
5. gotten
6. grown
7. become
8. ridden
9. flown

10. eaten
11. taken
12. beaten
13. eaten
14. sprang
15. were
16. taken
17. drawn
18. taken

19. become
20. eaten
21. gotten
22. given
23. driven
24. became
25. sprung

Exercise Three p 136

1. sworn
2. sunk
3. dragged
4. forgotten
5. sang
6. sank
7. threw

8. drowned
9. blew
10. sung
11. caught
12. forgotten
13. forgiven
14. gone

15. shaken
16. burst
17. hanged
18. threw
19. brought
20. forgiven

Chapter Review One p 137

1. did
2. sworn
3. gotten
4. stolen
5. sprung
6. were
7. drawn
8. torn
9. rung

10. burst
11. swum
12. thrown
13. caught
14. sprung
15. stolen
16. sworn
17. sunk

18. ridden
19. blown
20. broken
21. grown
22. ridden
23. thrown
24. given
25. saw

Chapter Review Two p 138
Incorrect/Correct

1. saw/seen
2. swam/swum
3. spoke/spoken
4. flew/flown
5. gave/given
6. threw/thrown
7. grew/grown
8. drunk/drank
9. sprang/sprung

10. been/were
11. wrote/written
12. drownded/drowned
13. drug/dragged
14. broke/broken
15. sunk/sank
16. busted/burst
17. forbid/forbidden

18. rode/ridden
19. stole/stolen
20. knew/known
21. ran/run
22. grew/grown
23. freezed/frozen
24. ran/run
25. saw/seen

Chapter Nine - Irregular Verbs

Chapter Review Three p 140
Incorrect/Correct

1. threw/thrown
2. wore/worn
3. seen/saw
4. stole/stolen
5. begun/began
6. stole/stolen
7. drove/driven

8. hid/hidden
9. forgot/forgotten
10. froze/frozen
11. seen/saw
12. come/came
13. ate/eaten
14. run/ran

15. swam/swum
16. drownded/drowned
17. became/become
18. fell/fallen
19. wrote/written
20. come/came

Exercise Four p 142

1. lay
2. lying
3. laid
4. laid
5. lain

6. laying
7. lies
8. lying
9. lies
10. lay

Exercise Five p 143

1. rising
2. raise
3. rises
4. raised
5. rose
6. raise
7. risen

8. rise
9. lies
10. lain
11. raising
12. lain
13. raise
14. lying

15. rising
16. worn
17. hidden
18. swum
19. forbidden
20. laid

Final Chapter Review p 144

Incorrect/Correct
1. swore/sworn
2. don't/doesn't
3. ran/run
4. took/taken
5. sung/sang
6. ate/eaten
7. flew/flown
8. become/became
9. chose/chosen

10. drug/dragged
11. rose/risen
12. seen/saw
13. sank/sunk
14. threw/thrown
15. ate/eaten
16. forgot/forgotten (you)
17. sprung/sprang
18. rang/rung

19. stole/stolen
20. hid/hidden
21. shook/shaken
22. went/gone
23. grow/grown
24. spoke/spoken
25. rode/ridden

Chapter Ten - Usage Glossary

Exercise One p 148

1. capital
2. capital
3. counsel
4. Council
5. peek
6. principle
7. counsel
8. peak
9. peak

10. cite
11. stationary
12. stationery
13. principal
14. principal
15. capitol
16. capital
17. stationary

18. Complimentary
19. counsel
20. sight
21. site
22. peak
23. council
24. compliments
25. Complementary

Exercise Two p 151

1. already
2. advise
3. anxious
4. except
5. between

6. effects
7. number
8. eager
9. affect
10. accept

11. advice
12. among
13. an
14. all ready
15. amount

Exercise Three p 154

1. led
2. bad
3. conscious
4. deserted
5. lead
6. figurative
7. can

8. conscience
9. dessert
10. take
11. literally
12. conscience
13. bring
14. badly

15. regardless
16. led
17. desert
18. may
19. badly
20. Bring

Chapter Review One p 156

1. number
2. regardless
3. badly
4. advise
5. conscious
6. eager
7. among
8. effects
9. may
10. takes
11. cite
12. except
13. advice
14. takes
15. already
16. lead
17. bad

18. amount
19. led
20. can
21. affect
22. dessert
23. accept
24. between
25. all ready
26. anxious
27. capitals
28. already
29. bring
30. literally
31. conscience
32. effect
33. Council
34. accept

35. advises
36. Regardless
37. desert
38. led
39. figurative
40. principles
41. Capital
42. peak
43. except
44. counsel
45. Complimentary
46. stationary
47. number
48 advice
49. except
50. conscious

Chapter Ten - Usage Glossary

Exercise Four p 161

1. effect
2. thorough
3. morale
4. imply
5. latter
6. through
7. later
8. advise
9. cited
10. accept
11. sight
12. moral

13. Loose
14. lose
15. take
16. quiet
17. advice
18. affected
19. infer
20. Figuratively
21. past
22. all ready
23. led
24. deserted

25. eager
26. deserts
27. led
28. disinterested
29. conscience
30. threw
31. figurative
32. among
33. passed
34. effect
35. lose

Exercise Five p 165

1. slowly
2. slowly
3. farther
4. closely
5. quickly
6. easily
7. further
8. poorly
9. loudly

10. further
11. smoothly
12. fewer
13. correctly
14. further
15. tightly
16. really
17. fewer
18. perfectly

19. poorly
20. prematurely
21. Fewer
22. dangerously
23. fewer
24. less
25. fewer

Exercise Six p 167

1. peeking
2. Capitol
3. through
4. morale
5. site
6. accept
7. affected
8. cited
9. capital

10. thorough
11. later
12. loose
13. Through
14. thorough
15. principal
16. thorough
17. moral

18. effect
19. effect
20. morale
21. site
22. accept
23. imply
24. already
25. lose

Chapter Review Two p 169

1. principal
2. compliment
3. sight
4. conscience
5. effects
6. later
7. Moral
8. Principle
9. stationery

10. Council
11. capital
12. complement
13. peak
14. site
15. thorough
16. conscious
17. sight

18. principal
19. stationary
20. affect
21. cite
22. Capitol
23. compliment
24. through
25. latter

Chapter Ten - Usage Glossary

Final Chapter Review p 171
Incorrect/Correct

1. led/lead
2. counciled/counseled
3. compliment/complement
4. desserts/deserts
5. advise/advice
6. moral/morale
7. sight/site

8. quiet/quite
9. Correct
10. passed/past
11. accept/except
12. infer/imply
13. bad/badly
14. later/latter

15. further/farther
16. conscience/conscious
17. stationary/stationery
18. irregardless/regardless
19. peek/peak
20. less/fewer

Chapter Eleven Double Negatives

Exercise One p 175

1. any
2. was
3. anything
4. anywhere
5. is
6. any
7. ever

8. could
9. can
10. anything
11. any
12. can
13. any
14. any

15. was
16. ever
17. any
18. could
19. ever
20. any

Exercise Two p 176

1. anything
2. ever
3. is
4. were
5. anything

6. could
7. anything
8. can
9. ever
10. ever

11. anywhere
12. either
13. anyone
14. can
15. ever

Exercise Three p 177
Incorrect/Correct

1. ain't/hasn't any
2. couldn't never/could never or couldn't ever
3. couldn't have no/could have no or couldn't have any
4. don't know nothing/don't know anything
5. couldn't hardly/could hardly
6. didn't have no money/didn't have any money
7. don't want no more/don't want any more
8. ain't seen nothing/haven't seen anything
9. isn't never/is never or isn't ever
10. hasn't never/has never or hasn't ever
11. wouldn't never/would never or wouldn't ever
12. isn't never/is never or isn't ever
13. ain't nothing/is nothing or isn't anything
14. weren't no/were no or weren't any
15. didn't see nobody/didn't see anybody

Chapter Eleven Double Negatives

Chapter Review One p 178
Incorrect/Correct

1. ain't/isn't
2. no/any
3. no/any
4. no/any
5. no/any

6. nothing/anything
7. no/any
8. no/any
9. no/any
10. couldn't/could

11. no/any
12. nothing/anything
13. hadn't/had
14. can't/can
15. no/any

Final Chapter Review p 179

1. without no friends/without any friends
2. hasn't done none/has done none or hasn't done any
3. no/any
4. doesn't have no/doesn't have any or has no
5. couldn't/could
6. hasn't done nothing/has done nothing or hasn't done anything
7. hadn't never/had never or hadn't ever
8. no/any
9. no/any
10. can't/can
11. wouldn't never/would never or wouldn't ever
12. haven't never/haven't ever
13. couldn't could
14. no/any
15. aren't never/are never or aren't ever

Chapter 12 - Successful Writing Strategies

Exercise One p 181

1. Neil Armstrong and Edwin Aldrin Jr. were the first two men to walk on the moon on July 20, 1969.
2. The car seemed to be in perfect condition when I bought it from my friend Garrett.
3. Anne Bradstreet was a Puritan poet during Colonial times.
4. Queen Elizabeth II became queen of England after the death of her father in 1952.
5. The Great Smoky Mountains are located in western North Carolina and eastern Tennessee.
6. George Washington was born in 1732 in Virginia.
7. It was an old black and white movie.
8. My father insisted that I clean up the yard and pull the weeds.
9. We moved the bed from my brother's room to the basement.
10. We boarded the Cog Railroad at Manitou Springs, Colorado, and rode it to the top of Pike's Peak.
11. The A&P was the first chain store business to be established in 1842.
12. Lonny and I listened to KLOL radio.
13. King Ferdinand and Queen Isabella were Spanish monarchs who had faith in Christopher Columbus and agreed to fund his exploration.
14. I have to rewrite my resumé and cover letter.
15. Ketchup is excellent for cleaning brass, especially tarnished or corroded brass.

Chapter 12 - Successful Writing Strategies

Exercise Two p 183

1. Maine is the only state in the U.S. that has just one syllable.
2. Although most people picture the Tower of London as a single tower, it is a group of buildings covering 13 acres along the north bank of the Thames River.
3. Although Emily Dickinson wrote more than 1,700 poems, only four were published in her lifetime.
4. Since there are so many smokers in the country, China must import tobacco.
5. Jacob is the best guitar player.
6. Many factors influenced Jimmy to major in theater.
7. Sigeru Miyamoto is considered the father of modern video games because of his successful Nintendo franchises.
8. Although most people believe the story of the little Dutch boy who placed his finger in the dike to save a town from a flood, it is actually an American fabrication.
9. Where will the class be offered?
10. Gasoline prices rose after the hurricane because the demand increased while production decreased.
11. Her mother seemed angry that we stayed out so late.
12. There are so many bicycles on the island of Bermuda because private automobiles were forbidden until 1948.
13. Although a suntan is considered attractive, a moderately severe sunburn damages blood vessels to the point that it takes four to fifteen months to return to normal.
14. Most people think fall is the most beautiful season on the year.
15. Motorists trying to conserve gas should not drive above the speed limit.

Exercise Three p 185

1. A kangaroo can't jump if its tail is off the ground because it needs its tail for pushing off.
2. The earth rotates on its axis more slowly in March than in September.
3. The mayor seemed angry that the sanitation workers had gone on strike.
4. Although Jamie had plenty of time to study for her history test, she didn't do it.
5. In spring many people suffer from allergies from pollen.
6. She wasn't a good singer because she sang off-key.
7. Although young people are generally considered healthier than older people, teenagers are 50% more susceptible to colds than people over 50.
8. Learning to write well is a necessary skill.
9. Because a diamond is exceptionally hard, it will not dissolve in acid.
10. I have given up looking for a job.
11. I would rather be on vacation than working.
12. Victoria has a great personality.
13. Classified ads in Tokyo are among the most expensive in the world.
14. In Puritan times to be born on a Sunday was interpreted as a sign of great sin.
15. The resort was poorly rated because of a lack of good restaurants.

Chapter Review One p 186

1. Shoppers spend an average of eight minutes waiting in line at the grocery store, and most would rather be doing something else.
2. Because ostriches can run faster than horses and the males can roar like lions, they are one of the most unusual creatures on the planet.
3. Approximately 55% of people yawn within five minutes of seeing someone else yawn.
4. David will take us to the concert on Saturday night if he doesn't have to work.
5. Mr. Lewis is well liked by all his employees.
6. During a serious recession most retail businesses lose revenue, but movie theatres often increase revenue.
7. The fire broke out at about three in the morning, but no one was injured and there wasn't much damage.
8. A person uses more than seventy muscles to say one word and three hundred muscles to balance himself or herself while standing still.
9. The Minnesota Vikings' player crossed the goal line and did a little dance.

Chapter 12 - Successful Writing Strategies

Chapter Review One con't. p 186

10. Texas prisons are saving six million dollars a year because they are reducing the number of daily calories served to prisoners.
11. We rented the house with a beautiful mountain view.
12. The Japanese keep birds and crickets as pets.
13. Harry Houdini, the world famous magician, died of a ruptured appendix on Halloween.
14. Zeke is clever and ingenious.
15. Because Venice is built on water, large motor boats are used as buses and small motor boats are used for taxis.

Exercise Four p 188

1. A
2. B
3. B
4. B
5. A

Exercise Five p 189

1. All the tickets for the Smashing Pumpkins' concert were sold in less than one day.
2. Brandon told James that because James was over six feet tall, he couldn't be an astronaut because that was too tall for NASA's height requirements. Or Because Brandon was over six feet tall, he told James that he couldn't be an astronaut because that was too tall for NASA's height requirements.
3. The newscaster said there is a serious flu epidemic sweeping the country.
4. *To Kill a Mockingbird* has a theme of racial injustice.
5. After Sophia and Tyler carefully wrapped the presents Mrs. Saunders quickly delivered the gifts (or Sophie and Tyler) next door.
6. Alyssa smiled when she was introduced to the group by Tanna. Or Alyssa smiled when she introduced Tanna to the group.
7. Some of the eyewittnesses to the robbery described the getaway car as gray and others said it was blue, and this discrepancy confused the police investigators.
8. We were upset by the messy apartment, but our attitude will change. Or We were upset by the messy apartment, but the apartment will be cleaned.
9. They were opposed to gun control because they believed every citizen should have a gun for protection.
10. When our cat crept into Mrs. Lock's house, the cat created such an uproar I thought our friendship was damaged forever. Or When our cat crept into Mrs. Lock's house, Mrs. Lock created such an uproar I thought our friendship was damaged forever.
11. Over 50 million tourists a year visit Italy, and tourism provides nearly 63% of Italy's national income.
12. Noah locked his laptop in his car and then the car was stolen.
13. A person's nose is connected to the memory center of the brain, which is why smells can trigger powerful memories.
14. Voters in San Francisco approved a ballot initiative that allowed police officer Bob Geary to take his ventriloquist's dummy, Brenden O'Smarty, on foot patrol.
15. Jackson told Liam, "I don't have enough money to visit Peru." Or Jackson told Liam, "You don't have enough money to visit Peru."

Exercise Six p 190

1. Reduce the amount of water you use by fixing leaking plumbing fixtures, ***using*** less water in toilets, and turning off the water while you brush your teeth.
2. Prescription medications are expensive because the pharmaceutical companies spend hundreds of millions of dollars developing them, testing them, and marketing ***them***.
3. The book explains how to build a safe, diversified investment portfolio and ***save*** for college tuition costs.

Chapter 12 - Successful Writing Strategies

Exercise Six con't. p 190

4. At the craft fair artists demonstrated glass blowing, pottery making, and *weaving*.
5. To lose weight, eat foods with fewer calories, eat smaller portions, and *exercise* regularly.
6. Electronic switches, computerized ticketing for passenger trains, and *electronic* signaling equipment have eliminated the need for cabooses on many trains.
7. To become an elite figure skater requires more than $130,000 a year to cover the cost of private lessons, ice time, custom made boots, blades, and *specially* designed costumes.
8. The committee is not only working to preserve historical buildings, but also *to develop* a local museum.
9. The tennis coach patiently taught her students how to serve, rush the net, and *win* the point.
10. Zachery was healthy, wealthy, and *athletic*.
11. NASCAR driver Brian Vickers said, "You'll never win unless you're willing to push everyone around you to their limit, to push your car to the limit, and *to push* yourself to your limit.
12. IKEA founder Ingvar lives in a small home, eats at IKEA, take the bus, and *flies* coach, despite being the 5th richest man in the world.
13. Standing while doing work increases productivity and *keeps* people focused.
14. Modern homing pigeons find it more convenient to follow highways and beltways and turn left and right at junctions rather than *use* their built-in navigational abilities.
15. On the day of the high school final exam in Korea, government workers can arrive one hour late to reduce traffic congestion, motorists can't honk their horns near exam venues, and taxis *offer* free rides to students who need them.

Exercise Seven p 191

1. A nanometer is to a meter what a hazelnut is to earth.
2. Advertising is used to make consumers aware of a product, feel positive about a product, and remember the product when they go shopping.
3. Creating recycled paper uses significantly less energy than creating new paper from wood.
4. Societies around the world expect parents to pass on the shared values, the role expectations, and the rules of the society.
5. Leah loves to read, dance, and talk.
6. Helicopters are unique flying machines because they can hover over a single spot, fly slowly, and fly backward.
7. People often judge others at first sight using stereotypes based on clothing, personal attractiveness, and behavior.
8. During recycling, plastics are collected, sorted, chopped, melted, and remolded.
9. More than one billion people worldwide use the Internet to send e-mails, search for information, listen to music, or shop online.
10. Political leaders try to increase employment, grow the economy, and control inflation (optional: at the same time.)

Exercise Eight p 192

1. The waiter distributed menus.
2. Khaled Hosseini wrote *The Kite Runner*.
3. Ben played the part of the Cowardly Lion.
4. Paul Revere warned the Massachusetts Minutemen of the approach of the British.
5. A runner consumes about seven quarts of oxygen while running a hundred-yard dash.
6. The cereal industry uses an amazing 816 million pounds of sugar each year.
7. Vietnam produces half the world's black pepper.
8. The gift shop sells reproductions of these great paintings.
9. George Washington was the only U. S. president to have been unanimously elected.
10. A Belgian company is producing ice cream specifically for dogs.
11. Charles Wilson Peale painted many pictures of George Washington.
12. Roman architectural grandeur reflected the growth in power of the Roman Empire.
13. Chickens lay more eggs when pop music is played.

Chapter 12 - Successful Writing Strategies

Exercise Eight con't. p 192

14. A McDonald's in New Zealand sells apricot pies.
15. Eating a few ounces of chocolate can kill a small-sized dog.
16. Many cultures use knots as symbols of eternal love.
17. Frederic Baur invented the Pringles can, and when he died, his ashes were buried in one.
18. Women invented the first bulletproof vest and windshield wiper blades.
19. Frank Lloyd Wright's son invented Lincoln Logs.
20. People around the world watch two billion You Tube videos a day.

Exercise Nine p 195

1. Of all the items at the auction of Star Wars memorabilia, which do you think is ***most*** expensive?
2. Liechtenstein, the world's sixth-smallest country, is the world's ***largest*** exporter of false teeth.
3. You're ***more likely (or likelier)*** to be killed by a champagne cork than by a poisonous spider.
4. The continent of Australia, with just 5% of the earth's land area, is smaller than any ***other*** continent.
5. Some psychologists believe that the person who tries to keep everyone ***else*** happy often ends up feeling the loneliest.
6. Of all the complaints about Internet dating sites, misrepresentation by both men and women is ***most*** frequent.
7. Both men and women are ***more*** likely to be attracted to someone wearing the color red than any other color.
8. Illinois has the greatest number of license plates than any ***other*** state.
9. Blind people smile despite never having seen someone ***else*** smile because it's a natural human reaction.
10. Researchers have discovered that people who regularly help others are usually significantly more ***happy (or happier)*** and less likely to become depressed as they get older

Exercise Ten p 197

1. b
2. a
3. b
4. b
5. a
6. b
7. b
8. a
9. b
10. b

Exercise Eleven p 199

1. Although Orcas live longer in the wild, in captivity Orcas live, on average, just 20 years.
2. In Egypt, even if you do not drink it, it's considered rude not to accept tea or coffee if it is offered.
3. To beat city traffic, wealthy Russians hire fake ambulances with couches and flat screen TVs.
4. Adults dream off and on for about one and a half hours to three hours a night.
5. Over a distance of about a mile, a carrier pigeon can deliver a message faster than a fax machine.
6. In England it's an act of treason to place a postage stamp of the Queen upside down.
7. Officials stated that a central Florida woman was attacked by just one bear, not five.
8. In Russia it's considered rude to stand with your hands in your pockets.
9. Earth has more than 8,000 pieces of space debris left over from previous space missions orbiting around it.
10. Cockroaches that were originally native to Asia are now able to survive New York City's brutal winters.
11. Playing poker with friends at the White House, President Warren G. Harding once gambled away a box of priceless presidential china.
12. At a southwest Wyoming power plant, security guards spotted a suspicious device with wires connected to a battery and called a bomb squad, but the device turned out to be a mosquito trap.
13. Emma was rushed by just three sororities, not seven.

Chapter 12 - Successful Writing Strategies

Exercise Eleven con't. p 199

14. From our backyard, we could see the city's amazing fireworks display.
15. Looking through a microscope, Alison and I were able to spot the bacteria.

Exercise Twelve p 200

1. The motion-activated singing fish "Big Mouth Billy Bass" apparently scared off a would-be burglar who ***broke*** into a bait and tackle shop, but left without stealing anything, including cash that had been left in a visible spot.
2. It is illegal to lock car doors in downtown Churchill, Manitoba, in case someone ***needs*** to escape from a polar bear.
3. In 2000 the KKK adopted a stretch of highway near St. Louis, but the Missouri government ***responded*** by renaming the road the "Rosa Parks Highway."
4. Correct
5. When *Jurassic Park* author Michael Creighton was a student at Harvard, he ***felt*** his literature professor ***wasn't*** grading him fairly, and to prove it Creighton submitted a paper written by *1984* author George Orwell and got a B- on it.
6. Flamboyant ex-NBA star Dennis Rodman visited North Korea in 2013 and ***called*** the ruthless dictator Kim Jon-un a "friend for life."
7. When "Elephant Whisperer" Lawrence Anthony died, a whole herd of elephants ***arrived*** at his house to mourn his death.
8. Correct
9. Guided by a few clues from Twitter, Stephanie hailed a cab to Central Park and ***started*** searching for money planted there by Hidden Cash, the scavenger hunt craze that recently made its way from California to New York.
10. Correct
11. The Strait of Dover separates France from England, and on the English side near the town of Dover, white chalk cliffs ***line*** the coast.
12. Correct
13. Two-thirds of people report they fell in love with someone they ***had*** known for some time rather than someone they just met.
14. American schoolchildren rank 25th in math and 21st in science out of 30 developed countries, but they ***rank*** first in confidence that they out-perform everyone else.
15. William Whipple ***freed*** his slaves when he signed the Declaration of Independence because he believed he could not fight for freedom and own slaves.

Exercise Thirteen p 202

1. Before becoming a popular talk show host, Montel Williams ***attended*** the U.S. Naval academy in Annapolis, Maryland, where he studied Mandarin Chinese.
2. During his second campaign for the presidency, Teddy Roosevelt was shot by a would-be assassin while giving a speech in Milwaukee, but he ***continued*** to deliver his speech with the bullet in his chest.
3. Cats are one of the few animals to domesticate themselves and ***approach*** humans on their own terms.
4. Correct
5. A study of more than 38,000 people in the U.S. and thirteen European countries ***found*** that Americans were more prone to developing depression if they became unemployed, compared to their European counterparts.
6. Correct
7. A Connecticut woman became concerned when she heard someone repeatedly calling "Daddy," but when she ***started*** looking for a child, she found a large green parrot in a tree, which had escaped from its home less than a mile away.
8. Both players and owners finally resolved the contract dispute when they ***reached*** a compromise on players' salaries.
9. A man received the transplanted heart of a suicide victim, married the donor's widow, and ***killed*** himself in exactly the same way the donor died.

Chapter 12 - Successful Writing Strategies

Exercise Thirteen con't. p 202

10. Partygoers attending a bachelor party at Elephant Butte State Park in New Mexico *found* a fossil mastodon skull with tusks that was more than 10 million years old.
11. Correct
12. Residents of Erie, Pennsylvania, *heard* a cat in a tree crying for two days, and 21-year-old Tara Dennis decided to rescue it, but she ended up needing to be rescued by firefighters herself, when she couldn't get down from the tree either.
13. Correct
14. A physically fit felon in a detention facility in Arizona *climbed* a 10-foor-tall basketball hoop and used it as a platform to lea over a high fence and escape.
15. Adele Laurie Blue Adkins is an English singer-songwriter who was offered a recording contract after a friend *posted* her demo on Myspace in 2006.

Exercise Fourteen p 203

1. the author of the Sherlock Holmes stories
2. celluloid
3. a mathematician and an astronomer
4. a primate found only on the island of Madagascar
5. the famous American artist
6. the *American Dictionary*
7. the upper class descendants of its original citizens.
8. a signer of the Declaration of Independence
9. one of the greatest hitters in baseball history
10. a balloon artist from New York
11. Ronald Wayne
12. a Greek mathematician born around 300 B.C.
13. the first new addition in nine years.
14. a British luxury ship
15. a 70 pound chocolate Labrador

Exercise Fifteen p 204

1. Paul Revere, a famous American patriot, was once court-martialed for cowardice.
2. The strongest bone in the human body, the thigh bone, is hollow.
3. The first macaroni factory in the United States, started by Antoine Zegera in Brooklyn, New York, was established in 1848.
4. The Sahara Desert, as large a land area as Europe, has a total land mass of 3,565,565 square miles.
5. The first ferryboat in America, established in 1630 between Boston and Charleston across the Charles River, charged riders one cent for every 100 pounds of goods transported.
6. The mosquito, one of the hardiest of the world's insects, can live comfortably at the North Pole and is at home in equatorial jungles.
7. Salt, the most widely used seasoning in the world, was given as monthly wages to Roman legionnaires.
8. Michelangelo, the greatest painter and sculptor of his time, was also considered a great poet by his contemporaries.
9. The shortest intercontinental commercial flight in the world, from Gibraltar in Europe to Tangier in Africa, is a distance of thirty-four miles and a flight time of twenty minutes.
10. The world's fastest dog, the greyhound, can reach speeds of up to forty-five miles an hour.
11. The border between Canada and the U.S., the world's longest frontier, is a distance of 3,987 miles.
12. Sue, the world's largest, most complete, and best preserved Tyrannosaurus Rex, made her grand debut to the public on May 17, 2000, at the Field Museum in Chicago, Illinois.
13. Health insurance for pets, a rapidly growing industry, guarantees that people can afford expensive veterinary care for their pets.

Chapter 12 - Successful Writing Strategies

Exercise Fifteen con't. p 204

14. The shortest British monarch, Charles I, was four feet, nine inches.
15. The largest employer in the world, the Indian railway system, employs more than a million people.
16. Dexter, a six-month-old pit bull, was rescued from the rubble of an apartment building nine days after a tornado struck Washington, Illinois.
17. The wreckage of *The Keystone State*, a wooden steamship that sank in a storm on Lake Huron in 1861, has been found by a crew of shipwreck explorers.
18. Heath Ledger, a famous actor who died young, won western Australia's junior chess championship at age 10.
19. Air pressure, the weight of the atmosphere pressing down on earth, is measured by a barometer in units called *millibars*.
20. The custom at weddings of throwing rice, a symbol of health and prosperity, goes back to the time when people thought rice would appease evil spirits so they would not bother the wedding couple.

Exercise Sixteen p 206

1. which is estimated to be 4.5 billion years old
2. which is larger than the state of Rhode Island
3. who was jailed in London for twelve years for preaching without a license
4. who made the offending remark
5. which is more than a thousand years old
6. who had tried to sell him the fake Rolex watch
7. which was an orange tree brought to France in 1421
8. which is the largest state in land mass
9. which I can't get open
10. which are important sources of vitamin C

Exercise Seventeen p 207

1. The girl who borrowed my cell phone disappeared.
2. Owls, which have huge eyes, have the best night vision of all creatures.
3. Leonardo DiCaprio, who first became famous as the star of *Titanic*, is passionately interested in reversing global warming.
4. The short-term memory capacity for most people is between five and nine items or digits, which is one reason that phone numbers are seven digits long.
5. Fingerprints, which were not accepted as evidence in U.S. courtrooms before 1941, are now considered an infallible method of personal identification.
6. *Gone With the Wind*, which was the longest film (238 minutes) to win the best picture Oscar, was also the first color film to win best picture.
7. Samuel got a job with UPS, which is a good company to work for, because it offers generous reimbursement for education costs.
8. The immigration bill, which was passed by the U.S. House of Representatives, did not pass the Senate.
9. The presidential one dollar coins are plated in brass, which gives them their golden tone.
10. The deadliest natural disaster in US. History, which was the Galveston, Texas, hurricane of 1900, killed between 8,000-10,000 people.
11. Methane gas, which can often be seen bubbling up from the bottom of ponds, is produced by the decomposition of dead plants and animals in the mud.
12. Lucy and Linus have another little brother named Rerun, who sometimes plays left field on Charlie Brown's baseball team.
13. The Slinky toy was invented by an airplane mechanic, who was playing with engine parts and recognized the possible secondary use of one of the springs.
14. Mark Twain, who thought fasting was a cure for illness, would cure his colds and fevers by not eating for one or two days.
15. Howard Schultz, who is the high-profile chief executive officer of Starbucks, was not one of the original founders.

Chapter 12 - Successful Writing Strategies

Exercise Eighteen p 209

1. George Custer was the youngest American officer ever to become a general in the United States Army, making his rank at the age of twenty-three.
2. My grandfather doesn't know how to send e-mails, preferring to send postcards instead.
3. The President recognized the need for immediate action, declaring the entire state a disaster area.
4. Tired from loading and moving his friend's furniture, Jacob was eager to finish and go home.
5. Winding through 14 states, the Appalachian Trail is 2,175 miles long.
6. The Golden Gate Bridge is an internationally recognized symbol of San Francisco, connecting the the northern tip of the San Francisco Peninsula to Marin County.
7. Dressed in a tight T-shirt and fitted jeans, Richard Gere was being interviewed about his new movie.
8. Filled with lavish sets and exciting dance numbers, *An American in Paris* is the story of a struggling American painter who falls for a French girl.
9. Shel Silverstein was a talented poet, playwright, screenwriter, and songwriter, best known for his popular children's books including *The Giving Tree, Falling Up,* and *A Light in the Attic.*
10. Made of gypsum, the biggest natural crystals in the world are found in a silver mine in Mexico called the Cave of Crystals.
11. Costa Rica, located on the Central American isthmus, is a middle income, developing country with a strong democratic tradition.
12. Some engineering students have come up with a device designed to prevent small planes from colliding on runways, using ultrasonic sensors that set off warning sounds and lights if a plane is in danger of clipping the wings of another plane.
13. The bee hummingbird is the world's smallest bird, weighing about as much as a teabag.
14. A Georgia man spent 15 hours in jail on charges of misdemeanor theft for plugging his electric car into an outlet at a school, drawing about five cents worth of energy.
15. One of Italy's biggest businesses is the Mafia, earning over $178 billion a year and accounting for 7% of Italy's GDP.

Exercise Nineteen p 210

1. The human attention span maxes out at abut 10 minutes, because people will revert to daydreaming after that.
2. Mexico City has sunk several feet during the 20th century, since the water table underneath the city is being drained for human consumption.
3. To study faster, read the first and last paragraphs of the material, since this is about as effective as reading everything.
4. Harvard uses Yale brand locks on their buildings while (or although) Yale uses Best brand.
5. The United States dominates film, television, pop music, the Internet, and business, which has increased the importance of the English language in recent decades.
6. Leap year occurs every four years because this is when all the extra hours, minutes, and seconds in the solar year are added up to make an extra day.
7. In the 20th century thousands of new, disposable goods were invented and fewer people had open fires to get rid of them, so more garbage was thrown away.
8. Pigs are generally thought of as being as intelligent as most dogs because pigs can be taught to accomplish almost any task a dog can perform.
9. Used car buyers are sometimes at a disadvantage because sometimes sellers don't give complete information about the cars they are selling.
10. Radio and TV serials about everyday life in the U.S. have been sponsored by soap manufacturers since the 1930s, so these serials have been called soap operas or just soaps.
11. Lucretia Mott, Elizabeth Cady Stanton, and Susan B. Anthony were all abolitionists, although they were more famous as pioneers for women's rights.
12. Bullies in the workplace harm not only the targeted person, but also the company as well, because bullying can lead to absences, decreased productivity, and even the loss of an employee.
13. The first regular phone service was established in 1878, when people answering the phone said "Ahoy."
14. Introverted people prefer to express differences of opinion by e-mail, while extroverts generally seek out face-to-face conversations.
15. College baseball players are allowed to use aluminum baseball bats, although professional players are not.

Chapter 12 - Successful Writing Strategies

Exercise Nineteen con't.p 210

16. A Hard Rock Casino security employee asked Ben Affleck to stop playing blackjack because he was "too good at it," although he is allowed to play other games there.
17. The 2013 government shutdown threatened to close a national program that gave medical attention and meals to children, so John D. Arnold donated $10 million to keep it afloat.
18. Most airlines have adjusted their flight arrival times because they wanted to have a better record of on-time arrivals.
19. Albert Einstein couldn't speak fluently until after his ninth birthday so his parents thought he was mentally retarded.
20. Under Chairman Mao, every Chinese family was required to kill a sparrow a week to stop them from eating all the rice, although the project was ineffective because sparrows don't eat rice.

Chapter Review Two p 212

1. The Concorde, the only passenger aircraft ever to fly faster than the speed of sound, made its last flight on October 24, 2004.
2. Thousands of extravagantly dressed fans of punk, Goth, Romanticism, and Victoriana celebrate the annual Goth Weekend in the English seaside town of Whitby, the fictional home of Bram Stoker's *Dracula*.
3. An important book about the Holocaust, *The Diary of Anne Frank*, describes a Jewish family's life in hiding until they were discovered and sent to a concentration camp, where Anne later died.
4. Robert Frost, famous for his poems about New England, was born in San Francisco.
5. President McKinley, the twenty-fifth president of the U.S., died of gangrene, after being shot by an assassin, and his wounds were not properly treated.
6. The besenji, an African dog, is the only dog breed that doesn't bark.
7. The U.S. has the world's largest geothermal resource, the Geysers, 72 miles north of San Francisco.
8. Ernest Hemingway, one of 20th century America's most respected writers, lived in Cuba for many years.
9. One of the largest beds in the world, the Great Bed of Ware, measures over 10 feet wide and 11 feet long.
10. Katia and Maurice Draft, two of the world's most famous volcano investigators, were killed in the eruption of the Japanese volcano Unzenin in 1991.

Chapter Review Three p 213

1. Jesse Owens, who was an American track star, outran a racehorse in 1936 over a 100 yard course, even though the horse had a head start.
2. The Passenger Rail Investment and Improvement Act, which will allocate more than $10 billion for Amtrak over the next several years, was passed by both the House and the Senate.
3. The Maglev train, which is named from combining the words magnetic and levitation, does not run on a track, but floats above it by means of magnetic repulsion.
4. One of the most famous Mongol emperors was Genghis Khan, who started out as a goat herder.
5. Snow, which is important in the wheat growing regions of America's Western states, provides moisture and protects crops from the intense winter cold.
6. The Australian koala bear, which looks like a toy teddy bear, is actually a marsupial, a mammal with a pouch for carrying its young.
7. Johnny Appleseed, who earned his name by planting apple seedlings over a large area of the Midwest, was really named John Chapman.
8. We crept cautiously around the deserted Warfield Mansion, which was rumored to be haunted.
9. Nearly 1.4 billion people live in China, which is over one-fifth of the world's population.
10. The Golden Raspberries, which were initiated in 1980, are joke awards presented to the worst films and actors, such as Sandra Bullock, who won in 2010 and the entire cast of *Sex in the City #2*, who won in 2011.

Chapter 12 - Successful Writing Strategies

Final Chapter Review p 214

1. The first real motion picture theater was called a nickelodeon, opening in McKeesport, Pennsylvania, on June 19, 1905.
2. A series of financial crises brought the Lehman Brothers firm to bankruptcy, caused by mismanagement in the company.
3. The test used to measure a newborn's health is known as the Apgar Score, named after its inventor Dr. Virginia Apgar.
4. Cliff found Botswana on the map, impressing all of us.
5. Twelve American astronauts have walked on the moon, exploring highlands and craters, taking photographs, and gathering soil and rocks for study.
6. Water expands as it freezes and contracts as it melts, displacing the exact same amount of fluid in either state.
7. The historic district of Williamsburg in Virginia has some of the most famous colonial buildings in America, dating from before the American Revolution.
8. During the storm, power outages were frequent, annoying utility customers.
9. Dinosaurs were among the most sophisticated animals that ever lived on earth, surviving for nearly 150 million years.
10. Sheepdogs have 220 million olfactory cells, enabling them to smell 44 times better than humans.

Index